PLOUGHSHARES

Fall 2001 · Vol. 27, Nos. 2&3

GUEST EDITOR
Donald Hall

EDITOR
Don Lee

MANAGING EDITOR
Gregg Rosenblum

POETRY EDITOR
David Daniel

ASSOCIATE FICTION EDITOR
Maryanne O'Hara

ASSOCIATE POETRY EDITOR
Susan Conley

FOUNDING EDITOR
DeWitt Henry

FOUNDING PUBLISHER
Peter O'Malley

PLOUGHSHARES, a journal of new writing, is guest-edited serially by prominent writers who explore different and personal visions, aesthetics, and literary circles. PLOUGHSHARES is published in April, August, and December at Emerson College, 120 Boylston Street, Boston, MA 02116-4624. Telephone: (617) 824-8753. Web address: www.pshares.org.

ASSISTANT FICTION EDITORS: Jay Baron Nicorvo and Nicole Kelley. EDITORIAL ASSISTANTS: Bess Newman and Patricia Reed.

FICTION READERS: Eson Kim, Wendy Wunder, Michael Rainho, Hannah Bottomy, Thomas Fabian, Emily MacLellan, Darla Bruno, Bart Cameron, Lisa Dush, Geraldine McGowan, Susan Nusser, Elizabeth Pease, and Laura Tarvin. POETRY READERS: Sean Singer, Scott Withiam, Ellen Wehle, Jay Baron Nicorvo, Joanne Diaz, Tracy Gavel, Kristoffer Haines, Jill Owens, Jennifer Thurber, and Christopher Hennessy.

SUBSCRIPTIONS (ISSN 0048-4474): $22 for one year (3 issues), $42 for two years (6 issues); $25 a year for institutions. Add $12 a year for international ($10 for Canada).

UPCOMING: Winter 2001–02, a poetry and fiction issue edited by Jorie Graham, will appear in December 2001. Spring 2002, a poetry and fiction issue edited by Cornelius Eady, will appear in April 2002.

GUEST EDITOR POLICY: Please see page 289 for information.

SUBMISSIONS: Reading period is from August 1 to March 31 (postmark dates). All submissions sent from April to July are returned unread. Please see page 289 for detailed submission policies.

Back-issue, classroom-adoption, and bulk orders may be placed directly through PLOUGHSHARES. Microfilms of back issues may be obtained from University Microfilms. PLOUGHSHARES is also available as CD-ROM and full-text products from EBSCO, H.W. Wilson, Information Access, and UMI. Indexed in M.L.A. Bibliography, American Humanities Index, Index of American Periodical Verse, Book Review Index. Self-index through Volume 6 available from the publisher; annual supplements appear in the fourth number of each subsequent volume. The views and opinions expressed in this journal are solely those of the authors. All rights for individual works revert to the authors upon publication.

PLOUGHSHARES receives support from the Wallace–Reader's Digest Funds, the Massachusetts Cultural Council, and the National Endowment for the Arts.

Retail distribution by Bernhard DeBoer (Nutley, NJ) and Ingram Periodicals (La Vergne, TN). Printed in the U.S.A. on recycled paper by Capital City Press.

CONTENTS

Fall 2001

Cover art:
Blue Birches by Emilia Dubicki
Acrylic on canvas, 16″ x 28″, 2000

DONALD HALL

Introduction

Editing my second issue of *Ploughshares*, in my seventy-third year, I look back on a life's worth of editing. It began in high school, continued at Harvard, then at Oxford. Late in my Oxford time, I took up editing poetry for the new *Paris Review*, and lasted nine years. I edited or helped to edit three anthologies of poetry by contemporaries: last was the Penguin *Contemporary American Poets*. In my fifties and sixties, I edited poetry for two monthly periodicals, and I did *Best American Poetry* with David Lehman in 1989.

Why did I spend so much time judging the poetry of others, when I might have been writing or watching college basketball? I know why. I edited, especially in the early years, in the urgent attempt to impose my taste on others, and to cut off at the pass any differing taste. It seemed to me imperative that *these* poems flourish and that *those* poems wither and die. Editing tries to assert power, such as it is, over the formation of a contemporary canon; the best editing is combative and passionate. I published people I had known: John Ashbery, Robert Bly, Geoffrey Hill, Thom Gunn. I published poets I found in other periodicals, and recruited: James Wright, Louis Simpson.

And I made gross mistakes. Working for *The Paris Review* back in the 1950's, I wanted to make it the voice of a generation—yet managed to reject Frank O'Hara and Allen Ginsberg, among others. Assertive editing makes for egregious error—both in accepting and in rejecting—but it is still preferable to passive editing. With passion, one puts pearls *and* boll weevils into the pancakes. Without it, one cooks a tasteless sludge of the merely *likely*.

At a certain age, such passion begins to wane, and with it the conviction of the vast importance of one's taste. Editing this *Ploughshares* was the most difficult editing I have done, and it is because of my age. I believe I can still discriminate—readers of this issue will decide for themselves—but I found judgment hard, in the matter of poems taken and of many poems turned away.

That judgment should deteriorate with age, or become less firm, is noted but little discussed. When I was in my mid-twenties, I was horrified when a fifty-year-old poet told me he could no longer tell the young poets apart. Since then, I have seen taste, or passionate preference, desert my contemporaries in their forties and in every decade thereafter. It becomes more difficult to summon or exercise the discrimination one had (or meant to have) when one was young, and I fear I am beginning to lose my old improbable fierce certitude. Before judgment begins to feel too arbitrary, one should leave editing. I will edit no more issues of journals. I will judge no more contests.

But... this final editing project pleases me greatly, as I hope it will please others. I am delighted that these writers—friends and strangers, some of whom are five decades younger than I am— have allowed me to print their brilliant work.

DAVID BARBER

Shades of Alexandria

Cosmologists, epic poets, holy men in exile—
They all found their way to the illustrious library.
All lovers of knowledge were welcome to a niche
In that bristling hush, no matter how shaggy or ragged.

There were the usual cynics and the inevitable stoics.
Some were sages without honor, scrawling out summas
In their mongrel dialects and inscrutable cuneiforms,
Working those little golf pencils right down to the nub.

There were the astronomers, who stayed up every night
Observing the movements of the firmament:
You could tell by their bloodshot stares and rumpled garb
How resolutely they pursued their lucubrations.

Some looked as if they'd studied under Aristotle—
Ancient souls, tottering about like crusty Nile tortoises,
Griping over the plague of errors infesting the card catalogues.
You'd hear them mutter darkly as they grappled with the drawers.

Sophists, peripatetics, soothsayers, tragedians—
None were turned away, you didn't question
This one's erudition or that one's chosen discipline.
The collections were open to scribes of every persuasion.

From the ends of the earth the seekers would come
Just to incline their heads over our long tables.
And if they slumped forward altogether on occasion,
Who could possibly object—the dream of reason

Is like unto the fathomless siftings of the sands,
Everlasting study is a weariness of the flesh.
You could tell by their soiled bundles and open sores
How profoundly they suffered for their great life's work.

One would think that there in the vaulted reading room
You could count on a modicum of classical decorum,
But you know how scholars are, jealous of their turf,
Forever denouncing their rivals as barbarians.

And to tell the truth, few of them were distinguished—
Whatever acumen they once may have possessed
They'd squandered on pedantry of dubious import.
Most seemed to be glossing corruptions in the texts.

And if you were a page—that's what we were known as then,
Back when the world was young—you picked up after them,
You reshelved the strewn compendiums and lexicons,
You inspected the rune-scored stalls at closing time

To make sure there were no thinkers lost in contemplation.
Satirists, orators, votaries of Ptolemy and Diogenes—
You'd shepherd them out the swinging double doors
Into the misty or sticky evening, the bay's salt bite,

The streets with their attar of dumpster and flask.
One day was like another in that seat of learning.
Creeping hours, turning leaves, cracked spines and paper cuts—
Here you spoke in whispers, and history held its breath.

Across from Grace

What had been hovering in the air all evening,
there, as near as the other side of the table—

No, not a woman, but so like a woman, turning away
and smiling privately. More like a man—a group of men—

who have found a way to draw the party to them.
Meanwhile I sit combing the spite from my hair.

My fingernails blunt back from poverty, risible
and public when the hand gets caught in the scarf.

Might as well just take this soupspoon and bang it
until the room clears. On second thought, don't.

I could sew the loops over the darning egg
where the pitiful hole has grown, but that, too,

would draw notice. Instead I must wait
as the fox waits for the hullabaloo to pass.

All

All bend
in one wind.

The Fact

After all these
analyses,
the fact
remains intact.

The Answer

What's it all about?
Don't ask
and then you'll know.

For the Record

The great sports hero can remember
When he thought sex was just for fun.
Now he's desperately affixed to woman number
53,671.

Injunction

As if the names we use to name the uses of buildings
x-ray our souls, war without end:

Palace. Prison. Temple. School.
Market. Theater. Brothel. Bank.

War without end. Because to name is to possess
the dreams of strangers, the temple

is offended by, demands the abolition of brothel, now theater, now
school; the school despises temple, palace, market, bank; the bank by

refusing to name depositors welcomes all, though in rage
    prisoners each
night gnaw to dust another stone piling under the palace.

War without end. Therefore time past time:

Rip through the fabric. Nail it. Not
to the wall. Rip through

the wall. Outside

time. Nail it.

Almost the Same

And then there was the night, not long
After my wife had left me and taken on the world-
Destroying fact of a lover, and the city
Roared in flames with it outside my window,
I brought home a nice woman who had listened
To me chant my epic woe for three
Consecutive nights of epic drinking,
Both of us holding on to the bar's
Darkly flowing river of swirling grain
As my own misery flowed past and joined
The tributary of hers, our murmured consolations
Entwining in precisely the same
Recitative, the same duet that has beyond
All doubt been sung in dark caves
Of drink since the very beginning
Of despair, the song going on until there was nothing
For it but to drive through an early summer
Thunderstorm in the windy night
To my little East Side apartment and gently
Take off her clothes and lay her down
On my bed by the light
Of a single candle and the lightning
And kiss her for a long time in gratitude
And then desire, and then gently kiss the full
Moons of her breasts, which I discovered
By candlelight were not hers, exactly;
Under each of them was the saddest,
Tenderest little smile of a scar,
Like two sad smiles of apology.
I had them done
So he wouldn't leave, she said,
But in the end he left anyway, her breasts
Standing like two cold cathedrals

In the light of the flaming city
And I kissed the little wounds
He had left her, as if I could heal them
And kissed the nipples he had left behind
Until they smoldered like the ashes
Of a campfire the posse finds
Days after the fugitive has slept there
And moved on, drawn by the beautiful
And terrible light of the distant city.

Adventures in the Simic Woods

I spent a night in the Simic woods.
I pulled my bed behind me through the trees.
I was a plowshare plowing ground mist.
Accordion players still playing their accordions
Were lying draped over the low branches;
And girls ran back and forth through the orchard
Tickling their bottoms with partridge wings.
"No matter what you give them," the undertaker said,
"The dead keep raising their right arms."
Communism and Capitalism are joined at the belly.
One sleeps while the other does immodest things.
Now the bridesmaids have climbed onto my bed;
They are throwing great loaves to the blushing parents.

Proteus

To take,
       like water,
whatever shape you flow through, fill, or rest in.
And to choose that shape.

*

As: Brian, become a gangster,
six feet from my face.
Voice no longer a caress
but a sharpened projection,
belly a ram in a buttoned vest.
The whole body shows
                  the thing done:
goat-song in the rites of a god,
transforming, starting to speak now
through him
          as he walks on stage.

*

Remember when you turned
into moonlight, the bark of an oak,
an orange going to shreds
in your own cold palm?
Everything you saw you *were,*
and you saw everything.
                No choice.
That face light gnarled around a tree
was your face.

*

Flesh is approximate.
We clothe it in dreams,
wrestling with our eyes closed

down through layers:
                              thug, wraith,
chieftain, devouring angel (held
by my shoulders I
am trying to make you
stay put) daddy mama breath
balm a man a woman in
separate desires
                              overlapped.

                                        *

Curious,
              cautious enough
to disguise himself as a woman,
the voyeur peeks at the rite.
Women, leaping, mothers and daughters—
their rapt beauty draws him out.
The god
          has tricked him:
they will tear him apart.

                                        *

As: a virus.
              Never alive,
but a frantic mimicry of life
to pierce the cell, makeover
its orders, move, repeat itself, mutate
in sped-up mini-evolution—
now it swims the blood, unravels
in light, never alive, now
                              it floats on air—
lost in the host a thousand years,
inert chemical mechanism
asleep in a rain-forest cave.

                                        *

To mime—
              not a statue
or a gray accountant picked from the crowd,

but a robot.
Steel jumpsuit and boots,
greasepaint turning the eyelids
aluminum. This hand a crank, this grin
the edge of a disk,
                    I am Mister
Silver Mister Silver—tape
loop syncopating
over the drum machine.

                              *

As: a child's toy,
its intricate language of joints and swivels,
creature within creature:
the robot
            a wolf on silver feet,
in his boxy jaw
the tiny half-robotic
head of a man
                    who will drive the car.

                              *

Who will drive the car
                    to the hospital
after the cancer has metastasized?

                              *

These knots rising in my palm—
look, in the photo album,
he grips the mower like a sad hawk.
Grandfather, father, son—flesh
tightens, branching genes
send up more
                    of the claw each year.
After the operation
skin comes back thick as bark.

                              *

A boy, a lion, wild boar,
snake no one will touch
holds the changes.
Dream he is a sea god,
                        and he is.
Dream he is a stone, a bull, no,
a tree
        rippling over
the waves' quick light, he is
shape always becoming, he is a flame
and the stream that drowns it.

The Rat Trinity

That rat's too smart to come
to the rows of crumbs I sowed
by the pond, he has the patience of true
hunger, he'll wait me out

    with the same tenacity I had
as a child, hungry to grow strong
enough to escape the nunnery
without being caught.

I loved the rats of Bruges
I watched from the study hall window,
how they slunk out the courtyard
sewer grill, slid along walls,

    slipped down the cellar steps
like whispers and vanished into gray.
I loved three in particular—christened
them the Trinity:

    the Father was slick, sullen,
the Daughter tense but lissome,
and the fat-bellied one, the Holy Ghost,
maker of miracles, was the Mother.

I imagined they came
from Antwerp, from the port's stinking
sewage by the Coal Wharf, last quay
before the wild, eager sea.

And there were times, when
beatings seared my skin with hues
of oil on the river Scheldt, and I
squeezed my thumbs

    in my fists through dormitory
nights, there were times I prayed
to the Rat Trinity. To show me the way
out of the convent,

    through Bruges sewers
and cobbled rows, then underground
to Ghent; out again through velour
wheat fields near Antwerp,

    and haste to my parents'
house where Mother wore silk,
and Father blew smoke halos
in the air. I prayed

    the rats to bring me back
to the young whispers of their bed
and into Mother's fat, white belly. To
crown them with

    the trinity they had hungered for:
Father, Mother, and from their fusion,
not I, but unscorned, chosen: one
divine being—a son.

The Men

Outside of town, back on that
one country lane, they work
down into the ground, pieces
of cracked road lie to the sides,
small black boulders. Deep brown
earth makes a rim around
the great opening, a moist lip.
Machinery sits on each side,
patient yellow creatures.
Lights are hung, making the men's
uniforms a stark tense blue.
They stand on the mounds of dirt,
looking down at the other men,
lowered now, and hidden. Night
peers over their shoulder
and squats at the hole's edge.
A passerby might think they scout
for the water line, but the men
don't really know what they look for,
though they sense the large low
trembling far under the surface.
They don't know it but as nights
grow colder, they get closer,
and one night they'll strike it,
split it down the middle,
not knowing how to climb back out,
not knowing how to smooth over
the great opening they made.
They thought they could find it,
manage it. They won't be able to stop
what is inside from gushing
into the dirt, rising like water.

HAYDEN CARRUTH

Something for the Trade

Please note well, all you writers, editors, directors
out there: when a phone call is terminated
by the other person you do not, NOT, hear
the buzz of a dial tone. You hear a faint click
and then silence, absolute silence, the Great
Silence, more eloquent than any electronic
buzz could ever be. In fact the dial tone
cannot be heard until you yourself hang up
and then lift the receiver again. Further
note this: you cannot tell from the click
if the other person has hung up reluctantly
or desperately, softly or violently. It is only
the sound of a disconnected circuit. I've read
this error in a thousand books, I've seen it
in a thousand movies, and how so many
of you can be so unobservant, you who
call yourselves artists, is beyond me.
Ah, my friends, you are becoming my
enemies, and I'm appalled by your irreverence
for the simple truth that should sustain us all.

TOM CLARK

Why Hillary Became a Goddess on the Night of Her Acceptance Speech

Because her hair looked cool
Because some of the best alien minds are watching
   developments closely
Because she is the traditional Daisy poised fragile before the
   masculine mills
Of production, yet wearing out six black pantsuits
To bring us to acculturation and consequence
Because the Nasdaq is plunging and there is a mandate for
   change
Sweeping through the gentle bacteria that make their home
   in her tireless campaign shoes
Because the worried market takes comfort in knowing what
   it must consume
Because choosing is not an issue except to the terrified
   cartoon eyeballs
In the takeout carton, wondering whose turn is first
Because some of the best alien minds consider "us" the
   shrill-voiced uncertainty factor
That threatens to bring the whole cosmic chorus to its
   whispering knees
Because Utopia is the island in time that forgot itself as it
   lifted its utensil
At the altar of its great consuming goddess No Memory,
   with her sadclown smile strained
Because her lofty position at the social fulcrum which is the
   mercy seat
Takes a terrific toll on black pantsuit bottoms
Because some of the best alien minds are surveying
   developments in numb disbelief
Because sixty-five percent of the wood lice aren't losing any
   sleep at all
Because retreat in the face of even greater problems,

While not a bad idea, won't solve anything
Because acceptance and consumption are just what the
    market needs
To shake it out of its trance-like belief in what it thinks
    alien minds are saying
Because acceptance means acculturation to the masculine
    mills
Because happiness is merely their invention anyway,
    because Dame Pleasure is wearied
Of Earth, has taken to the air, faded, fluttered down in a
    still, snow-
Like inwardness to spill, scatter, and be raked up with all
    the sibyl's other fallen leaves
In this enchanted-recount self-enclosure, like a small-town
    autumn
Where the commoners lie down nightly with what they
    have made
Happen, amid the bedded reeds of the vigilant event
    horizon
Because in this collapse its truths are received
By their souls, because of what this means to the odd
    weightlessness they feel
Because they have no way to grace their laurels
Beyond filling up the best alien minds, intent upon those
    peerless screens
With the black pantsuits of our resident historian
Who's just keeping a chair among the blond clouds warm
    for them.

Okay, Let's Not Have Sex

And who could play it well enough
If deaf and dumb and blind with love?
—Yeats

Let's not pretend we could be less
complicated than millions before us.
Let's be *just friends*, be *Platonic*, only
look at the bottoms of each other's feet,
or skin on inner forearms, where the sun
has done almost no damage. But let's not
say we wouldn't drop to our knees in praise.
Why else would we drop to our knees?

No, let's not have sex—let's just learn
curves of each other's fingers, all the way
to the cuticles, nails, tips; touch every
bony prominence on each other's faces,
supraorbital tauruses, chins, jaws, teeth,
sinewy cartilage of nostrils, all
the hairs inside the nostrils, the satin
nap of your beard, the dark down on my cheek.

But let's not have sex—let's just talk
about *bones*, listen to patellas grind.
I'll show you where I broke my arm once, twice,
where three pins held my elbow together;
my hysterectomy scar. You'll show me
where a CO_2 cartridge ricocheted
its way into your chest, a pain that was
nothing compared to a broken heart once, twice...

Agreed, though. No sex—let's just lie
side by side after late picnics, fireflies
settling, bullfrogs croaking, and wise us
talking about stars we can't name
though they seem almost touchable.
Knowing that abandonment, alone, is
a great argument for not having sex,
we'll lie there and lie there, not having sex.

On the Outskirts of the Lost Cities

1.
That the wandering
would be the more-favored part,

this was unexpected, exceptional.
Even the gnaw of the harness,

faces shawled
against the dust, nights

without fire—sweet to him now—
even this.

Who could find that point again,
at the canvas steppes

where exhaustion forced them on
into the serrated mouths of grass

rather than return
to what they knew,

the lush blur
too thick to show the way they came.

2.
That when they couldn't go on
that place looked like every

other place, but now
familiar. Where later the trees bent

like wind stopped in mid-breath
that would make him miss the wandering.

That the children and their children
would flourish, then sicken and die here,

very near here, he had known that
in stopping—it was always implied.

This only meant they cherished
the fields of their hunger, their dirt

and why they spoke, instead,
of joy. Just as, in beginning, he left

his own house, praising the road
that took him from the walls

where a son assumes
his father's face, separated

only by years and anger.

Visited

There's joy for the well-turned
shinbone, praise for the wrought
torso, we were warned
      when he opened
those gray eyes.

      What gifts we gave
we gave for virtues—a white stone castle
to teach him courage, small guns
to set the blood. A storybook,
illuminated, kept him close, hard
against the fire.

      He was one
with fitful sleeps, strife with milk,
a rude, colicked baby, satisfied
in solitude. Knit of slurred, imperfect
purpose, he has come to dream. After-
math, blood puppet or my salvation,
he is come to dream.

Art History

Two Italians painted on both sides of the grand marble staircase
in the Scuola di San Rocco—The Plague.
The great equalizer.
In this democracy of the dead, a woman and her baby
are flung over a pallet on wheels, a man with sinews
and massive calves pushes them, and it could be
almost tender how her arm trails toward him.
And then it will happen to him,
rough trade that he is, getting cleanup money.
Bodies.
Bodies in the 1630's. On the left it's the price
of decadence—all breasts, and fleshy arms,
jewelry, loosened bodices, and hair swept up, revealing a neck.
Luscious.
It swallows—this staircase, and as you ascend
the sprawling, heavy limbs fall forward, reaching for each other,
for you, for someone
to take them away from the pain where they've been painted
    forever.
Never has death been so active.
It's fairly surging in a wave down both sides—
a sea, parted, and I'm in the middle, fleeing.
Antonio Zanchi and Pietro Negri took pleasure in such
    voluptuous disgust.
Their humanity roils—an orgy, not sexual, but the press
of flesh is there. It happened.
Punishment. The painters reek of the high ground
while loving the low. One leaves himself a boat
in the quay. This is Venice.
Who makes it, who doesn't, is an arbitrary matter

of who gets there first, and if you can keep the dying out.
The boat must be clean
because God is not there,
not in the equation.
We are alone with our appetites, and our consequences,
read to us inexorably, from the great book of time.

The Morning of the Morning

Why let it matter so much?: the morning's morningness,
early dark modulating into light
and the tall thin spruces jabbing their black outlines at dawn,
light touching the slope's outcroppings of rock and yellow grass,
as I sit curled under blankets in the world
after the world Descartes shattered,
a monstrous fracture
like the creek's water surging through broken ice.

A silent wind bounces spruce branches
in that motion that sets molecules vibrating latitude by latitude
to crack the absolute
of feeling, of knowing what I know, of knowing who I am,
while down the road the town wakes to hammer and saw—
a sound that says to some, if you don't grow you're dead—
and then farther down the elk and deer gather
at a farmer's fence for his handout of hay.

Late January: just outside Rocky Mountain National Park:
a high branch of ponderosa offers a rosette
of needles blackgreen and splayed as in a Japanese scroll painting,
which is beautiful if I focus there and not on the sprawl I'm part of
in this rented condo where I don't want to live since I, too, need
more rooms to haul my coffee to, more bookshelves for books
I haven't time to read—bird chatter!—I shouldn't make one more
   resolution
I can't keep to spend more time with friends.

But it's morning and morning's my time of day
as spring's my season; more light, I say.
I do regret some things I've done and if I could,
I'd do things differently: start sooner, say, look deeper.
One flake of snow drifts down slantwise,

a lovely interruption to my tirade—
as each aspen is to the larger groves of taller firs—
and brings me back to what's happening here.

Tires rumble as a jeep passes,
rumble that in hours will crescendo into a roar
and, down on the plains, into that background drone
I don't hear even when I hear it penetrating my walls and sleep
because I've learned—haven't you?—to live without one
    square inch
of silence. But it's morning light filling the skies if you're up
    to see it,
sky washed white with thin clouds
the ground white with last night's snow.

The Nun on the Bus, Florence

Black drape like a solid shadow,
as if the shade won't slide from her. Veil,

abstracted hair lifting on the breeze.
Around us heels, furs, and scarves like swatches

of Las Vegas, a twitch of liner
on a pair of eyes, men in the cut of coats,

the usual, long-faced inspection
of each other's clothes; mine unpressed, I creep

toward her. I like her sandals, try
to look at what she sees: flitting gardens,

cracked salmon, fitful ochre, moon-green
olive leaves, and the massings of overcast days

in the age-blown stone. I follow her
off the bus, and in black windblasts of her gown,

move a finger out where it might be
brushed by that day-lit, midnight tempest

descending to the piazza.
As she hurries toward San Marco and folds

into the heavy doors, I don't move.
The boy beside me watches a beauty

going by. Suspended and free
of intent, he pauses before resuming his stride

negotiating the crowds that course
between the pleasant and the tragic.

A snatch of blue above a broken wall.
The being picked up and swiftly returned.

Private Life

Little Kaiser, the parrot
in our local headshop's sidewalk cage,
confronts an unceasing daily stream
of whistles and coos and hellos,

waspish buzz of film on auto-wind,
the sudden, minor lightning
of a flash. He doesn't seem to mind.
Not a headshop exactly:

years ago the police swept away
the ranks of bongs and rolling papers,
leaving behind sex toys
and a universe of tie-dye arrayed

beside every conceivable kind
of bead; the tourists stream in,
in search of something wild,
and everyone looks, at least,

at Kaiser's cage; he chews
his parrot toys, he speaks,
or rocks from side to side
behind a sign which reads,

I bite. He couldn't be said to be
lonely; all day the world comes to him,
endless procession of faces,
only a few of them known.

We pass him every day.
Irascible acrobat, he's half the time

upside down, marvelous feet
commandeering the narrow wires,

or hanging from his roof,
lost in thought till he looks out
and begins his coloratura tape-loop
of whistles, cut and paste

of copycat cries: bicycle bells,
miaows, squeaky brakes, a brilliant
rendering of a cell phone's trill,
low in the throat. In the evening,

he's still there, up late, clicking
and preening at his oyster gleam.
(He is an African gray,
which means his modest cloak

is lined, beneath the tail, in stunning red,
a frank indulgence of the private life.)
Tonight it's a little chilly, late in the season,
bedtime soon. What does Kaiser dream?

Probably no original paradise;
this little trooper was born in a shop.
A soul mate, come to him
out of the daily stream? Why

should he prefer a single,
perfect other? Maybe he'd rather
give and give himself away;
maybe the pilgrim line of visitants

continues in the echoing landscape
of his night, one human form
after another bent over him
in momentary delight, while he takes

their measure, and mouths
a limited vocabulary,
all greeting and praise:
Hello, Pretty, Howdy-do,

speech enough for our dear,
promiscuous singer, whose tongue
lifts and curls out to the world, performing
all night in his blanketed cage.

Mercy

An absolute sound,
this soughing above
the tops of trees.
For the longest while
I couldn't look up, so much
did I long to see the ocean,
rough and whitened.

Such soft ululations,
such a drumroll of feathers!
Yet it was no other weather
than Wind. I looked up; the sky
lay blue as always, Biblical
and terrifying, just where
it was supposed to be.

The Sisters: Swansong

We died one by one,
each plumper than the mirror
saw us. We exited obligingly,
rattling key chains and
cocktail jewelry, rehearsing
our ghostly encores.

Glad to be rid of pin curls
and prayers, bunions
burning between
ironed sheets—we sang
our laments, praised God
and went our way

quietly, were mourned
in satin and chrysanthemums,
whiskey and cake, old gossip
evaporating into cautionary tales.
Does it matter who went
first? Corinna or Fay,

heartache or coronary,
a reckless scalpel or
a careless life—whoever was left
kept count on the dwindling
rosary: Suzanna, Kit.
Mary. Violet. Pearl.

We all died of insignificance.

Now the Dead Will Dance the Mambo

—Achill Island, County Mayo, Ireland, June 2000

Last night the shadow of a cloud rolled off the bare mountain
like a shawl slipping from the shoulder of a giant.
Shirts on the clothesline sagged in rain.
We burned turf, fists of earth blackening in the fireplace,
room full of poets' books leaning rumpled, half-asleep.
All night a radio sang in Irish, tongues sod-hard with lament
or celebration. Then the BBC news, and the announcer's lips
pinching the name: Tito Puente, The Mambo King, dead in New York.

I would listen to Tito's records and see my father years ago:
black hair shiny as the spinning disk, combed slick
before the dance. I learned to spy on his mambo step,
drummed the pots and kitchen tables of Brooklyn.
I saw Tito Puente, too, hammering *timbales* on the Jazzboat
in Boston Harbor, brandishing drumsticks overhead
to scatter the malevolent spirits that grabbed at his hair.
Guadalupe pushed backstage to return with Tito's drumstick,
splintered from repeating, always repeating the beat of slaves.
Here, on this island, I rehearse the Irish word for drum:
bodhrán, gripped by hand like the *pandereta*,
circle of skin and wood for the grandchildren of slaves
to thump as they sang the news in Ponce, Puerto Rico.

Again today the rain grays the graying stones.
We shake away drizzle in the pub dwarfed by mountains.
In brown Guinness light we squint to see
the posters of their Easter dead: James Connolly
bellowing insurrection to the Citizen Army,
the year 1916 ablaze above his head, numbers torched
like the pillars of an empire's monuments to itself.
The bartender says Connolly eyed the firing squad
strapped to a chair in the stonebreakers' yard,

gangrene feasting on his wound so he could not stand.
I tell the bartender that Puerto Rico has its Easter dead:
a march on Palm Sunday, colonial police intoxicated
by the incense of gun smoke, Cadets of the Republic
painting slogans on the street in their belly-blood.
That was Ponce in 1937, and Rafael still says:
My mother left in a white dress and came home in a red dress.

Tito Puente is dead, and we are in a pub on Achill Island
plundering the jukebox, flipping between the Wolfe Tones
and the Dubliners till we discover Tito's *Oye Como Va.*
The beat is a hand slapping the bar, heads nodding
as if their ears funneled a chant of *yes-yes, yes-yes,*
and when we shoot a game of pool in his memory
the table becomes a dance floor at the Palladium,
cue ball spinning through a crowd of red and green.
Now James Connolly could dance the mambo,
gangrene forever banished from his leg.

Roma Caput Mundi

Their place is now taken
by ruins, but not by ruins
of themselves but of later
restorations, Freud said
of the Senate and People of
Rome—otherwise known
as *SPQR,* inscribed
above the arch of Septimius Severus:
Senatus Populus Que Romanus
Silk Pajamas Quietly Rule Us
Seven Peaches Quite Ripe
Some Passing Qualm Resurfaced
Some Private Quarrel Revived
Same Palatial Quiz Revisited
Some Possible Quiet Remains

At the place

where three roads met, ancient
Romans posted news: *trivia*
they called it, for the way
that all roads lead only
to roam until we end up
at memory and find not
what we left there
but the history of how we wanted it
to be. We might as well call
the fine line finishing off
each letter of Roman type
seraph, the peonies lifting
up from the loam
and the sheaves of hosannas
we call hostas, *Romans,*
every one, rising from the
ruins of what we've become.

ROBERT FARNSWORTH

A Classical Education

None of us would have admitted having sentiments
or fears, but we had to have the right loafers, wide
belt, sober tie, a madras jacket, hair just too long,
and a studied slouch, suggesting bored intelligence

and the athlete's effortless grace. It was 1967, part
and not part of what's called now, with more than a hint
of weariness, an era. Under old class photographs
we read Cicero and Homer, and robotically recited

Tennyson. Spindle-legged or fat as seals, we spent
our vanity and love and bravado on battering each
other, or on obsessively averaging our grades.
The proud and pretty among us were so certain of their

futures—they would have it all. But there rose
in some of us, beyond the endless posturings
and performance checks, the hope of both indulging
and mastering desire: what *The Theogony* told us had

transformed the void, what football players claimed
as ultimate virtue, what us bookish types would figure
and refigure in long, loose sentences of waterfront
description. Tonight, reading Ovid brings back all our

fuddled groping at the world's ancient body, our
giggling over what myth was letting us in on: capricious
hungers, awful prides, crazy, jealous passions played
through to death or ecstasy. We thought dead languages

dead, just the stuff of make-work: it was 1967 after
all—everything was changing. But our gathering

blood knew better than we how mysteries would ravish
and transform us. So I meditated on the irresistible

lust of Zeus, Diana's ferocious chastity . . . those coils
of slippery skin, desire weaving earth and flesh
together—laurel, mulberry, seafoam. Gods lay down
with the human until the human became divine: those

shuddering loins we craved and feared were a holy
profanation, if only we could have known. And though
they were watching, knew all of our confused desires,
they would only confirm, not answer them. *Of bodies*

changed I sing. O Siren songs. Now this is what we
feared, unaware, isn't it, while yearning became a kind
of hatred, or subtler corrosive in our hearts. Tonight
I heard again the harsh, tuneless chant of bonding boys

before a game, and the old rock 'n' roll pouring down
from dormitories. Now that I've come home, and decanted
Ovid's ancient songs, I can read again my life's
gradual translation into hours of literate silence,

into one affection that must assuage knowing at last
how the body is singular and brutal. Almost, almost
redeemed by a lover's hand in the dark—that wild,
transfiguring touch the desperate boy I was desired.

Conjecture Number One Thousand

If I loved him—I loved him—
I cannot remember the whole middle part
where the gods never go, they'd be bored.

Of the beginning—how many poems
to describe his buoyancy,
and gaze, and hands—

how many times can the act of whispering together
be a remonstrance to the underworld?

And the end is completely remembered—
flinging his clothes in the driveway,
like a movie—domestic comedy they call it.

Okay, finito.

But no, I want to know, still, what it was
there in the everyday
that turned the connection into threat.

If I could I would blame the blameless
spoons, or the air where springtime bluebirds
—all rufous breasts—returned.

They had been to the Amazon.

Maybe we went wrong—we lacked
a winter vacation—never gambling in Miami,
never asking some beautiful Cuban

to deflect the ordinary.

This cold light—New Hampshire fall—
illuminates a trembling,
probably the wind. Or something with a purpose.

Baci, Of Course

The walking on alone of it, stooping (I could say I was picking
     flowers)
the birthday near Easter when the word, girl, seemed foolish,
the resistance to make the past read like Rilke when it read like
     KRAZY
KOMICS, the adoration of Rembrandt despite the vogue away
from Rembrandt, the feeling of kinship with the criminal,
Caravaggio,
the interior city: wanting to get the secrets,
the leveling at sea level,
bluish marks because love was rough or I couldn't eat red meat,
no cigarettes, finding a spider, *Brown Recluse,* in the cellar
and knowing fear where once brutal insects were excitement,
the white powdery eye shadow look of all Sienese in paintings,
a rising moon preferable to one that wanes, a full sea preferable to
low tide's drifting dead,
and the always razzle-dazzle of a man's
walk, hips turned not in increments but turned, an iota of
turning, meaning, *Yeah, I could,* meaning skin,
the sweet small of the back, and kisses, *baci, baci,*
I think God abandons me not in an explosion, but, Himself, tired,
like wind over the hills early evening where the heat still is—

TERRI FORD

Song for Two Bodies

Lumber me up, my licky bloke,
my one so far unseen, my limbered
timber boy. What luck

to bucky suck till sated,
luminous tuneful body
to play on, even now long play

me on. I hanker for
the slow bang of my love,
his howl and cheek, shebang, the

flaming oh's of his moany
mouth. There will be tongues,
I think, and bells.

CHRIS FORHAN

Lonesome Tableau

Tacked on the wall, a map of my sad luck,
places self-pity has planted its flag.
In the bed, my body, a book in its hand.

In my skull, a voice reciting the words
on the page one moment—an exegesis
of a bungled kiss—and then the next

enumerating the canyons and cliffs, the familiar
indigenous flowers and patterns of weather,
in the vast mapped reaches of my despair.

There are things it is best not to speak out loud:
deepest being, conscience of God,
though sometimes one desires to read them

in a book, then set the book down while the mind
wends its way around a sentence's sense,
but the mind is sorrow's topographer—

it wants as well to ponder the sheer
slopes on the map. It flatters itself
that its talent is being two places at once

when it hasn't the will to be anywhere at all
for long—certainly not in this book
I cannot finish, so thick, so difficult,

with its flashbacks, its too many women and men,
each attached to a hope, an intention.
In every room of my house, the same

distracting map of my own lost chances
but thousands of books to choose from. Perhaps
it's time for the tale of a ghost ship, timbers

groaning as it drifts with cracked mast
and tattered sail for months on the open sea.
Perhaps it's time for a poem with no people in it.

Flamingo

Libby killed herself just before the holidays, and so the flamingo stayed where it had been hidden—in the rotten shed at the edge of our yard. I'd often sneak out to look at it. The flamingo seemed incredibly big, its wooden neck reaching up past the shelves of potting soil and garden shears. It stood six feet tall, was painted a brilliant pink, and back then, when I was nine years old, I thought it was the most beautiful thing I'd ever seen. I'd close the door and stand there in the shed, the smell of lawn-mower gas making me dizzy. The flamingo's wood had been sanded smooth, and I'd lay my cheek against the curve of a wing, or wrap my hands around the sturdy pole legs.

Sometimes I told the flamingo things that were upsetting me. I never planned on doing this, it just happened. I told it about things that went on in school, or my dreams, or if my mother was going through one of her bad times. I might describe how she had called in sick to work again from her job as a secretary at the local high school, and was in the house, right that moment, still in her nightgown, even though it was four-thirty in the afternoon. I would explain how if I went to her she would want me to hug her as she cried, or hold her hand as she slept. Or I might tell how on some mornings my mother would wake me singing "High Hopes" or "You Are My Sunshine." How she'd throw open my curtains, laughing, then scoop me into her arms and carry me down the stairs before I fully woke up. On those mornings, her hazel eyes were bright, and her blond hair was clean and shiny, swept up with a few pieces curling at her neck. Her frosty lipstick was perfect. And it would seem, for a moment, as if those other mornings—when she could barely bring herself to get out of bed, much less hold a comb in her hand—had never really happened.

My mother and her two friends, Dee and Loretta, had originally bought the flamingo with the plan of leaving it in Libby's yard late Christmas Eve night, decorated with lights and tinsel. Before Libby died, the four of them had a joke which involved leaving embarrassing lawn decorations in each other's yards. My mother had planted her share of tacky windmills and wooden cutouts of geese or squirrels. One morning we woke to find a rock garden, made from stones painted orange and pink, gracing the area around our mailbox.

Of all of my mother's friends, I loved Libby the most. She was strong and sure, never weak. She wore tailored dresses and heady perfume. She smoked, drove fast, and flipped the finger at anyone who got in her way. She was the first woman, the first adult, I'd ever heard say the word "fuck." She called me "kid" and would touch me lightly on the head, a touch that said she understood how things were, and I loved her especially for this.

Libby had always known how to talk my mother up from her low times, or down from her craziness. Besides me, Libby had been the only other person who really understood how bad my mother could get. Even though they had other friends like Dee and Loretta and some neighbors, the two of them were the closest, and only Libby really saw my mother at her worst. Neither had much of a family—Libby was divorced with no children, and my mother just had me. My father was never mentioned, and if I asked my mother, which I rarely did, she'd say, "He came and he went," or "I knew him for a short time and then he was gone." That was it. So she and Libby were on their own. They were always there for each other, or rather Libby was usually there for my mother.

But then Libby was diagnosed with a disease that had been winding through the women in her family; she'd seen her grandmother, and more recently a younger sister, die slowly and full of pain. And so when she realized her life was over, she didn't wait until she was forced to bed. Instead she secretly planned out her death, detailed and thoughtful. A few days before Christmas she overdosed on medication, leaving notes and gifts for her loved ones, explaining her actions, asking them to understand and not be angry. For my mother she left a box containing an angel made of paper and dried leaves painted gold, as well as a picture of Libby and my mother when they were twelve, the summer they first became friends, posing in their bathing suits in the backyard. Libby is looking at the camera straight on, her lips puckering into a kiss, and my mother is whirling around beside her with her hands held up, the sun shining on her skin. Across the bottom Libby had written, *Don't forget what that felt like—the sun on your face.*

After Libby died, my mother fell into a series of downswings, each worse than the one before. Sometimes she would stay in bed for an entire day, the velvet curtains in her room drawn. I tried to do things like the laundry or dishes. I'd bring food to her—soup or cereal or toast with cheese, which was the extent of what I knew how to make back then.

"Get in bed with me," she'd often say. "Please."

It was usually late afternoon, after I'd come home from school. I'd crawl under the flowered sheet and press myself against her. I'd feel the way the flat of her back fit mine perfectly, but she'd be shaking with sobs and hiccups that wouldn't let her breathe, and so it was scary, not comforting, to lie so close.

"I can't stand it," she'd say in the darkness. There would be light hinting around the edges of the closed heavy drapes, and I'd wish I were a simple wisp of air, that I could rise and slip through that crack of light into what was left of the day.

"I can't stand that every night for those last few weeks, she must have climbed the stairs to her bedroom, alone with all that *fear*. And there was nothing I could do."

She was talking about Libby, although now I think it was also a way to talk about herself. I am convinced fear had something to do with her taking to bed for days, and the mania that often preceded or followed. Back then, I had fears of my own, but there was no one to listen. Only the flamingo, and even after what happened with Mr. Schenley that summer, even after I lost my voice and could not speak, still I went out to the shed. I would close the door and sit in the dark beside the flamingo's feet. The large bird would stand silent, tilting its head toward me, its glass eyes watching steadily.

I stopped speaking because of a car accident a few days after the school year ended in June. It happened on the way home from swimming practice at the YWCA. Mr. Schenley, a man who lived a few neighborhoods away, was driving the car. He came to take me and two other girls home. It was his turn in the carpool, even though his daughter hadn't been there that evening, which wasn't unusual, since she seemed to be sick a lot. I hadn't missed his daughter, who I didn't especially like, although I felt sorry for her. She was a tall, big-boned girl who hunched her body to appear smaller, but only appeared hunched. She kept to herself. And even though she was a fine swimmer, she'd often panic in meets, having to crawl out of the pool halfway through her race and run to the bathroom, where she'd throw up. Then she'd come back out and sit away from the rest of the team, holding her stomach, tears in her eyes.

That evening I was the last girl to be dropped off, and by the time it was only Mr. Schenley and me in the car, it had become quite dark. The sky filled with black clouds, and rain began to pound on the roof and windshield. It was one of those sudden, angry summer storms, completely unexpected. Mr. Schenley was acting strangely. He was perspiring heavily from the time he picked us up; I noticed the wet stains under his arms. And once we were alone he seemed to have trouble breathing. He coughed and cleared his throat and made snort-like noises. I politely ignored all of this.

What caused the accident was simply that the car skidded out of control and across to the wrong lane. We'd been going fast on a curvy back road with no guardrails, a few miles from my house. Trying to avoid an oncoming car, we slid off the road altogether and were airborne, dropping for what seemed a long while, until I heard a booming clap, like the earth was caving in, and I realized we had crashed and rolled into the rocky stream below. My eyes were open the whole time. I saw everything. I saw Mr. Schenley's body flopping around like a rag doll, because he didn't have his seatbelt on like I did. I saw his head crack the windshield, and blood spray out of his nose and mouth. Then he looked as if he were doing some kind of strange acrobatic flip in the front seat, so his feet were on the ceiling, and one of his fists shot over and slammed my jaw, at which point I must have blacked out. When I regained consciousness, it was strangely quiet except for the rain on the roof, and the hiss and click of the cooling car parts. I could hear water running somewhere close-by. The inside lights were on, and there was smoke drifting through the car, but I couldn't see a fire. It was then I realized that I had lost my voice, because I tried to scream for the first time as I noticed that Mr. Schenley was upside down in the seat beside me, his head craned around facing me, his neck in a crazy, twisted position. His eyes were wide open but completely flat, like those of a doll or stuffed animal. His nose was a bloody, purple mess.

I did not tell my mother or police or doctors any of this. I let them think I was too frightened to remember, and so they accepted my silence a little more easily. And so I also did not tell them what happened before we crashed, in fact the reason that we even did crash. That Mr. Schenley was taking the long way home, and that at some point during the drive he began to act even more nervous, and finally rested his hand between my legs. I looked over, and his fly was open, so I could see a part of him that was terrifying, that I couldn't believe was real. I closed my eyes then, and even though my heart and head and stomach began to thump with panic, I sat very still, as if I had suddenly fallen asleep. I thought that perhaps if I did not move, if I pretended to ignore Mr. Schenley's now erratic breathing, and the way his hand had begun to make the smallest nudging motion, then it might all go away. I might be somehow able to slip out and float above it all until whatever was done was done.

I didn't tell anyone that actually the crash was, in a way, a huge relief, the escape I desperately needed. That after it happened I wondered if I had somehow wished it into being, and if I should feel guilty, like I often do about anything. I didn't tell anyone that his last words were, simply and stupidly, *Oh shit,* and that I would later hear him shouting those words in the middle of the night, loud and clear in my bedroom, and each time I'd wake with a start and smell the burning stink of the wrecked car, see his white hand dangling across the seat, the hand that had been on me just before, and that even then, even when I knew it was dead, I was still very scared of that hand.

Luckily the school year was finished, so it was fairly easy to exist in my silence. Except for the summer swim team, which was no big deal, I was out of my normal loop of activities and friends. The doctors at the hospital said I had gone into some kind of psychological shock. They told my mother I'd speak when I was ready. But after a few days she began to worry. She'd sit on my bed and hold my hands saying, "Not even one word for *me*?" And when I didn't make a noise she would lie across my legs and weep into the bedspread.

A week after the accident she took me to my regular doctor, a wise, older man who was respected in the community, and who was one of the few people in my life who made me feel safe. My mother was in a stern mood that day. She wore a serious gray dress with long sleeves, even though the early summer air was hot and humid. Her thick, blond hair was yanked back into a tight bun. Since my accident she had collected herself, but was still acting irritated—muttering under her breath and swearing a lot. She was likely to explode at the smallest things, like her cereal getting soggy, or the clasp of her purse not working quite right. She acted as if my not speaking were a heavy burden upon her, as if it somehow made me unmanageable. At the doctor's office she put a hand on each of my shoulders and directed me into the examining room, saying, "Well, sir, I'm sorry to say, but we do have a problem here."

The doctor glanced at her and then turned his attention to me. He examined my healing minor injuries and nodded with satisfaction. He touched my neck and peered down my throat like they'd done when I was in the hospital. I liked his hands—cool and gentle on my skin. They were hands that could tell when something was wrong. After he finished examining me, he looked into my eyes, and it was as if he'd been in Mr. Schenley's car with me and knew what had happened. The way he looked at me made me want to cry with relief. But I didn't, and he sent me out into the waiting room while my mother stayed in to talk with him. When the door finally opened about fifteen minutes later, she emerged with a stiff smile that made her look much less pretty. She took me by the arm and walked me briskly to the car, so I stumbled trying to keep up with her fast-moving feet. She was wearing low-heeled pumps that made a sharp, clacking sound. A few times she wobbled as an ankle gave way into a crack in the pavement.

Once we were in the car, she turned to me, but her eyes looked over my head to the parking lot beyond us. It was as if she were onstage and looking past the faces of the audience, or she'd lose her nerve.

"Damn," she said, and I thought she was going to start crying, but she just pressed her lips together and paused. Then she shook her head and started again. She told me clearly and slowly that I didn't have to speak if I didn't want to, that she could wait this out, but that under no circumstances was I to think that I couldn't talk to her, because she was listening, she really was, and I should know that.

I nodded.

"And," she said after thinking for a moment and tapping her fingers on the steering wheel, "I just hope you're through with this by September. You can't go back to school without talking, you know."

I nodded again.

"Okay, then," she said and drove us home.

I knew she was right, that if I still wasn't talking when school began it would be a problem. The other kids would not quite believe it. They'd sneak up and scare or tickle me to see if I would scream. They'd taunt me since I had no defense. But somehow I expected to be talking by then. My silence didn't feel like something that was to last a lifetime. It was more like a temporary relief, a chance to rest. Like when you're sick and are glad to have a good reason to stay in bed, pulling the covers up to your chin. I knew quite well that my ability to speak was not gone forever, it was just that I couldn't bear to do it right *then*.

I also felt on some level that if I spoke, then difficult things would be expected of me. I would have to say what really happened in Mr. Schenley's car. Or I would be asked over and over what it was like to stay silent for so long. Or my mother would say, "I just can't, honey," if I asked her to please get out of bed, please get dressed. She'd say, "It's just too much," and I'd have to sit beside her in her darkened room and let her lean on me. I'd have her towel in my hands, and the water would be running in the bathroom where I'd turned it on a few minutes before. I'd help her take off her nightgown and place a robe around her shoulders.

"Don't worry," I'd have to tell her. "I'm here. You'll be just fine."

In July, a month after my accident, my mother and her friends decided to have their own kind of memorial service for Libby. Back when Libby died before Christmas, they could stand to do nothing more than attend the required ceremony and burial, and so they had intended to have their own kind of service, when they felt the time was right. They finally decided on July 15th because it was Libby's birthday. In their eyes, the flamingo was a symbol for everything they loved about Libby, and so they wanted to plant it on her grave, a final gift, a last laugh.

The week before the memorial service, my mother's mood changed drastically. She was suddenly riding high, energetic—a string pulled tight and getting tighter. As usual, I did not trust her manic bursts, and watched her cautiously. For the past few mornings she had risen early without my waking her, and showered before I even came downstairs from my bedroom. Since her job was finished for the summer, she had time to do a number of day-time projects. She sewed a light blue cotton dress. She embroidered daisies on several pairs of my socks. And one afternoon I came in from the yard where I had been playing for a few hours to find she had painted the bathroom yellow, not a soft color, but the more orange shade of cheddar cheese.

On the night before the memorial service, I could not sleep. I thought about my mother's burst of energy, and a terrible hope began to tug at me, a hope I didn't want to give into, but couldn't resist. I had watched my mother all day as she ran around our small house, cleaning and pushing things in and out of the oven because the next day the "girls" were coming over to have dinner and drinks before they all went to visit Libby's grave. As I lay in bed I began to hope that perhaps her recent bout of dark moods had passed. I imagined her back to her old self, which, although moody, now seemed incredibly stable compared to how she'd been since Libby's death. I thought maybe her depression had run its course. Maybe this memorial service for Libby was breaking her spell of grief. She'd spent the whole day getting things ready. She'd even gone to the grocery store herself instead of calling for delivery. Food was stacked in our refrigerator: sliced roast beef, ham salad, potato salad, pickled eggs, upside-down cake, a tray of assorted cheese and crackers.

I rose from my bed and walked barefoot through the house. As I passed my mother's bedroom, I heard her mumble in her sleep, then turn over and sigh. I unlatched the kitchen screen door and crossed the damp grass to the shed. The flamingo was there in the darkness, its body and part of its oversized beak illuminated by a crack of moonlight.

Now, outside in the shed, my hope disappeared. I began to

believe what I feared most: that my mother was on a temporary high, that she'd probably be fine the next day, and maybe the next, then she'd crash again. This knowledge sunk low in my gut, so I could feel it pulsing there, like a heart that belonged to a desperate part of myself. At that moment I somehow understood that each time my mother would sink a little deeper. And I was right. Up until I graduated from high school, I would see her in and out of hospitals, undergoing counseling and medications. For most of that time, I would live with a retired schoolteacher across town, who in the past had taken foster children into her home. Her name was Miss Mildred, and she would turn out to be patient and kind. For years, until her death long after I was grown, Miss Mildred would remain one of my closest friends, and more than once she would save me from spiraling down myself, if only by listening to me.

But I couldn't know any of this as I stood alone in the shed that night. All that was ahead of me was another day, and each day had begun to feel like a wall that needed to be unbricked, piece by piece, and if I could get through without it all crumbling, then it was a good day.

I squinted in the darkness to look more closely at the flamingo. My mother had tied a white ribbon around its neck for the memorial service, and it fluttered in the light breeze from the open doorway.

I felt a little guilty for not speaking to it since I had lost my voice, even though I knew it didn't matter. The flamingo knew what I wanted to say. In fact I wondered if I had ever really spoken out loud to the flamingo at all. Maybe those other times in the shed, before I stopped speaking, I had just thought so hard that I imagined I heard my own voice.

I'm sorry, I said, but the sound was somewhere deep inside of me, and what came out was barely a whisper. Still I moved my mouth to give the silent words shape, send them through the air. I had no desire to hear my voice right now. The quiet of the shed and the flamingo's steady stare felt like peace to me. But I knew it would not last. I knew that words I was not speaking were somehow building up inside of me, and at some point I would have to let them out. I pictured a small sac in the very center of me that was growing heavy and tight, like a balloon filling with water, eventually bursting. But for now I was trying to ignore it.

Mr. Schenley was a creep, I told the flamingo. Then I went over how happy I was in the hospital bed when I woke and found out I was okay and, in fact, not in very much pain, and that they were burying Mr. Schenley two days later.

The flamingo looked back at me and did not flinch. Its eyes, steady and black, never left my face.

I silently told it other things then, like the only person I'd ever known to die besides Mr. Schenley was Libby, and that the night after her funeral she came to visit me in a dream. She sat at the foot of my bed in her white burial dress and smoked a cigarette. Her dark hair was brushed away from her face, and her lips were painted movie-star red. I loved seeing her there. The dream was so real I could smell the smoke that seemed to hover around her head like a halo, and feel her hand, which was warm, not cold, as she stroked my face and said, "Hang in there, kid."

I also told it how scared I felt when my mother's hands shook as she tried to do anything delicate, like put on mascara, or thread a needle, or put a key in a lock.

My mother might die, too, I told the flamingo. Then I turned around and went back inside the house to bed.

Early the next evening, Dee and Loretta showed up on our doorstep. As I expected, my mother was still riding her wave and had been up early, doing laundry for most of the day, washing everything from curtains and rugs and pillows to old Halloween costumes stored in the top of my closet. She'd ironed all of it, and our house had a clean, starched smell. For the memorial service she put on a polka-dotted dress that she often wore to work during the school year. Her hair was pulled back by a wide cotton band, except for a few pieces that escaped and clung in curls to her sweaty forehead and cheeks. She looked pretty and fresh but tense, the bones in her jaw locked tight, the muscles in her neck rigid. I'd kept out of her way for most of the day, although occasionally she'd walk by and tousle my hair. "I feel good today, sweetie," she'd say. And once, as a joke, she looked over her shoulder and said, "What was that? Did I hear something?" as if I had spoken. Then she came to where I was sitting on the couch with my book and gave my hand a squeeze.

Dee and Loretta looked something like sisters. They were both short and plump, with hair they wore in tightly curled perms. Dee, however, was more fair and had a soft, high-pitched voice, while Loretta was darker and had the kind of voice people get from smoking since they were young. My mother invited them in, and they stood around in the kitchen, looking at the flamingo and its white bow with reverence. That morning she had dragged it from the shed into the house. The flamingo seemed much thinner and delicate out of its familiar habitat. I did not feel at ease with it like I did in the shed. Seeing the flamingo in the kitchen was like having a friend over to your house for the first time—a friend you'd been so comfortable with at school, but once they enter your house, you both act differently, and you notice things about your friend that you may not have before, like they talk too much, or use a silly voice when they address your mother, or they look in your closet too long.

My mother and her friends stood around eating and drinking brandy out of delicate little glasses. Whenever my mother lifted her glass to her mouth, I could see the way her arm shook, as if she were shivering in the heat. I stood quietly among them, but Dee and Loretta paid attention to me anyway. They petted my hair or laid their hands on my face.

"You're becoming beautiful," Dee said in her high, breathy voice. "Just like your mother."

"Cat still got your tongue?" Loretta asked with a husky guffaw. She pinched my ear and offered me a sip of her brandy, which felt like it was burning a hole straight into my heart.

After an hour or so, they took to the task of fitting the flamingo into the back of Loretta's station wagon. They packed Libby's favorite brand of scotch and some paper cups in a basket, which they gave me to hold on my lap. I noticed my mother was becoming anxious, her eyes moving a little too quickly, and once or twice filling with tears. On the ride there, she sat with me in the back seat, the flamingo poking between us. She laid her hand on my knee and looked out the window.

At the gravesite, they steadied the flamingo on the grass, which had grown thick and tough from the summer rains. Loretta found a rock and wedged it under the large feet on one side so it was level. They looped a string of cheap, battery-operated Christmas lights around its neck and wings, and straightened the white bow. I stayed close-by, sitting on the hood of the car, watching.

Dee handed out paper cups and poured scotch. She raised her glass. "Happy birthday, Libby," she said, lifting her arm higher. "I'm toasting this day which honors your birth"—she paused for a moment and thought hard, squinting into the grass at her feet—"because I want to remember your time here with us, alive, and how you made each of us better in some way." She downed her scotch then, throwing back her curly head, wiping a hand across her lips when she finished.

Loretta followed, toasting Libby's laugh, and the unexpected humor she found in the worst of situations. She toasted her toughness, and recalled the time Libby woke as a young man was trying to break into her house, and chased him in her silk robe clear down the street. She said that Libby was brave, and even her suicide was not something weak, but a way to die with dignity. "I know you live on!" she shouted suddenly, looking into the sky as if she might see Libby floating there. For a moment I looked up, too, and imagined I saw Libby wearing a pink gown, with wings instead of arms. Then Loretta gulped her scotch, leaving a few drops in the bottom of the cup, which she sprinkled onto the grave near the flamingo's feet.

When it was my mother's turn, she raised her cup and said, "She always stood by me." She bit her lip and closed her eyes. She whispered, "She held me up," and began to cry big, rolling tears down her cheeks, so that Dee and Loretta turned their backs to the flamingo and put their arms around my mother, swaying side to side.

Finally Loretta took a step back and pulled out a pack of cigarettes from the pocket of her long skirt. She handed one to each of them, and they smoked silently, a last tribute. No one said anything about the way my mother's shoulders were still jerking with sobs, even though no sound was coming from her throat, or that her tears had dried in long, black trails of mascara down her face.

They filed back to the car, leaving the flamingo on the grave with the lights still lit. It was beginning to get dark, and the tiny lights seemed as if they were twinkling. Dee and Loretta climbed into the car, sniffling and patting their eyes, but my mother's eyes were now dry and wide open. Her chest was rising and falling quickly, but her breathing was shallow and raspy. She held her hand over her throat.

I stood there for one last second before I climbed into the car. I felt like something bad was on the verge of happening, and yet I couldn't think about anything but how beautiful the flamingo looked, glowing against the darkening summer sky. Its neck reached thin and high, its head tilted slightly down, looking toward where Libby lay. A few fireflies mingled with the colored lights, as if they were falling in love.

"Goodbye," I felt I should say, but instead raised my hand as if I held a glass in it. I toasted the flamingo, silently saying thank you, and that I would miss knowing it was out in the shed night after night. I would have even gone to it and wrapped my arms around its body, but Loretta was starting the car, and in the back seat my mother was stretching a hand toward where I stood, just out of her reach.

By the time they dropped us off, my mother was trembling noticeably. "You all right?" Dee asked as she opened the back door. "Oh, fine," my mother said, but I could see her face doing strange things.

That night I stayed up late, putting food back in the refrigerator, wiping off the table and counters, standing on a footstool in front of the sink to wash the dishes and brandy glasses in warm soapy water. My mother lay in her bedroom, curled up in a ball, still in her dress. I changed into my nightgown, brushed my teeth, then went upstairs and lay on my bed. I thought of the flamingo in the graveyard. It seemed a million miles away, and I became sure that I'd never see it again, and this thought seemed to open up that same desperate place that beat inside of me—the part that hoped when it knew it shouldn't, the part that made me want to cry when I looked into the doctor's eyes, or saw Libby in a dream at the foot of my bed. I gave into a feeling of dread that I'd been trying to ignore for days, but now it was too heavy, like a wet, woolen coat, and I could do nothing but lie there sobbing and shaking. I had been turned inside out, and I felt so completely awful that all I could do was let it happen. That's when a broken, husky sound came to my ears; it was like a shout being strangled, so only bits and pieces of it came out. And it took me a few seconds to realize that it was my own voice, coming from deep inside me.

I fell asleep then, and dreamt I could not swallow. A terrible dream of wandering around alone with my hands gripping my neck. I understood quite clearly that the blockage in my throat was a baby bird, I could feel it shuddering and chirping, and although I wanted it gone, I knew I had to feed it. I dropped flowers and tiny beetles into my mouth until I felt the bird grow calm, then it slowly emerged, a tiny crow that was wet and sticky. I held it in my hand, and it looked up at me, its black eyes unblinking.

I woke early in the morning to yellow light slanting across the wooden floorboards of my attic bedroom. I was exhausted, my body heavy on the bed, but I pushed myself up on an elbow, then to a sitting position, and finally stood. I walked over to the night light and switched it off, as I had done every day I could remember. I opened my bedroom door, stepped through, and closed it. I was being careful, although I don't think I knew why at the time, but now looking back, it seems I had some sort of premonition of what was about to happen. That I was about to find my mother half-naked in the bathroom, passed out but nowhere near death from the pills she had swallowed, which only amounted to half a bottle, and the one small slash she had made on her wrist, not even cutting into the biggest vein there.

But still. There was my mother with her dress unzipped, exposing her shoulders and breasts, collapsed in a puddle of blood on the bathroom tile. The tub was half-filled, and the arm that was not cut was hanging into the water. I screamed then, a choked, scratchy sound, which only made her open her eyes groggily and close them. But what I screamed surprised and alarmed me, not only because I had not heard my voice for so long, but because of the word that came out of my mouth. "Mother!" I'd screamed. I'd never called her "Mother," which had always seemed formal to me. But as soon as it came out of my mouth, I knew that it was what I'd call her from then on.

I went to her and lifted her hand out of the tub. Her fingers were white and shriveled. I pulled her dress up to cover the front of her, and laid a towel over her head and shoulders. In the hallway, as I dialed 911, my hands were shaking and my breathing rattled in my

ears. "My mother wants to kill herself," I whispered to the opera-
tor. Her voice was clear and calm on the other line while she asked
me questions and waited through my deep breaths before each
answer. After she hung up, with the promise of an ambulance on
the way, I stayed there for a minute with the receiver still to my ear,
because the sound of her voice had comforted me.

That evening a lady from the hospital took me to Miss Mildred's house for the first of many long visits. This time it would
be for two months, until my mother was finally released from the
rehabilitation home where she'd been staying. Miss Mildred's
house was large and creaky and surrounded by shady trees that
rustled outside of the windows all day and night. Her clothing
always smelled like lavender. She was quiet, and we took our time
getting to know each other. Often we passed the hot summer
afternoons just sitting and drinking iced tea. For dinner she'd
prepare fine meals of meat and salad, and she'd make sure I drank
a tall glass of milk. I was relieved that even though I had my voice
back, I wasn't being pressured to say anything at all. And on those
nights when bad dreams woke me, Miss Mildred and I would sit
out on her patio with blankets wrapped around us. It was there I
told her what really happened in Mr. Schenley's car. I also told her
that I thought if perhaps I had come downstairs that morning
and found my mother dead in the bathroom, I wouldn't have
been so sad. Miss Mildred would wait until I was finished, and
then she would pick me up and carry me back to my bed, where
she'd sit close in her lavender-scented nightgown, a hand on my
forehead or cheek, until I slept.

But that's a different story. That's a story of being saved.

This is a story about my mother. She is the one I am trying
most to remember—how in her hospital gown a few days later,
lying in bed, she held her arms out to me as she saw me in the
doorway, which a nurse gently pushed me through. My mother
held her arms out to me, and I went to her. And in each step I recognized something new in myself. That I could go to my mother,
stand still in her embrace, remain steady as she rocked me and
wept on my shoulder, and not feel the slightest bit of hope tug at
me. Even as I was taking steps toward her, I was also stepping
away, my need for her already lessening. I had Miss Mildred to

whisper to in the night, and soon there would be others: a babysitter named Fran who would teach me to smoke and convince me I was pretty, a dog named Buddy who would sleep on my feet in bed. There would be a high school teacher who'd stay after class to read my notebooks filled with tediously long poetry. A best friend named Charlotte who'd never waver.

I took steps away from her my whole life, into the arms of others, until now, a grown woman, I finally want to look back. She has been dead ten years, but I have turned around to see her, understand her, write her until she is perfectly clear. And now I find something most surprising, breathtaking even. I find that I recognize her completely, there is little mystery involved. She was simply a woman in need of rest, silence, and someone, anyone, to stand beside her.

MARILYN HACKER

Paragraph for Hayden

Quadruple bypass: yes, he had it.
What happens next is anybody's guess.
After the surgeon's pre-op visit
he pulled the tubes and needles out, got dressed
and stalked outside to smoke a cigarette.
The surgeon threatened not to operate.
Old heart, old curmudgeon,
old genius, terrified old man
who more than anyone knows form
is one rampart of sanity,
your mind is ringing like a fire alarm
and you still smoke three packs a day.
Not lover, barely friend, from this distance
I break your rule and say,
Stay in the present tense. Stay in the present tense.

JEFFREY HARRISON

The Pond of Desires

"…most desires end up in stinking ponds…"
—Auden

The water, if you can call it that, is black
as tar, and the lily pads are seared at the edges,
curling up as if trying not to touch it
more than they have to. The lilies themselves have gone
to seed, their pure white petals only a memory,
like the bass that used to cruise in the shadows.
The only fish left are suckers, kissing the same muck
that a lone duck upends itself to peck at:
so there must be some nourishment yet in these
jettisoned desiderata. Somewhere down there
is your brief, secret crush on a student,
the time you came within a kiss's width
of seduction, fantasies you hardly notice
yourself having before letting them sink
into this stinking pond. Slowly it fills up
and thickens into a swamp, where, some nights,
during the bullfrogs' lewd reverberations,
the effluvium bubbling up through the ooze
flickers elusively with a bodiless light.

Kickers

Listen to me, said the boys' grandfather. When I was a boy, you had to be smart or you could get hurt.

Their grandfather had already sat down in his old swivel chair. He lit one of his cigars and took a big puff. The boys made themselves comfortable on the floor.

We milked by hand in those days, he said. And you had to look out for kickers. It was hard to tell which heifer was a kicker until you tried to milk her. Kicking seemed like an instinct to some of them, but some of them got better with practice. And just like with a good bucking bronco, you couldn't predict a good kicker's moves.

He laid his cigar down and rubbed his hands together. You had your four types of kickers, he said. There was your sidewinder kicker who'd catch you in the stomach. You have to think of a hind leg going up about two feet and then making a U-turn out to the side at about forty miles an hour.

He made a quick swing of his arm. That's your sidewinder, he said.

Then you had your jackhammer kicker. She'd lift a leg straight up and come down with it straight in the bucket you had under her.

Sort of like your jackhammer kicker was your pogo-stick kicker. She liked to bounce on her rear legs and could just as easy break your jaw with her hip as smash your foot with her hoofs. Main difference between your jackhammer and your pogo stick was that the jackhammer kicker tried to give you a knockout punch and the pogo-stick kicker tried to get you with quick jabs.

But then you had your fourth kind of kicker. Here's where you get your art and finesse. The bumblebee kicker. Maybe you could spot a young heifer as a bumblebee-kicker type, but it usually took her three or four years to perfect her style. The bumblebee kicker's hoof would come up a little off the straw and sort of hang there. Then it would start jittering and bouncing around in the air like it was looking for a target. All of a sudden, Blam! Maybe she'd go for the bucket. Maybe for your wrist. Sometimes she'd take out somebody who was standing behind her. You never knew for sure. Whatever it was she went for, she'd hit it, and it had a real sting!

Wow! said the oldest boy. How'd you learn to keep from getting kicked?

The grandfather relit his cigar.

Now that's another story, he said. You had your factory-made shackles you could hook on the legs of the easy ones. There was rope that you could tie in different ways around the rear legs. Or you could tie a rope tight around the middle. This was supposed to paralyze the rear legs a little bit. Then there was kindness. You don't like to tell too many people about this method because they'll think you're a softy. But I always gave kindness a try. I'd pet and feed a kicker until she trusted me.

Did kindness always work? asked the youngest boy.

Their grandfather looked toward the window, as if he could read all of his memories out there. I'm afraid not, he said. A real kicker just made a profession of it. Kicking is the only thing that interested her, and she made no secret of it. That's why milking was so dangerous when I was a boy.

I've never been kicked by a cow, said the youngest boy.

No, no, said the grandfather. And you probably won't, either.

Because I am nice to them? he asked.

No, no, said the grandfather. Because kicking has been bred out of them. You hardly have to keep your guard up at all anymore when you're around cows.

That's good, isn't it? said the youngest boy.

What do you think? said the grandfather.

The Corn Bin

The shelled corn bin was like a huge box over the alleyway of the corncrib. Millions of crisp and yellow corn kernels, ten feet deep, and ten feet square at the top. The boys liked to dive into it, letting it sting their hands and faces as they squirmed until they almost disappeared into the golden wonder of it all.

Sometimes they pretended it was quicksand, swaying back and forth in it as they slowly sank down to their armpits, and another one of them would fling them a rope in this great but pretend rescue mission.

None of this was dangerous. But the boys were told not to play in the shelled corn bin when it was being emptied. You could get sucked down in a whirlpool of shelled corn. You could get buried in corn so far that you wouldn't be able to get out. You could choke. You could drown in corn is what could happen. You'd be four feet under the corn before the corn chute would be stopped when a wagon under the grain bin was full. Then what? Nobody would know what happened to you. If a boy disappeared, people always looked in the wells and cisterns first to see if he had fallen in. But who would think of looking for a boy in the middle of a big corn bin? It might be months before anybody found you. And then you'd probably be half-eaten by rats.

The youngest boy knew that the problem with doing something you're not supposed to do when the other boys were around was that one of them would always tell—and blame him. They'd say that it was the youngest boy's idea. It's not our fault, they'd say. We tried to stop him, they'd say.

So the youngest boy waited until none of the other boys were watching to go play in the shelled corn bin while it was being emptied into a large wagon beneath it in the corncrib alley.

At first the moving grain was like a golden funnel forming before his eyes, and the small cave-in at the middle was like the center of the flour in a sifter as it slowly indented, or the way the center of a milkshake caves in if you have the straw in the middle. Then he saw the corn start to swirl a little. This is where the grown-ups got that whirlpool idea. But it was no fun if you couldn't feel the kernels of corn moving against your body. There was no way a person could drown in shelled corn, he knew that. It was just another one of those things grown-ups said to keep kids scared. So the youngest boy jumped into the middle of the whirlpool of shelled corn. It was great. It was like having somebody rubbing you softly with a back-scratcher all over your body. Gently scratching you and turning you over at the same time. He lay back and moved his arms the way he would if he were trying to swim on his back. The moving and gently swirling yellow corn was a million little fingers moving across his body, making every inch of him tingle.

Then something grabbed both of his feet from the bottom and started pulling. He thought of the time he hooked a big mud turtle on his fishing line and slowly dragged the stubborn weight to shore. Now he was the mud turtle and something was pulling him. He tried moving his legs the way he would if he were running, but the suction from the opening at the bottom of the corn bin was pulling him down. His hands were still free, and he beat at the corn with them, but all of the kernels were working together now, working against him, working to pull him down under. At first it was the corn dust in his nostrils and eyes, and then the sting of the kernels on his face. He tried to take a deep breath. And couldn't.

It was as if his body exploded then, and light came back as quickly as it had gone out. He pushed corn away from his face and rolled with the swirl of the corn, cupping corn and pulling toward the light, turning over and over the way a log might turn over on the surface of water, but with his arms moving all the while, beating at the corn as he pulled himself against the suction. And then the sucking stopped.

He crawled out of the half-empty corn bin and looked down at what he had conquered.

I'm not four feet under the corn, choked, dead, and drowned, he said to himself. That wasn't so bad, he said to himself. I could do that again if I wanted to.

He stood up and looked down at what he had survived, more proud of himself than he had ever been in his life. He looked around smiling, ready for applause and praise. But there was no one to either punish him for doing what he was not supposed to have done, nor to praise him for surviving the sucking corn.

All right, he said to himself. All right, all right, he said again and again, trying to understand whatever it was he was trying to understand about all this.

Winter Chores

On freezing winter nights, the boys had two chores before going to sleep. They had to tie the blankets down to the bed frames so that they would not toss their covers off in their dreams and get frostbite on their hands and feet. And they had to empty their chamber pot so that what was in it would not freeze and need thawing on the stove in the morning.

One night they remembered to tie down the blankets but forgot to empty the pot. When they were all settled in, someone remembered the pot, but it was so cold that night that no one would get out of bed to take it out. Storm windows had already been put on so they could not even cheat by emptying it out the window.

They argued for a while about whose turn it was to empty the pot and then argued about who would have to thaw it out in the morning if nobody emptied it that night.

If we keep arguing like this, it is going to freeze before we even go to sleep, said one boy.

At least arguing is making it nice and warm under the covers, said another.

That gave the youngest boy an idea. Let's keep the pot under the blankets with us tonight—then it won't freeze, he said.

It will have to be in your bed, said the oldest boy.

All right, said the youngest, if you will be the one who gets out of bed to get it.

The oldest boy jumped out of bed and ran across the cold linoleum floor to get it.

The youngest boy had to loosen his blankets a little bit to get the pot in with him. He put it right under his feet so that he would not trip on it. At first, the metal pot felt cold, but soon it warmed up with him and seemed to keep his feet warm. He told the other boys about this, and within a few nights all the boys were willing to take their turn with the pot in bed with them. Sometimes they even fought over who could have it in his bed— but not so much that they spilled any of it.

Bonsai

One morning beginning to notice
which thoughts pull the spirit out of the body, which return it.
How quietly the abandoned body keens,
like a bonsai maple surrounded by her dropped leaves.
Rain or objects call the forgotten back:
the droplets' placid girth and weight; the dresser's lack of
    ambition.
How strange it is that longing, too, becomes a small green bud,
thickening the vacant branch-length in early March.

The Mountain

One moment, the mountain is clear
in strong morning sunlight. The next, vanished in fog.
I return to Tu Fu, afraid to look up again
from my reading and find in the window moonlight—
but when I do, the fog is still there,
and only the ancient poet's hair has turned gray
while a single wild goose passed, silently climbing.

CYNTHIA HUNTINGTON

The Rapture

I remember standing in the kitchen, stirring bones for soup,
and in that moment, I became another person.

It was an early spring evening, the air California mild.
Outside, the eucalyptus was bowing compulsively

over the neighbor's motor home parked in the driveway.
The street was quiet for once, and all the windows were open.

Then my right arm tingled, a flutter started under the skin.
Fire charged down the nerve of my leg; my scalp exploded

in pricks of light. I shuddered and felt like laughing;
it was exhilarating as an earthquake. A city on fire

after an earthquake. Then I trembled and my legs shook,
and every muscle gripped so I fell and lay on my side,

a bolt driven down my skull into my spine. My legs were
swimming against the linoleum, and I looked up at the underside

of the stove, the dirty places where the sponge didn't reach.
Everything collapsed there in one place, one flash of time.

There in my body. In the kitchen at six in the evening, April.
A wooden spoon clutched in my hand, the smell of chicken broth.

And in that moment I knew everything that would come after:
the vision was complete as it seized me. Without diagnosis,

without history, I knew that my life was changed.
I seemed to have become entirely myself in that instant.

Not the tests, examinations in specialists' offices, not
the laboratory procedures: MRI, lumbar puncture, electrodes

pasted to my scalp, the needle scraped along the sole of my foot,
following one finger with the eyes, EEG, CAT scan, myelogram.

Not the falling down or the blindness and tremors, the stumble
and hiss in the blood, not the lying in bed in the afternoons.

Not phenobarbital, amitriptyline, prednisone, amantadine, ACTH,
cortisone, cytoxan, copolymer, baclofen, tegretol, but this:

Six o'clock in the evening in April, stirring bones for soup.
An event whose knowledge arrived whole, its meaning taking years

to open, to seem a destiny. It lasted thirty seconds, no more.
Then my muscles unlocked, the surge and shaking left my body

and I lay still beneath the white high ceiling. Then I got up
and stood there, quiet, alone, just beginning to be afraid.

COLETTE INEZ

Winter Thoughts

Nights turn a hairpin curve
to dreams:
I need to find our child
a country or a name. I forget which.
Jung remembered the smell of milk
from his high chair,
Woolf, red and purple flowers
sprawled on her mother's dress.

A nun's pink nose
swoops towards me like a bird
in my first recall. Yours?
Papa's pockets bulge with gifts.
Mameh's no, no, hands on hips.
The moon's milky C sits over the gorge.
A child standing on her toes
I scratched my name in chalk,
commenced with a capital C.

Bootprints in snow.
Crows call: "We are crow."
My voice can't bring you here.
When I curve my last letter
at the edge of the page
your ghost breath skims
the back hairs of my neck
close as ink clasped to my pen,
wick bent to flame.

We burn apart.
North, Cassiopeia's W tips to the side.
Dear S., the small M of your lips
whistled what was it in Maine

when red-violet shadows on water
promised us days
mirroring blue bees in the lobelias—
our footprints vanished under stones?

KATIA KAPOVICH

Gogol in Rome

Annoyed with the parochialism of the "fantastic city"
of St. Petersburg and close
to the unexpected end of his life,
Gogol escaped to Rome.
He settled in a colony of Russian artists,
shared lodgings with his bosom friend,
the painter Alexander Ge.
On their long walks they discovered
"the inner meaning of everything."
Gogol, a perpetual titular councilor,
was almost happy there: he could forget
the petty insults of the civil service
and a failed career at the University. He was secretly
working on Book Two of his magnum opus,
Dead Souls, stealing bits of furniture and parts
of the domestic atmosphere
from paintings of late-Romantic friends
into the mansions and orchards
of his grotesque characters. His own
descent into madness occurred in strongly marked stages.
He saw that everything was alive in Mother Nature—
trees, stones, sand on the beach, seashells—
and everything called for his empathy.
He stopped eating, stopped drinking wine
(that blood of grapes), turned almost into a Jainist.
His friends were appalled; his mother freaked
whenever she received another of his
strange and ambiguous letters,
full of advice for improvement of the Fatherland.
His doctors prescribed enemas, hazardous treatment
which seeps potassium out of the body,
causing a deterioration at the heart. He destroyed
his novel, throwing four hundred pages

into the fireplace, and would now spend his days
mostly in bed, covered with three woolen blankets.
"It's cold in Italy, it's dark!" he complained to his servant.
The doctors bled him with leeches until he was dead.

14th Street

In the apartment next door, a boy plays the piano,
Chopin, mostly, though sometimes notes he's made up.
Through the woman's window climbs the noise of 14th Street:
merciless horns, squealing bus brakes, carnival-like music
from an ice cream truck belting "She'll Be Coming Round
the Mountain" over and over and over.

The phone rings: her lover coos, Can I come over?
She hesitates, weighs her desires: company, or listening to
 the piano,
spending the evening with her books. Can you come around
nine? she concedes. How about eight? he counters. I'll cook up
some pasta, open the red Bordeaux, put on a little music—
Eight-thirty, she sighs. Pick up some bread at Palermo's on
 14th Street.

She settles on the couch with *Take Heart* by Molly Peacock.
 14th Street
begins to fade like an old grief. She turns the book over;
the cover: "Hummingbird and Passion Flowers"; inside: the music
of poetry, intelligent passion of form, not so unlike the piano
sonata walking through her wall like a ghost. Upstairs a neighbor screams for quiet. The ice cream truck begins
 another round.

How many times can one listen to "She'll Be Coming Round
the Mountain"? And how *could* a woman ride six horses at once?
 14th Street
is no place for country songs, or a girl from LaGrange. Up
where she's from they play a song once, and then it's over.
She closes the window, eases back on the couch. The piano
overwhelms the street noise; she can return to poems,
 the true music.

In "Blue and Huge," Peacock describes the ocean: "It's like
    music, /
a substance that can't be cut up." The woman smiles. Unlike
    a round
that divides a card game, the ocean doesn't end by chance.
    The piano
is silent. She doesn't notice, so absorbed even 14th Street
can't touch her. She uses sticky notes to mark poems she will
    read over.
Just then, the door buzzer. He croons, Can I come up?

She's regretting their date. I'm not sure I'm up
to this tonight, she says as he selects a CD, puts on some music.
He pulls her toward him. Are you saying it's over
between us? he teases, knowing how to bring her around.
She presses closer, confides: I guess I have to get away from
    14th Street.
That's why I'm here, he whispers. It's just you and me, and
    Monk on the piano.

Later, alone in bed, she thinks about home, wonders if her
    mother's still up
then decides it's too late to call. She can't sleep, keeps replaying
    that music
from the street, thinking about a girl riding six white horses,
    over and over and over.

Thawing Out

1.

You'd brought a hand-carved toy, a wooden ring
Tied by a thong of leather to a stick
And demonstrated with a stab, one quick
Thrust through its circle. Shaken by the thing,
My gaze slid from your freshman composition
Down to your sandals and enameled toes.
Come on, you said, let's cut out—what's to lose,
Why not go get our noses full of spring?

The more fool I. In the botanic garden
You flung your body on me, and I fell
Under your little bitter kiss, your spell,
Sprawling upon the leaf mold, growing ardent
Though premonitions rattled in my bones
Like the freak storm that pelted us with stones.

2.

I can't get over your teeth, nor how that moment
Persists like cooties from a stranger's comb:
Your bare-soled feet fluttering above the dome
Of your small rump. More heavy than cement,
That hailstone-drenched wool skirt you'd not remove,
Barring all access. Thrall to April's law,
I shivered in your arms, began to thaw
A cold susceptibility to love.

Like a dull mule team I'd conveyed you home.
What if I'd lugged you airborne like a bride?
Instead, no sooner did we step inside
Than I took wrangling phone calls, and alarm
Bells jangled in my head—what, fuck your student?
Unlucky Joe, born priest-watched, slow and prudent.

3.
Things eked their way downhill. In arid June
You penned one letter. Soon you'd volunteer
For some dire needy country far from here.
I lived for when your classes would resume,
But in September, though I tried to meet,
My phone calls drew no answer. Still, my heart
Fluttered a moment when along State Street
You strolled in my direction, but apart

From me you kept your eyes, denied your buns
Their usual squirming. Wiser far than I,
You'd known enough to let that day go by,
Yet your brief bonfire had delivered me
From lifetime glacial stasis, set me free
To love, to sow a daughter and four sons.

Hark, Hark

The phones, the long-distance phones are ringing.
The satellite phone from the field camp in Kosovo.
The lawyer's phone in a complex in Palo Alto.
The car phone conveying a child to baseball practice.
In this way the siblings converse and condole

much as the now-vanished Carolina parakeets
with their sunflower-yellow heads and radiant green backs
swooped down to their captured kin
and fluttered all night in noisy flocks
against the cage, their opposing breasts
marked with the wire grids that kept them apart
until the last ornamental bird was extinguished

as we will be, but not without having first
listened in to the ongoing shrill, with all of its
anxieties and triumphs taking place among
the offspring we raised, pre-analog transmission
and the ones they are raising in a cacophony of connection.

LAURIE LAMON

You Think of the Loss of Paradise

When you stood up and walked past the rows
of desks and windows, seeing the yellow and green

trees you had already admired, praising
even the door where you stood before entering,

imagining yourself reading passages of sin or love
or the earth or moon's ashen birth—

what amazement you must have felt
later, looking back down the sunlit aisle

to the blackboard chalk-marked and dry as a cough
the body tires of, tired of nature's aging

catastrophe—you were right to think of the loss
of paradise, on the street folding the ends

of your scarf against your ears so that you could hear
yourself singing, so the tongue's nomenclature

could mean nothing else: not the end
of the century, not the sea's dazzle and hieroglyphs

still beckoning, not the roar of traffic
or the language of signs ground into the dim scene's

capacity for light and darkness. Not darkness.
Not the wind that was there.

Pain Thinks of the First Thing

without sleep without history the first thing
without sound without memory of sound

Pain thinks of origin's trespass *hoof* and *cochlea*
earth without blossom without axis

or column the Yangtze without passage the sea
without apparition and the animals let loose

at Peloponnesus Pain thinks of the first thing
without temple water black as burial's

locust and palm without fruit without water
Pain thinks of the first thing and drinks it

DAVID LEHMAN

March 30

Eighty-one degrees a record high for the day
which is not my birthday but will do until
the eleventh of June comes around and I know
what I want: a wide-brimmed Panama hat
with a tan hatband, a walk in the park
and to share a shower with a zaftig beauty
who lost her Bronx accent in Bronxville
and now wants me to give her back her virginity
so she slinks into my office and sits on the desk
and I, to describe her posture and pose,
will trade my Blake (the lineaments of a gratified
desire) for your Herrick (the liquefaction of
her clothes) though it isn't my birthday and
we're not still in college it's just a cup of coffee
and a joint the hottest thirtieth of March I've ever

PHILIP LEVINE

My Fathers, The Baltic

Along the strand stones,
busted shells, wood scraps,
bottle tops, dimpled
and stainless beer cans.
Something began here
a century ago,
a nameless disaster,
perhaps a voyage
to the lost continent
where I was born.
Now the cold winds
of March dimple
the gray, incoming
waves. I kneel
on the wet earth
looking for a sign,
maybe an old coin,
an amulet
against storms,
and find my face
blackened in a pool
of oil and water.
My grandfather crossed
this sea in '04
and never returned,
so I've come alone
to thank creation
as he would never
for bringing him home
to work, defeat,
and death, those three
blood brothers

faithful to the end.
Yusel Prishkulnick,
I bless your laughter
thrown in the wind's face,
your gall, your rages,
your abiding love
for women and money
and all that money
never bought,
for what the sea taught
you and you taught me:
that the waves go out
and nothing comes back.

Felix Culpa

Down on all fours.

The breaking of rules
the only rule.

Cut off from clear lines
of retreat.

Beguiled by excess.

By like-minded folk
enthroned

in ever tinier courts.

Marsh Marigolds

in memory of Penny Cabot

Decades ago you showed me marsh marigolds
At Carrigskeewaun and behind a dry-stone wall
The water-lily lake's harvest of helleborines.

As you lie dying there can be only one lapwing
Immortalizing at Dooaghtry your minty
Footsteps around the last of the yellow flags.

The Pine Marten

That stuffed pine marten in the hotel corridor
Ended up on all fours in nineteen-thirteen
And now is making it across No Man's Land where
A patrol of gamekeepers keeps missing him.

The Bat

They kept him alive for years in warm water,
The soldier who had lost his skin.
                                    At night
He was visited by the wounded bat
He had unfrozen after Passchendaele,

Locking its heels under his forefinger
And whispering into the mousy fur.

Before letting the pipistrelle flicker
Above his summery pool and tipple there,

He spread the wing-hand, elbow to thumb.
The membrane felt like a poppy petal.

Edward Thomas's Poem

I
I couldn't make out the minuscule handwriting
In the notebook the size of his palm and crinkled
Like an origami quim by shell-blast that stopped
His pocket watch at death. I couldn't read the poem.

II
From where he lay he could hear the skylark's
Skyward exultation, a chaffinch to his left
Fidgeting among the fallen branches,
Then all the birds of the Western Front.

III
The nature poet turned into a war poet as if
He could cure death with the rub of a dock leaf.

ALICE MATTISON

In Case We're Separated

You're a beautiful woman, sweetheart," Edwin Friend began. His girlfriend, Bobbie Kaplowitz, paid attention: Edwin rarely spoke up and complimented her. He tipped his chair against her sink and glanced behind him, but the drainboard wasn't piled so high that the back of his head would start an avalanche today. He took a decisive drink from his glass of water and continued, "But in that particular dress you look fat."

It was a bright Saturday morning in October 1954. Edwin often visited Bobbie on Saturday mornings, and she had dressed up a little, anticipating. Now she didn't bother to speak. She reached behind to unfasten the hook and eye at the back of her neck, worked the zipper down without help, stepped out of the dress, and in her underwear took the sharp scissors. She cut a big piece of brown wrapping paper from a roll she kept next to the refrigerator, while Edwin said several times, "What are you doing?"

Bobbie folded the dress, which was chestnut brown with a rust-and cream-colored arrow-like decoration that crossed her breasts and pointed fetchingly down. She set the folded dress in the middle of the paper, wrapped and taped it, and addressed the package to her slimmer sister in Pittsburgh. Then she went into the bedroom and changed into something seriously gorgeous.

"Come, Bradley," she called, though Edwin would have babysat, but Bradley came quickly. He was a thin six-year-old with dark curls and the habit of resting his hands on his hips, so from the front he looked slightly supervisory and from the back his pointed elbows stuck out like outlines of small wings. They left Edwin looking surprised. At the post office, a considerable walk away, the clerk said the package had to be tied with string, but lent Bobbie a big roll of twine and his scissors. Bobbie was wearing high-heeled shoes, and she braced herself on the counter with one gloved hand. She was short, and the shoes made her wobble. She took the end of the twine in her mouth, grasped it between her teeth, and jerked her head back to pull it tight. It was brown twine, now reddened with her lipstick, and its taste was woody and dry. Fibers separating from the twine might travel across Bobbie's tongue and make her gag. For all she knew, her poor old teeth might loosen.

Much was brown: the twine, the paper around the package (even the dress inside, if one could see it), and the wooden counter with its darkened brass decorations. The counter was old enough to have taken on the permanent sour coloring possessed by wooden and metal objects in Brooklyn that had remained in one place—where any hand might close upon them—since the century turned. But Bobbie's lipstick, and the shoes she'd changed into, and her suit—which had a straight skirt with a kick pleat—were red. She wore a half-slip because she was a loose woman. Joke. Edwin's hands always went first to her bare, fleshy midriff. Then he seemed to enjoy urging the nylon petticoat down, sliding the rubber knobs up and out of the metal loops that attached her stockings to her girdle, even tugging the girdle off. She never let him take off her nylons because he wasn't careful.

Bobbie tied a firm knot. Then she changed her mind. She poked the roll of twine and the scissors toward the clerk with an apologetic wave, called to Bradley—who was hopping from one dark medallion on the tile floor to the next, flapping his arms—and went home. As Bobbie walked, one eye on Bradley, the package dangled from her finger on its string like a new purchase. At home she found Edwin taking apart her Sunbeam Mixmaster with her only tool, a rusty screwdriver.

"Didn't you say it wasn't working?" Edwin asked.

"There's nothing wrong with it. I didn't say anything."

Edwin was married. He had told Bobbie he was a bachelor who couldn't marry her because he lived with his mother, who was old, silly, and anti-Semitic. But his mother lived in her own apartment and was not silly or anti-Semitic, as far as he knew. Edwin had a wife named Dorothy, a dental hygienist. She'd stopped working when their first child was born—they had two daughters—but sometimes she helped out her old boss. Now, fumbling to put Bobbie's mixer back together, Edwin began to wonder uneasily whether it wasn't Dorothy, dressing for work in her uniform, who happened to mention a broken mixer. He had never confused the two women before in the years he'd been Bobbie's boyfriend.

Edwin's monkey business had begun by mistake. He was a salesman for a baking supply company, and Bobbie was in charge of the payroll at a large commercial bakery. Though Edwin didn't wear a ring, he believed that everyone in the firms through which he passed assumed he was somebody's husband. However, a clerk in Bobbie's office had moved to Brooklyn from Minneapolis. When this young woman, who had distinctive habits, asked him straight out, Edwin misheard the question and said no. He had heard, "Mr. Friend, are you merry?"

Edwin was good-natured but not merry, and the question puzzled him until he found himself having lunch with Bobbie, to whom the young woman from Minneapolis had introduced him. He realized that he was on a date. Bobbie seemed eager and attractive, while Dorothy liked to make love about as often as she liked to order tickets and go to a Broadway show, or invite her whole family for dinner, and with about as much planning. Not knowing exactly what he had in mind, Edwin suggested that Bobbie meet him for a drink after work, nervous that she'd refuse anything less than dinner and a movie. But she agreed. Drinking a quick whiskey sour in a darkened lounge, she suggested that next time he come to her house. So his visits began: daytime conversations over a glass of water or a cup of coffee; suppers followed by bed. Bobbie was always interested. She only needed to make sure Bradley was sleeping.

Bobbie rarely spoke of her marriage. Her husband had been a tense, mumbly man, a printer. He'd remained aloof from her family. At first he said she was nothing like her crude relatives. "I felt refined, but I didn't like it," Bobbie told Edwin. Later her husband began to say she was *exactly* like her family, and at last he moved her and Bradley, an infant, into a dark two-room apartment where nothing worked and there was hardly ever any hot water. He said he slept at his shop, and at first he brought her money, but soon that stopped. "I didn't have enough hot water to bathe the baby," Bobbie said. "Let alone my whole self." Edwin imagined it: naked Bobbie clasping a thin baby and splashing warm water on herself from a chipped, shallow basin. She'd moved back with her mother and got a job. Eventually she could afford the apartment on Elton Street where Edwin now visited her. When Bradley was two, she had taken him on the train to

Reno, lived there for six weeks, and come home divorced, bringing her sisters silver pins and bracelets with Indian designs on them, arrows and stylized birds.

Bobbie's family wouldn't care much that Edwin wasn't Jewish, she assured him, and they'd understand that he couldn't be around often because of his mother. But they did want to know him. So Edwin had consented to an occasional Sunday lunch in Bobbie's kitchen with her mother or one of her sisters, eating whitefish and kippered salmon and bagels off a tablecloth printed with cherries, and watching the sun move across the table as the afternoon lengthened and he imagined Dorothy wondering. After the bagels they'd have coffee with marble cake from Bobbie's bakery. He'd tip his chair against the porcelain sink and consider how surprised his wife would be if she knew where he was, being polite to another woman's relatives. His own house was bigger and more up-to-date.

Dorothy would be even more surprised if she knew, right now, that Edwin was in that same kitchen, less sunny in the morning, fixing a mixer that wasn't broken. Edwin would have preferred to be a bigamist, not a deceiver. When he reassembled the mixer, it didn't work. He left the bowls and beaters and took the big contraption home in the trunk of his car. He'd work on it when Dorothy was out. She had promised Dr. Dressel, her old boss, a few hours in the coming week.

The day Edwin carried off the mixer, Bobbie's sister Sylvia and her kids, Joan and Richard, rang Bobbie's bell after lunch because they were all going to the Hayden Planetarium. Sylvia, a schoolteacher, had said, "Bradley's ready," as if she'd noticed blanks in his eyes where stars and planets belonged. Her own kids had often been to the planetarium. So the sisters walked to Fulton Street, urging along the children, who stamped on piles of brown sycamore leaves. Climbing the stairs to the elevated train, Bobbie was already tired. She'd have changed her shoes, but she liked the look of the red heels. They waited on the windy platform, Joan holding Bradley's hand tightly. She and Richard were tall, capable children who read signs out loud in firm voices: "No Spitting." "Meet Miss Subways." They had to change trains, and as the second one approached, Sylvia said, "Does Bradley know what to do in case we're separated?"

"Why should we get separated?" said Bobbie.

"It can always happen," she said as the doors opened. The children squeezed into one seat, and Sylvia leaned over them. She had short curly hair that was starting to go gray. "Remember," she said, "in case we get separated, if you're on the train, get off at the next stop and wait. And if you're on the platform, just wait where you are, and we'll come back for you. Okay?"

Joan and Richard were reaching across Bradley to slap each other's knees, but Bradley nodded seriously. Bobbie rarely offered directives like that, and he probably needed them, yet she felt irritated. At the planetarium, Bradley tried to read aloud words on the curved ceiling that was covered with stars. The theater darkened. While the stars revolved swiftly, a slightly spooky voice spoke of a time so far back that Bobbie felt disjoined from herself: she in her red suit would surely never happen. Anything at all might be true.

Then Bradley whispered something. "Do you have to go to the bathroom?" Bobbie asked. "I can't go in with you." If Edwin would marry her, he'd be there to take Bradley to the bathroom! The size of Bobbie's yearning, like the age of the stars, was suddenly clear. But Bradley shook his head. "No. No. I can't remember what I do if you get off the train without me."

"I wouldn't do that, honey," she said, but of course he continued to worry. She could feel his little worry machines whirring beside her.

"You scared him," she said to Sylvia later as they shuffled toward the exit with the crowd. "About being lost on the subway."

"He needs to know," Sylvia said, and Bobbie wondered if Sylvia would be as bossy if she didn't have a husband, Louis—an accountant, a good man; although Sylvia said he was quick in bed.

They spent an hour in the natural history museum—where Joan held Bradley's hand, telling him what Bobbie hoped were nonfrightening facts—before taking the long subway ride home again. At the stop before theirs, Bradley suddenly stood and ran toward the closing doors, crying out. Richard tackled him, knocking him to the dirty floor, and Bobbie took him on her lap. Bradley had thought a departing back was hers. "Oh, sweetie," she said, brushing him off and kissing him. She carried him as far as the stairs.

"Well, I shouldn't have said anything," said Sylvia as they reached the sidewalk and turned toward home. The train's sound grew faint behind them.

Bobbie said nothing. If she agreed, Sylvia would change her mind and defend what she'd said after all. Bobbie glanced back at the three kids, who were counting something out loud in exultant voices—passing cars, maybe. "Seven! No, nine!"

"I have chopped meat," said Sylvia at last, when their silence had lasted for more than a block. "I'll make mashed potatoes. Lou will drive you later, okay?"

"That would be nice," said Bobbie. They reached the corner of Sylvia's street and turned that way.

"Unless you have a date?" Sylvia added.

But it was cruel to make Bobbie say what was apparent. "No such luck."

"That guy has a problem," said Sylvia. "It's Saturday night!"

"Edwin says I look fat in that brown dress," Bobbie said. She never let herself think about Saturday nights. Edwin said his mother cooked corned beef and cabbage then, and minded if he went out. "Remember that dress? With the design down the front?"

"That gorgeous dress!" Sylvia said. "To tell the truth, you do look a little hefty in it, but who cares?"

In the dark, Bobbie cried. She hoped her sister would notice and maybe even put an arm around her, but that wasn't their way. Maybe Sylvia did notice. "I'll make a nice salad. You like salad, don't you?" she said soothingly.

Edwin's house was empty when he came home on Tuesday. Dorothy was working, and the girls were at a neighbor's. He spread newspaper on the dining-room table and fixed Dorothy's mixer, the one that had been broken in the first place. It was not badly broken. A wire was loose. Then it occurred to him that the mixers looked alike, with bulbous arms to hold the beaters, and curved white bases on which bowls rotated. He'd bought Dorothy's after seeing Bobbie's. Edwin set aside Dorothy's bowls and beaters. He carried Dorothy's fixed mixer out to his car, then returned and put Bobbie's broken one on the sheet of newspaper.

He jumped when he heard Dorothy and the girls arriving, but there was nothing to worry about. Dorothy asked, "Did you fix it?" and Edwin truthfully said, "Not yet." She stood behind him watching as he took apart Bobbie's mixer. By this time it was hard to remember that the broken mixer was the one he had broken himself, not the one Dorothy had reported broken, and he listened attentively while she told him what she'd been about to mix when it didn't work. As he listened, his back to his wife, he suddenly felt love and pity for her, as if only he knew that she had a sickness. He looked over at Dorothy in her thin white hygienist's uniform, her green coat folded over her arm. She had short blond hair and glasses.

The girls had begun to play with a couple of small round dentist's mirrors that Dorothy had brought from Dr. Dressel's office. Mary Ann, the younger one, brought her mirror close to her eye. "I can't see anything," she said.

"Wait a minute," said Eileen. Her light hair was in half-unraveled braids. Eileen turned her back on Edwin and Dorothy, and positioned her mirror just above her head. "I'm a spy," she said. "Let's see...oh, Daddy's putting poison in the mixer." Eileen would say anything.

"I'm a spy, too," said Mary Ann, hurrying to stand beside her sister and waving her mirror. "Show me. Show me how to be a spy."

Edwin couldn't fix Bobbie's mixer, and it stayed broken, on a shelf in Edwin and Dorothy's kitchen, for a long time. Meanwhile, Dorothy's working mixer was in the trunk of Edwin's car, and it was a natural thing to pretend it was Bobbie's and take it to her house the next time he visited.

On many Thursdays Edwin told Dorothy a story about New Jersey, then arranged a light day and drove to Brooklyn to visit Bobbie. Bobbie prepared a good dinner that tasted Jewish to Edwin, though she said she wasn't kosher. Little Bradley sat on a telephone book, and still his face was an inch off the plate, which he stared at, eating mostly mashed potatoes. "They're better the way Aunt Sylvia makes them, with the mixer," Bobbie said on this particular Thursday, the Thursday on which Edwin had brought her his wife's Sunbeam Mixmaster and pretended it was hers.

"I'm sorry I couldn't bring it sooner, babe."

"Oh, I didn't mean that. I just don't bother, the way Sylvia does."

Edwin watched Bradley. With the mental agility born of his mixer exchange, Edwin imagined carrying Bradley off in similar fashion and replacing him, just temporarily, with talky Eileen. If her big sister was out of the way, Mary Ann would play with Bradley, while Bobbie would enjoy fussing with a girl.

"What are you thinking about?" said Bobbie.

"I wish I could take Bradley home to meet my mother."

"Take both of us. She won't be against Jewish girls once she sees me," said Bobbie. "I don't mean I'm so special, but I don't do anything strange."

She hurried to clean up and put Bradley to bed, while Edwin, who hadn't replied, watched television. He couldn't help thinking that his family was surely watching the same show, with Groucho Marx. Over the noise of Groucho's voice and the audience's laughter, Edwin heard Bobbie's voice now and then as she read aloud. " 'Faster, faster!' cried the bird," Bobbie read. Soon she came in, and Edwin reached for her hand, but she shook her head. She always waited until Bradley was asleep, but that didn't take long. When she checked and returned smiling, Edwin turned off the set and put his hands on her shoulders, then moved them down her back and fumbled with her brassiere through her blouse. Dorothy wore full slips. Edwin pulled Bobbie's ruffled pink blouse free and reached his hand under it. Even using only one hand, he'd learned that if he worked from bottom to top, pushing with one finger and pulling with two others, he could undo all three hooks of her brassiere without seeing them. In a moment his hand was on her big round breast, and she was laughing and opening her mouth for him, already leading him toward her bed.

Edwin forgot that Dorothy had promised Dr. Dressel she'd work Saturday morning. As he dressed in Bobbie's dark bedroom on Thursday night, she asked, "Will you come Saturday?"

"Sure, babe," he said. He had fallen asleep, but he could tell from Bobbie's voice that she'd remained awake, lying naked next to him. He leaned over to kiss her, then let himself out, rubbing his hand on his lips and checking for lipstick stains.

But on Saturday he had to stay with Eileen and Mary Ann, then pick up Dorothy at Dr. Dressel's office. He was more at ease with the girls in the car than at home. Made restless by his broken promise to Bobbie, he left too early, then had to look after his children in the dentist's waiting room. He didn't know how to braid Eileen's hair, and it had not been done that morning; Edwin noticed as he reread the dentist's posters, which urged him to eat carrots and apples, that one of yesterday's rubber bands still dangled off Eileen's mussed hair. He called to her and tried to remove the band without pulling. "You're hurting me," she said, though he didn't think he was.

At last Dorothy came out in her coat. "I heard them whooping it up," she said, but she sounded amused. She took two rubber bands from the receptionist's desk and swiftly braided Eileen's hair. Leaving the car where it was, they walked to a nearby luncheonette. Dorothy took Edwin's hand. Sometimes she spoke to him in baby talk; it was a kind of game. "I am going to teach you to bwaid hair," she said. But he didn't know how to answer, so she spoke again, now taking his part, in a gruff voice like the Three Bears. *"How on earth do you braid hair?"* He let go of her hand and put his arm around her shoulders as she answered with elaborate patience, "Well, first you make a center part..." Edwin imagined Bobbie watching them, not jealously. "Squeeze," the imaginary Bobbie said, and Edwin squeezed his wife's taut shoulder through the green coat.

Bobbie didn't use her mixer often. She was not sufficiently interested in its departure and return to put it away, so she left it on the extra chair next to the kitchen table where Edwin had put it. On Saturday morning she put on makeup and stockings, but he didn't come. Ordinarily, if Edwin didn't appear by a quarter to ten, Bobbie took Bradley out, rather than brooding. This Saturday, though, Bradley had a cold. To distract herself, Bobbie called Sylvia, who asked, "Does he have a temperature?" Bobbie's thermometer was broken, so Sylvia brought hers over. Bobbie made coffee. Bradley sat on the floor in his pajamas, wiping his nose on his sleeve while putting together a jigsaw puzzle, a map of the United States.

Bobbie offered Sylvia a cookie, and she and Bradley said together, "Before lunch?" but then everyone took a Mallomar, since Bobbie said a cookie might cheer her up. Bradley licked his fingers and then placed Florida in the puzzle correctly.

"Edwin didn't come today?" Sylvia said, playing with her spoon.

"Sometimes he's busy on Saturdays."

"You need more."

"I manage," Bobbie said. If Sylvia knew all Edwin's ways, she thought, she wouldn't object to him. "He's worth it."

Sylvia laughed, stretching her arm and actually taking a second cookie. "Oh, I know what you mean," she said. She interrupted herself to supervise Bradley's placement of California. "I know what you see in your Edwin. I see the way he looks at you."

"When you've been married a long time," Bobbie said, "I guess it's not so exciting."

Sylvia laughed. "I know how you feel," she said again, not scolding.

"You mean you felt that way about Lou once."

"Well, I suppose."

"What *did* you mean?" Bobbie said.

"Oh, I shouldn't say anything," Sylvia said. She tipped the bowl of her spoon with one finger, making the handle rise.

"He's not listening," Bobbie said, tilting her head toward Bradley. "You mean—someone?"

"Someone I met at an in-service course."

"Another teacher? A man."

"He teaches at Midwood."

"A high school teacher. You—have feelings?" Bobbie said.

"Did this ever happen to you?" Sylvia said, now glad—it seemed—to talk. "At night, you know, picturing the wrong person?"

Bobbie thought she knew what Sylvia meant. She wasn't sure what an in-service course was, whether it consisted of one occasion or several. "How many times have you seen him?"

"Wait a minute," said Sylvia, but then she crouched on the floor. "Doesn't Colorado belong where you put Wyoming, Bradley?" Wyoming was nice and tight. "Could the map be wrong?"

"Did you have lunch with him?"

"Oh, I'm exaggerating, it's nothing," Sylvia said. She remained on the floor, helping Bradley with a few more states. Then she got up, reaching out a hand to steady herself on the extra chair. She gave the Mixmaster a pat. "Hey, you didn't just buy this, did you?"

"No, I've had it for a while."

"I might have been able to get you a discount. A client of Lou's…"

"I bought it last year."

"Oh, right." Sylvia seemed to expect Bobbie to explain why the mixer was on the chair, so Bobbie told in full the story Sylvia had heard only in part: the story of the dress, the walk to the post office, and her return to find Edwin fixing a mixer that wasn't broken.

"He took it home? Why did he do that?" Sylvia asked.

"At home he has tools."

"Maybe he took it to a repair place."

"Oh, no. I'm sure he fixed it himself," said Bobbie.

"You're sure he brought back the same mixer?"

"You mean he bought me a new one? I hope not!" Bobbie said.

"Or he could have bought a used one," said Sylvia.

"Oh, stop being so suspicious." She liked the more tremulous Sylvia who had spoken of the teacher from Midwood High School. She wasn't ready, yet, for the usual Sylvia. "Of course it's mine."

But as she spoke, as she insisted it was hers, Bobbie suddenly sensed that the mixer on the chair might never have been in her house before, and then, looking hard, she was certain. It was the same, but somehow not the same. It had been cleaned differently, maybe with a sponge, not a dishrag. But that thought was ridiculous. It had been handled in a way that was not Jewish. An even more ridiculous thought.

Bradley had abandoned the puzzle and left the room. Maybe Sylvia would say more. "Did you have lunch with him?" Bobbie asked again.

But Sylvia would not be deterred. "Maybe Edwin has another girlfriend," she said, "and this is her mixer. Hey, maybe he has a wife!" She gave a short laugh.

"He has a mother…," said Bobbie. His mother didn't sound like someone who'd plug in a mixer and mix anything. She now remembered that the metal plate with the Sunbeam insignia on her mixer was chipped. She looked, and this one was whole. She looked again. "I *trust* Edwin," she said.

"I know you do. Boy, that would be something," Sylvia said. "If it turned out Edwin was married."

But Bobbie was experiencing one of those moments when one discovers the speed of thought by having several in an instant. First she felt ashamed of being stupid. Of course there had been plenty of hints that Edwin was married. Once she allowed herself to consider the possibility, she was sure it was so. Bobbie didn't need to know whose mixer it was to know that Edwin was married. Then, however, Bobbie felt something quite different. It wasn't anger at Sylvia, at her sister's gossipy curiosity.

She was not angry at Sylvia. She felt sorry for Sylvia, a little superior to Sylvia. All her life, Bobbie had known that Sylvia was smart, so Bobbie must be smart, too, even Bobbie who carried her clothing back and forth to the post office. Once they knew Edwin was married, Sylvia would imagine there was only one way to behave—to laugh bitterly—but Bobbie understood that there were two.

That there were two different ways to think about Edwin's marriage—like thinking about the stars, which might be spots of light, close together, and might be distant, wild fireworlds—struck Bobbie with almost as much force as her sorrow. Sylvia's way would be to laugh bitterly and tell everyone the story. Edwin's marriage might be a bad joke on Bobbie, but then Edwin would no longer tip his chair against her sink, or walk her to her bed while his hands grasped all of her body he could reach under her loosened clothes. His marriage might be a bitter joke—or it might be something Bobbie just had to put up with.

Bobbie would never marry Edwin, but Bobbie had the mixer that worked. She stood and plugged it in, and it made its noise. The years to come, during which she'd keep Edwin's secret, not letting him know she knew—because it would scare him away—and not letting her sisters know she knew—because they'd scream at her to forget him—became real in her mind, as if she could feel all their length, their loneliness, at once. She would be separated from Edwin, despite Thursday evenings and Saturday mornings. Bobbie turned off the mixer and wept.

"Oh, of course he's not married," Sylvia said, and Bobbie didn't say that wasn't why she was crying. "Me and my big mouth, as usual," Sylvia continued. She stood up and put her arms around

Bobbie, and then the sisters were hugging and smiling. "Edwin married," Sylvia said. "If there's one man on earth who couldn't manage being a two-timer, it's Edwin. Sorry, baby, I love the guy, but that swift he's not." And she went on and on, hugging her sister and calling her baby. Baby! The unaccustomed sweetness, like the cookie, comforted Bobbie for a while. Maybe she and Sylvia both had secrets, like Edwin. Maybe life required secrets. What an idea.

WESLEY MCNAIR

The Rules of the New Car

After I got married and became
the stepfather of two children, just before
we had two more, I bought it, the bright
blue sorrowful car that slowly turned
to scratches and the flat black spots
of gum in the seats and stains impossible
to remove from the floor mats. Never again,
I said as our kids, four of them by now,
climbed into the new car. This time,
there will be rules. The first to go
was the rule I made for myself about
cleaning it once a week, though why,
I shouted at the kids in the rearview mirror,
should I have to clean if they would just
remember to fold their hands. Three years
later, it was the same car I had before,
except for the dent my wife put in the grille
when, ignoring the regulation about snacks,
she reached for a bag of chips on her way
home from work and hit a tow truck. Oh,
the ache I felt for broken rules,
and the beautiful car that had been lost,
and the car that we now had, on soft
shocks in the driveway, still unpaid for.
Then one day, for no particular reason except
that the car was loaded down with wood
for the fireplace at my in-laws' camp
and groceries and sheets and clothes
for the week, my wife in the passenger seat,
the dog lightly panting beside the kids in the back,
all innocent anticipation, waiting for me
to join them, I opened the door to my life.

History of Talking on the Phone

Once the phone, called the "telephone,"
was a voice one heard by pressing
what looked like a stethoscope
to one's ear, answering by shouting
at a device on the wall.

This was before talking on the phone
was invented—a more intimate exchange
using a receiver that allowed one to speak
to the voice while holding it in the hand.

Everyone held it and spoke to it.

In stereoscope movies of the period, starlets
lounged on beds talking on the phone
as they stroked its long cord. Men in high-rise
offices commanded, "Put her through!"

or sat in bedrooms on a split screen
talking on phones that matched their pajamas.

In the small towns of America, the tender gesture
of hunching one shoulder to talk on the phone
became popular with housewives washing dishes

and men in the workplace, whose big shoulders
balancing the voice as they smiled and talked to it

while turning the pages of a parts catalogue
or toweling grease from their hands
made a poignant moment
in the history of talking on the phone.

In the cities, meanwhile, where phones
had begun to resemble miniature

PC keyboards, so square and flat
not even teenagers practicing on private lines
in their rooms could balance them,

talking on the phone rapidly advanced
to contacting someone on the phone,
or explaining what one wanted into a machine.

The voice, now a filed message,
was what one listened to all alone,

like the starlet in the movie
coming home all smiles after a week away
to the ominous dark of her apartment
and releasing voices

until she gets to the one
she can hardly believe and plays it

over and over, unable to stop crying.

Miss Waldron's Red Colobus Is Extinct

Any afternoon on the brink of extinction
there they were: lolling in the canopy,
loud-mouthed with abandon, red-cheeked,
eating the topmost leaves. Where the monkey

prospered, the Ghana forest now slumps
into stillness, the way a dying man suddenly
sees something in the distance and gives it
his complete and stony attention. I can't ponder

the loss of Miss Waldron's red colobus
without pondering the woman for whom
it was named. "Traveling companion to the
collector P. Lowe" is all most sources

wrote, leaving us mysterious Miss Waldron
to conjure: red-cheeked with exertion,
ever more alarmed or bored as the expedition
brokered the forests of West Africa

and her first rush of feeling for P. Lowe
wore down. The afternoon he spied it, they'd
paused to drink, listening into the birdsong,
snapped twigs, heavy cinch of snake on bark.

And there it was, a red monkey with coltish
long limbs and tail, special features he
claimed in her name, though they'd
quarreled not two hours before. Today,

they're saying we've lost Miss Waldron's
red colobus for good, the way we'll soon lose
the golden lion tamarin and silly sifaka,
white-naped mangabey and Cross River

gorilla. Somewhere out there, the last
of the northern muriquis peels a banana,
and a Cat Ba Island golden-headed langur
makes short work of a fistful of leaves.

In a clearing, the ghost of Miss Waldron
stoops to retrieve the wreath
of her maiden name from a short-
lived wonder from the lost world.

PAUL MULDOON

The Stoic

This was more like it, looking up to find a burlapped fawn
halfway across the iced-over canal, an Irish navvy who'd stood
   there for an age
with his long-tailed shovel or broad griffawn,
whichever foot he dug with showing the bandage

that saved some wear and tear, though not so much that there
   wasn't a leak
of blood through the linen rag, a red picked up nicely by the
   turban
he sported, those reds lending a little brilliance to the bleak
scene of suburban or—let's face it—*urban*

sprawl, a very little brilliance. This was more like the afternoon
   last March
when I got your call in St. Louis and, rather than rave
as one might rant and rave at the thought of the yew
from Deirdre's not quite connecting with the yew from Naoise's
   grave,

rather than shudder like a bow of yew or the matchless Osage
   orange
at the thought of our child already lost from view
before it had quite come into range,
I steadied myself under the Gateway Arch

and squinted back, first of all, through an eyelet of bone
to a point where the Souris
had not as yet hooked up with the Assiniboine,
to where the Missouri

had not as yet been swollen by the Osage,
then ahead to where—let's face it—there are now *two* fawns
on the iced-over canal, two Irish navvies who've stood there for
    a veritable age
with their long-tailed shovels or broad griffawns.

Lunch at the Blacksmith

I think at last I will give up the Blacksmith House. I've liked the place since college, when my best friend, Celia, and I would meet for coffee in those frugal, scrubbed pine rooms, full of the feel of long-dead Puritans, which we were not. You could smoke in public in those days, and we sucked unfiltered Pall Malls, the most kick for the buck, making sure that there was paint on us somewhere. Celia was beautiful, part Indian, part imp, with Coke-bottle green eyes and skin that somehow let you know it wasn't white, though it was nougat-pale, creamy. Her father and older brothers fished in Maine, and she liked to wear ripped jeans, flannel shirts, and stroll along beside the tweedy Harvard crowd with languid grace.

Underneath, hidden to everyone but me, she had a conscience worthy of Aquinas, and a deep God streak. She wanted to discuss the moral implications of our every act. Was it right to buy paint when you could give all your money to the poor? Was a portrait of a dying homeless person just sensation for itself? For years we wondered what she could do with a certain married professor that would be morally correct, yet satisfy her raging need to get into his pants.

"He tucked the label in my shirt," she said one day, upstairs in the Blacksmith House. "I felt his fingers on my neck. He went on staring at my canvas like it was nothing. I think he has some casuistical system worked out, wherein he can do anything so long as his motives are pure. He pretended to be calm and said something about Gauguin. 'What was his crime against perspective?' as if I might do it, too. As if his mission were to prevent me."

"What did you do?"

"I didn't know *what* to do. Do I have to say something, to keep from being wrong? Like *Keep your mitts off, buster*? Not as if I *mind*. Do I have to lie, to keep from tempting him?"

"Yes, you do," I said and gave her a hard look. It was one of our big subjects—lying from kindness, to protect someone, lies of omission. When did they become the same as any other lie?

She took the cigarette out of my hand and sucked on it. "But you never lie, do you? And you know it. Would you tell him you wanted him, and *therefore* he should keep his mitts off you?"

I reached across the table, pushed a silky lock out of her eyes. We touched each other all the time in public, made a point of it. We held hands, or stood with one arm draped around the other's neck. I was what some people would call a tall cool blonde, and we must have been a sight, Celia soft and dark, me all bones, entwined. Not even lesbians did that in public yet, and we weren't lesbians. I'd had a parade of men and boys, a new one every two months. Celia was not a virgin, but she wanted to get married, have a baby sometime soon. I wanted that life, too. It's just that our approaches were a little different.

"You can't tell him unless you want to seduce him. Because you know it would. He'd go insane." I had seduced a married professor myself, the year before, as Celia well knew.

Her laugh was soundless, like a bellows puffing in and out.

"Knowing I felt the same? But I keep thinking—what if he'd be happier with me? His marriage is hollow. He never sleeps. He reads all night. He drives me home three nights a week."

I nodded. Celia lived about three blocks from him, in a house with other students.

"And that's fine. So long as you never do a thing you couldn't look back and approve of fifty years from now." It was our principle, the one that stood to every test.

She closed her eyes. "Oh, God. Of course I can't. The guilt is even too much now."

She leaned forward, searched my eyes.

"You know what I wish? I wish we could be Catholics. They know exactly what a sin is and how to get absolved. Protestants have to obey the *spirit* of the law, and that's endless, because it's vague. And no one hears your confession. You carry the same sin year after year, and never get absolved. 'We are forgiven,' says some minister who hasn't heard your sin, and what is that supposed to do? It hasn't been removed. Not like when a priest has heard the whole earful, and he frees you from it. Go in peace and sin no more. Then it is truly gone."

I held my hand over her head. "Go in peace, my child, and sin no more."

She caught my hand and gazed into my eyes. "You laugh, but you know it helps, even if it's you. Do you really think I am absolved?"

"No one was ever more innocent than you."

"That's *now*." She laughed her soundless laugh. "How will I ever keep from telling him?"

I grinned. "Just stare at that little bald spot on his head and think about Gauguin."

Celia stopped riding home with him. We graduated, wondered what to do. We both wanted to paint, but how were you supposed to eat?

There was art history, and we got fellowships to read a million books while grading freshman essays on the Post-Impressionists. We spent more years on Levi-Strauss and Baudrillard and Lyotard than anyone who'd ever held a brush. We took the same classes, and dominated them. Celia hated abstract art, except Rothko and Franz Marc, in whom she thought the spirit moved. She could say words like "numina" and "grace" with a straight face, while I tried out the tougher faiths of Marxism and cultural historicism.

"Art is hoax," I said, "and surplus capital, effluvia of luxury. Art is imperial aggression, very thinly veiled. The sun never sets on Jackson Pollock's empire anywhere."

Then I retired with Celia to the Blacksmith House, to discuss the hierarchical behavior everywhere in academe, and how there was no way to escape judging constantly. We wondered if we could foster our students without hurting them, and read each other's seminar papers before we turned them in. We talked an hour on the phone at night, even if we'd met that day. We wore each other's clothes.

"We need another year," she said one afternoon. "For this friendship to jell."

"To jell?" I said, a little hurt she could think so. How much more jelled could it get? She was already the best friend I'd ever had.

"I mean, for it to become strong and flexible, the reed that bends in gale-force wind. So even if one of us had to commit murder, we'd defend each other automatically. Three musketeers."

I picked a tobacco flake off my tongue. "You planning to murder someone soon?"

Her green eyes shone. She laughed her puffy gasps. "You never know."

Our second year in grad school, Celia met a future minister named Daniel, moved in with him, and took two incompletes. Her back hurt, she said, from so much reading, and she couldn't paint. She carried a pillow into class, and went to chiropractors instead of to the library.

"Paint gives me hives," she said. She went to herbalists, who made her give up cigarettes and coffee. She quit going to class. One day I saw her disappear into the big brick church on Harvard Square.

"We're off art, and into God," she told me when I asked.

"Okay. But what will you do now?" As far as I could tell, she wasn't doing anything.

I was too busy to pay attention for a while. I finished coursework, studied for my doctoral exams. I had to memorize the history of Western art and every theory about it. For a year, I hardly slept. I read. I smoked three packs a day, and knew what time it was by counting butts.

People fainted in the course of their exams and threw up in trash cans. The written part was sixteen hours long, plus three oral, two more when the art department challenged every word. By the time I finished, I knew nothing about anything, and staggered out to Celia in the hall. She waited with me while the art department debated my fate inside. Finally, the tall, gray-haired chairman came out from behind the beveled glass.

"It was a pass, but not as good as we expected it to be," he said mournfully.

Celia gripped my arm and led me out of there. She took me home to the apartment she now shared with Daniel, a decent place in an old house in Somerville. Daniel was extremely thin, with deep lines in his face, though he was only twenty-five, like us, with a blond shock of surfy hair. He gave a wry smirk as he held a champagne glass toward me. I reached for it, began to sob.

"It was too hard."

Celia crouched beside me, pressed her cheek to mine. "I know," she said.

And it was true. She did.

That summer, Celia married Daniel at her parents' seaside church, and stopped taking my calls. Daniel answered every time.

"She isn't here," he'd say. Or, "She's resting now."

"Resting?" I said. *"Resting?"*

Had Celia become an invalid? Did Daniel keep her locked inside their room? Even prisoners got one phone call. I phoned every day for weeks, but she did not call me.

"Hey, Daniel. Tell Celia I'm not calling back again. She'll have to get in touch with me."

"Okay," he said. But when my phone rang, it was never Celia.

A year later, I caught a glimpse of her in the chilly reaches of the Harvard swimming pool. She was hugely pregnant in a green tank suit stretched tight, and I watched her underwater do a dreamy breaststroke back and forth. In the locker room, we both stood at the mirror, several women in between, while she drew a faint brown line beneath her eyes and smudged it with a fingertip. I'm sure she saw me in the frame of her vision. But she did not turn her head.

I supposed it was the saga of my life, the way the boyfriends came and went, that looked especially boring from her new position on the inside of a wedding ring. I could almost understand.

But when I knew that Celia was gone for good, I was more crushed than I had ever been by any man. You *expected* that from lovers, but not from your best friend. I caught the flu, kept smoking, and it turned into pneumonia. I spent a month in bed, unable to catch my breath. I wasn't sure I wanted to. I wanted to find a deep woods, crawl inside a big black garbage sack, and put a gun inside my mouth. I wanted to dispose of my remains and never be identified. I had no messages to send to anyone.

Instead, I found a psychiatrist who took me on for charity at half the going rate, and spent a year weeping for Celia in his red wingchair. Dr. Douhomet was hairless as a frog, and hardly said a word, except "Time's up" and "Thirty-five dollars, please." Once, when I described the way that Celia and I had touched in public, he gave a small, superior smile.

"It was erotic, but not genital," he said and nodded with a click.

I shook my head. "It wasn't erotic. It was playful, and about defying categories. It wasn't easy to freak out the art department, but we tried. We wanted to show them even straight girls could do that. That there were more things in heaven and on earth than were dreamt of in their philosophy, Horatio. Or in *your* philosophy," I said with sudden energy.

He went on beaming his Olympian grin, and didn't say a word.

One afternoon I saw him drive his BMW convertible through Harvard Square, and I lit up like the preteen fan of some rock star. I ran a block to try to catch him at the light on Church, and when his car was gone, I laughed and laughed. So that was transference—and if I felt that way about a frog, of whom I knew nothing, it was a very strange experience. I supposed he wanted me to transfer onto him and somehow feel what I had felt for Celia, and cure myself by understanding it.

But the feeling I had on the street was nothing I had ever felt for Celia. I loved Celia, but I would not have chased her up the block. Sex was what gave you that crazy energy, and I had done stranger things for men I hardly knew. And after I had slept with them, I felt related to them, forever and ever, amen. It must be because my genes got mixed up in it, trying to fulfill their evolutionary destiny.

But I didn't feel that way for Celia. Evolution wasn't interested in friendship, and that gave it a democratic feel. Friends loved each other voluntarily, no matter how close they got. And that meant Dr. Douhomet had nothing he could do for me.

"I'm not coming back," I said the next week, in his chair.

His cheeks went purple.

"But you're finally getting somewhere!" he shouted. It was the first time he'd expressed emotion, while I'd been weeping for a year.

"That's okay. I feel much better anyway."

And it was true, when I walked out of his office, it cheered me up. I didn't need a shrink. I needed a friend to talk things over with, share the details of my life.

But I was wary, and I had a dissertation now to write, on the New York School. It took me five more years, and I was over thirty, so lonely I thought I might implode, before I had the heart to find another friend.

It was the week I broke up with my sweetest lover ever, a handsome pipe welder who sculpted on the side. Ricky had made me an eight-pound valentine of inch-thick sheet metal, with a small arrow he had somehow made to pierce right through. He'd done it tenderly, precisely, using his blowtorch. He made love like that, too. But he had gotten a vasectomy at twenty-three, and he was never going to marry me.

"You're never going to marry me, are you?" I said, one night on the phone.

"No," said Ricky in a voice of mild surprise. "Did I ever say I would?"

He hadn't, that was it. Now what was I supposed to do?

I needed someone I could tell it to. I thought of Katie, who was art director of a Boston magazine. Katie was thirty-eight, and lovely, confident, good at what she did. We had met socially, and she took pity on my student poverty, gave me castoff clothes. They were the best things I had ever owned, a wool Ralph Lauren skirt, a hand-knit harlequin sweater, fawn-brown Gucci loafers light as glove leather. For the shoes alone, I ought to call Katie.

We made a date for lunch at the Blacksmith House. I hadn't smoked since the pneumonia, and half of Cambridge had quit, too. Most restaurants around the square ignored the trend, went on as smoky dives where you could swill martinis, chew on fat and gristle in the dark. Only the Blacksmith had clean air, mesculin salads, homemade soup—which meant it would be packed with parents, kids in strollers, diaper bags. So I put on the Guccis early, dodged the icebergs crossing Harvard Yard, as snow began to swirl.

The tall, lean windows of the Blacksmith steamed, as frostbit people packed inside. Puffed coats stood eight-deep to the counter, babies squalled. I tried to wiggle into line. But someone dropped a bowl of lentil soup down the staircase, and the crowd recoiled, slipping on the oak floor.

I waited half an hour, and was almost to the register when Katie wedged inside. She looked about nineteen in a hooded car coat, tall suede boots, hair sprung out around her face in bright banana curls. She worked out hours every day with weights, got massages, facials, manicures. She had her pores vacuumed, hair lightened with special weaves. Unwinding her long scarf, she cried out in a cheerful voice, inches from a woman trying to pull a toddler out of its snowsuit.

"Sorry! The gynecologist ran late. I asked him to check out the bacteria in there, you know, take a smear and look under the microscope. And he said, '*Whew!* Have you got bacteria in there!'"

Katie was from Manhattan, and I'd noticed that New Yorkers could say anything in crowded restaurants, sure they'd never see the same people again. But Cambridge was about the size of an Upper West Side block, and I cringed as she shouted on.

"And I have this *thing* on my shoulder, this little nothing red spot. I showed it to him, hoping he would say it's definitely not herpes, and I should forget it right away. Know what he said? 'Yep! Sure looks like herpes to me!'"

Mortified, I stared into the deli case. What did I care what these people thought? I did, though. I cared. Holding up one foot, I pointed to the Gucci loafer, trying to distract her.

Katie smiled and nodded, shouted on. "He said it can be years in incubation, so there's just no way to tell who gave it to me. It could be some guy ten years back, who didn't know he had it. He may just be getting symptoms now, and *wham,* it's got me, too. The doctor says I shouldn't bother notifying guys I've slept with in the last few years, since they'll find out soon enough. Oh, lentil soup, how perfect, don't you think?"

The girl behind the counter had six rings through her upper lip, and she lifted it as if she hadn't realized women our age still had sex. I had once given that look to my mother and her friends, when they fixed their hair or shopped for clothes. Why do they bother? I had wondered then. Who's going to look at them?

"Two lentil soups," I said. I turned to Katie loyally. "I bet you're going to be fine."

She seemed to strain to hit a high note that went through walls. "No way. He said there's herpes now in half the single population. But even married people aren't quite safe, are they? Think of Bob's poor wife. You know, that guy I slept with last year? She's probably got herpes, too!"

The girl behind the counter slopped our soups in haste. Hoisting the tray, I turned to fight my way into the crowd. But it parted like the Red Sea, averted eyes on every side.

Upstairs, no one knew how dangerous we were. All the babies had been crowded into two small rooms, like steerage class in a potato famine year. The only empty table lay buried in coats, children squirming all around. We worked our way in, settled down beside a young blond woman with her sweater pulled up, one pink breast exposed. She looked like a Swedish grad student, and her tiny red-faced infant suckled audibly, so close I could smell milk.

I smiled at Katie, rolled my eyes. Of course we'd have to talk on neutral subjects here. Katie knew a lot about the art scene, and she had explained to me the process of full-color printing and the problem with the greens. Shaking out my paper napkin, I held my spoon above the soup.

"So, did you see that thing on Caravaggio, in *Art in America*?"

She brightened with delight. "By that dick Howard James? Oh, sure, you know who he is. He did those burning scarecrows under glass. 'American Gothic.' You know, you saw that. I knew him in SoHo, when he was sealing dead seagulls in Plasticine. And he not only *was* a dick. He had this huge one that he thought you were supposed to die for. He thought it was about pumping, you know? Pumping! Half an hour, in-out, in-out, in-out, on and on and on!"

Crowd noise ceased, and Katie could be heard in the next room at least.

"Does that do anything for you? You know, pumping?"

I took a slurp of soup and gestured to my full mouth. She leaned forward, yelled.

"What's that you're mumbling? I bet it's no. It doesn't do a thing for me, either. *Oral sex* is what I like. Licking, I mean. But most guys only seem to like it for themselves. It's been an age since I found anyone who'd give me cunnilingus, more than two minutes anyway. Have you? Do you have trouble finding men willing to lick you properly?"

She waited for an answer, as did everyone at every table on the second floor. A pierced and tattooed, gender-non-specific busperson paused with a tray nearby, pretended to scan the room.

"Let's not talk about it here," I whispered.

"What?" She gaped at me. "Not talk about it here? Why ever not?"

I was miserable for days. I was not cut out for friendship, that was clear. Why couldn't I have talked to Katie and forgotten all those people listening? I was raised to be inhibited, by unhappy Protestants. Why couldn't I have shouted pump! lick! herpes!, told a few tales of my own? Maybe then I'd have a friend.

But I didn't have one, and now I was even more alone. I missed Ricky terribly. I'd been invited to an opening in the Back Bay, and he might be there. I knew I shouldn't go, but I put on his favorite dress, a knitted cream silk sheath, and the three-inch heels he said made my ankles unforgettable. Wrapped in my somewhat shabby overcoat, I took the T to Arlington and wobbled through the slushy streets.

I had almost reached the gallery when a cab pulled up in front and Ricky bounded out. He looked devastating, wide shoulders in a tweed jacket, curls on his strong brown neck. He turned back toward the cab, and Katie stepped out in a tight black dress and heels. Her ankles looked extremely good. Laughing, he put an arm around her, and they disappeared into the gallery.

My toes froze as I stood, and certain memories came back to me.

"You and Katie, what a team," he'd said, the night I introduced them, warm brown eyes gleaming. Once I went up to Vermont to see my family, and when I got back, neither of them told me they had met. Then Katie had a party, and I took Ricky. It was a November night, cold in her living room, and Katie shivered in a shimmering tube top. She fiddled with the radiator valve.

"Ricky!" she cried. "This thing doesn't work. You're the only one who ever made it put out any heat. What did you do?"

Ricky blanched, and so did I. He rushed in, and the two of them fussed with the valve, animated as if onstage. They shouted about a painting on the wall, which someone had given Katie. Ricky thought that it was bad.

"Really bad!" he cried. "Wretched!"

"Oh, not that bad!" she yelled.

"No, really bad!"

They laughed frantically. Now all I could think of was how Ricky's favorite brand of sex did not involve *pumping.*

I had a friend once, loyal and true. I was five, in a mill town, and Sue Ellen's family lived next door to mine. Two years older than I was, she still stuck with me all through elementary school. We talked for hours on her brick front stoop, about the strange things people did, and where pets went when they were dead, until she graduated into junior high and started to wear nylons and French heels, and smelled like Campbell's soup when it was warm. Then my father lost his job, and we had to move to my grandparents' farm. I never saw her after that, though we wrote for a few years, on the perfumed stationery our brothers gave us every Christmas and birthday.

In the country, I had cousins but no voluntary friends. Then Radcliffe took me on for charity, let me wait tables in the dorm. I made friends with Amy, a small, dark, quiet girl I waited on, who was smart and funny when you got to know her, privately, and had the finest taste I'd ever even seen. She was from the Upper East Side of New York, and she got married after our sophomore year and moved back home.

I heard from Amy sometimes and had been to visit her and her husband, Alex, and their little boy. Amy had a gift for friendship, and I often cried when we talked, as if I were in therapy. She had in fact become a therapist, but had to limit her practice, while Alex was chief surgeon of a major hospital, and wrote books in his spare time, about medicine and ethics, life and death. "Poetry," *The New York Times* had called his last, which spent a few months on the bestseller list.

Why didn't I call Amy more? I picked the phone up, punched her number in.

"But how did you know?" she cried. "I'm coming up to Boston for a conference. Let's have lunch at the Blacksmith House."

I had no qualms. Amy was the most discreet person I knew, and she never even gossiped or said mean things about anyone. Merely being seen with her should raise me in the eyes of all those supercilious pierced persons in the Blacksmith House.

The day she met me there, she looked the way that I remembered, lovely and well-dressed. She could look natural inside a tailored skirt, a cashmere sweater, pearls, at eleven in the morning, in 1998, and I felt tasteless in my tight black pants and chunky shoes, like some fake teen. My hair had never once been so well-cut as hers, in a simple shape from some hairdresser whom you needed a hereditary link to see.

"You look wonderful," I said. "Mind if I just go shoot myself?"

"Don't do that, please. I like the way you look. It's so . . . *caj*," she said, meaning casual, and I felt a rush of pleasure. The last time I had seen her, we decided that should be the term for suave, cool style. I was touched that she remembered what we'd talked about.

We carried tea and mesculin salads up the stairs, and at first we had a good few feet between us and the nearest mothers with children. But soon a troop of Japanese tourists came shyly in. The Swedish grad student wedged next to me and flashed her young pink breast, as if we had agreed that she should always nurse by me.

"Are you all right?" Amy murmured. "Everything okay?"

I felt the urge to cry, because I missed Ricky and had no money for haircuts. But I held it off a moment, almost happy, knowing I could tell it all to her.

Suddenly she gave me a big blazing look. Her eyes looked huge and black, intense.

"Well, I'm not all right. Alex told me last weekend he doesn't want me anymore. We've only made love about twice in the past year, and I asked him why. I took my clothes off, waved my breasts around, and nothing happened. I asked if he has any sexual feelings, and he just looked uncomfortable." Her voice rose to a seagull's cry. "I think he's fucking someone else!"

At tables nearby, conversation ceased. I tried to notice only what she'd said. Alex was urbane and charming, asked intelligent questions about my work. The last time I saw him, he'd started to go bald and grown his hair long on one side to comb across. I caught a glimpse of him emerging from the shower, a wing of hair about a foot long jutted from his ear. Was that some kind of danger sign I should have recognized?

I kept my voice down. "Maybe he's just getting middle-aged. You've been married a long time."

Her voice stayed loud. "But I'm still horny, and why shouldn't he be, too? Bald guys have lots of testosterone. I bet he's having tooth-and-claw sex with some nurse right now. It makes me so angry! And horny! You know that awful kind of horny you get when you think that everyone is having sex but you?"

She gasped, and dropped her head back on her neck. Around the room, no one moved. The tattooed bus-nerd lingered near our table, stared. If Amy noticed, she didn't care.

"You know what I want to do? I want to masturbate some guy while telling him how much I hate him. Doesn't that sound great? Go fuck yourself, you say and yank on it. Go fuck yourself!"

Sometimes life presents you with a test, and you have ten seconds to pass or fail. I had failed most of them so far. Did it matter that I'd never wanted to do what she'd said?

"Wow, sure does!" I cried. "Jerk off the jerk! Only you shouldn't do it all the way. Just almost, and then say, 'My hand is tired.' Tell him you're going to find some guy who doesn't have to comb his hair across his big bald spot!"

She whooped. "Some guy about nineteen who wants it all the time!"

"He'll beg for it!"

"He'll be your slave!"

"And you can tie him up and torture him!"

Amy giggled, stared at me, along with everyone else in the Blacksmith House.

"Well, I suppose, if that's what you like," she said demurely, sipped her tea.

A week later, another therapist told Amy that Alex did indeed have someone else. Not a nurse, but a psychiatrist whose name was practically a household word. She wrote articles for *The New Yorker* and commentaries for *All Things Considered,* and Alex had been seeing her for years. All the therapists in New York knew, except Amy. When she confronted him, he seemed relieved. He moved to an apartment near his hospital.

"Everyone knew but me!" Amy shouted on the phone. We had been talking for so long, the phone burned against my ear.

"Why didn't Alex tell you? What exactly was his plan?"

"He says they thought I was too vulnerable. *They* thought! Him and his concubine, like I'm this patient in their care! I think everyone's been doing that to me. Did you know he was seeing her? Would you have told me if you did?"

"No way." I felt a qualm. Could I have lied and kept it to myself, and would that have been better? I wished with sudden violence that I could talk to Celia.

"Are you glad you know? Do you still like the person who told you?"

"I do. I like her more. Where would I be without her? In the dark! When I think of everyone who knew and kept the truth from me!"

I took the train down to New York and sat up half the night on Amy's couch, talking it all through. Punchy in the dawn, we told each other jokes, about how many therapists it takes to change a light bulb, and how many art critics. I told the one about the penguin who tried to drive across a desert, but its car broke down. The penguin took the car to a garage and went into an ice cream parlor to cool off, and covered itself in vanilla ice cream.

"Looks like you blew a seal," said the mechanic, coming in.

"Naw," said the penguin. "This is just ice cream."

We laughed and squeaked. Amy tried to speak.

"What do you call that ugly piece of flesh on the end of a man's penis?"

I didn't know.

"That's . . . the man!"

A few weeks later, back in Cambridge, my phone rang at one a.m.

"I have to find a man," said Amy, in a panicked voice. "I want to have sex right this minute! How do you find men? Tell me quick!"

All the men I knew were either married, or untrustworthy, or recently divorced and needed time in the emotional deep freeze. Half of them were my old lovers anyway, and I'd already told her what was wrong with them.

"I don't care! He can be a jerk, and live in Timbuktu. So long as he'll fuck me!"

Two weeks later, Amy had found Steve, a nice genetic researcher at NYU, younger than she was. She didn't call me for a week. I left messages, and she called back a few times. But she was busy now with Steve, and her divorce, and juggling her practice and her son. Soon we only talked to each other's answering machines.

I understood, though I was shocked to realize how few resources I had left. I had nothing but my dissertation, and even that was getting done. I applied for jobs, and went down to a conference in New York for interviews with two Midwestern schools. I called Amy, and she said she'd be with Steve all afternoon. But could I meet her around six at her favorite sushi place?

The sushi bar was tiny and crowded, and Amy was half an hour late. They wouldn't seat me until she arrived, so I had to stand. At last she breezed in through the bamboo-decorated door, flushed and grinning in a rumpled tweed suit, and they put us at a table about two feet wide, in the center of the tiny space. She looked great, but she'd been drinking martinis all afternoon and seemed unable to talk quietly. Her voice was high and powered by a laugh.

"God, isn't sex great?" she yelped. "Is it always so great for you? Is that what you've been doing all these years, fucking every afternoon?"

I murmured that, as she knew, I had not seen anyone for several months.

She shouted sympathetically: "But you have to find someone! If only I had known, I never would have waited for Alex to fuck me twice a year. I would have fucked the FedEx man. Surely you know someone you can fuck!"

I wondered if such things were shouted all over the country now, wherever women met. I couldn't take it anymore. I snapped.

"Let's not talk about this in a sushi bar, okay?"

"Okay, sure. Sorry."

Sake, she gestured to the waitress from across the room, holding up her hands to imitate the china bottle and the cup.

"If it makes you uncomfortable. But just tell me one thing." A giggle squirted out of her. *"Don't you think sex is great?"*

After that, I did without close friends. Sometimes I did talk to another grad student, Lisbeth, who was English and even more bitter than me about the years we'd spent in school. When we started, Lisbeth had been glamorous and willowy, but now she drank, and she was shapeless as a tube of pudding, with a red face and broken vessels in her cheeks. She liked to say things like, "Mmmmm, Dom Perignon, and such a *full* bottle!" She liked to slander women we both knew. She insisted so-and-so "would screw a bush if she thought there was a snake in it," or that no inch of someone else was untouched by the surgeon's knife. A man we both knew had a lovely wife, who happened to be rich, and of course Lisbeth said he'd only married her for money. I knew Lisbeth's intentions were not especially good, and I mostly steered clear of her.

My final year at Harvard came down to a pinched, reluctant spring. In June the sun burned through, and lilacs opened, sweet enough to make your temples pound. I got a job at one of the Midwestern colleges, where I would know no one. But my fellowship was over, and I had to go. I filed my dissertation, packed up my few things.

A few days before I had to leave, I walked through Harvard Yard. It was hot summer now, and I could smell cut grass, Chinese restaurant, hints of sewage from the Charles. Circling the square, I visited the stations of my youth. On the brick sidewalk, I could see Celia ahead of me look back laughing, in a ripped tank top and ragged cutoff jeans. The bricks were there, the yellow light on them. But where was Celia?

I'd been invited to a party, in a loft in Watertown. Everyone I knew in Cambridge would be there, and I was tempted not to go, avoid saying goodbye. But I had nothing left to do. At nine o'clock, I dressed and took a cab.

The loft was in a warehouse with big clanking metal doors, the room high-ceilinged as a barn, a hundred people packed inside. The first person I saw was Lisbeth, face already splotched. She held a drink in one fist and a burning cigarette.

"Fancy running into you like this!" she cried and kissed me on the lips, which no woman had ever done before. Startled, I stepped back. Her voice rose as if eager for an audience.

"And to think that I just had a call this very afternoon from Celia!"

Arrested, I stared like a cow unaware it has been shot in the head. Celia called *Lisbeth*?

"Oh, but how tactless of me. What a shock it must be for you to hear that. Can you ever forgive me? Here, let me get you a drink."

She took hold of my arm and dragged me off to find a double scotch. Then she backed me in a corner, stood too close, and offered me a cigarette.

"Pardon me, it slipped my mind. Your marvelous pure lungs, like Celia's. You two were always quite the pair! But you seem rather sensible, next to her. Poor Celia's *quite* batty, you know, up there in New Hampshire with those eight or nine small boys. I thought the worst was when she needed to be Born Again, as if once weren't bad enough. Tent meetings, all that, passing out for God, that sort of thing. And of course she's always been a positively *devoted* hypochondriac, exists on rice and greens."

She took a drink, and her shoulders shot up with eagerness to swallow it and tell me more.

"And now! The horror! She's become a Catholic. *A lay nun,* no less, part-time bride of Christ, and scribbled a book to enlighten the rest of us. *God Is My Co-Dependent,* I believe it's called, or perhaps it's *Going All the Way with God.* Still married to the country parson, though, alas."

I tried not to show that every word of this was more than I had ever heard. Lisbeth shrugged my murmurs off and stared into my eyes, as if she knew this news would hurt but still be good for me.

"Now, you do realize, I trust, my dear, that she is nothing to disturb yourself about. She has become a very ordinary housewife."

"Disturb myself about?"

She shook her head, as if to dislodge a fly. "Oh, you know, your lesbian period. We all knew about it at the time. Such a good idea, I always thought. So sensible of you! It's just that Celia couldn't bear it, though, you see. She *recoiled,* in fact. Oh, dear, I fear I *have* stepped in it, haven't I? Can you ever forgive me? Let me take you out to lunch, say, Thursday at the Blacksmith House?"

I escaped, and made no dates. I went home and tried to blot out Lisbeth's voice. Had everyone believed I was in love with Celia? Had Celia thought I was? I knew it wasn't true, and yet I couldn't sleep. I dreamed of sneering faces, murderers outside my door, and woke up every twenty minutes all night long.

In the morning, big white cruise-ship clouds stood motionless against a hot blue sky. I packed up my last things, and the phone began to ring. I had forgotten to unplug the answering machine. A woman's voice began to speak.

"I had to call. I had a message. It was very clear."

It was a dry Maine voice, full of salt cod. It took me several moments to be sure.

"It was the strangest thing. I was just praying, and I knew. I had to call."

I picked up the phone. My tongue wouldn't move.

"So, Celia. How've you been for six or seven years?"

Sharp intake of breath. "It hasn't been that long."

Who was I to argue with someone who heard from God?

"Okay. What did the message say?"

"They're not in words. It was just a feeling, that I had to talk to you. But when it happens, I don't question it."

I felt impatient with the call. Had she had my number all this time, like when I was plotting to dispose of my remains?

"So, hey, Celia. Why did you stop speaking to me?"

She seemed to expect this. "That's too big a question to answer on the phone. Meet me in an hour at the Blacksmith House."

"Okay," I said before I thought, and Celia hung up.

So she was in town. She had swooped in, and now I was to report as ordered. Had she come to prove me wrong about the democratic nature of friendship? Was I supposed to just eat mesculin salad with her as if nothing had happened?

Sweating, I drifted to the Blacksmith House. The moment I saw Celia, I felt calm. She did not look the way that I recalled. She *did* look like a nun, or an old-maid clerk in 1956—stick-thin, in a Peter Pan collar and lace-up shoes. Her hair was bowl-cut, but her eyes were still Coke-bottle green, and when she saw me, something impish flashed through them. She walked toward me with languid grace.

"But you look wonderful," she said, as if she had heard differently. She kissed my cheek, and laughed her airy laugh.

"Hey, thanks. Want some lunch? They make good salads here," I said, as if she'd never been there before. "I mean, they've gotten better lately."

"Sure." She laughed again, breathless, as if this were hilarious. She seemed astonished to be there with me.

We carried salads up the stairs. The place was packed, but without piles of snowsuits, there was more room. The baby of the Swedish grad student could now sit up. Most of the other mothers looked familiar, too. Even the Japanese tourists could be the same.

Celia showed me pictures of her two small sons, and Daniel, and the white church where he led the flock. Daniel was even thinner than before, his face ashen, as if he'd been incinerated from within. He looked ill in his white collar, and even in the Santa suit he had put on for a children's party at the church. But their boys were round and rosy, cheerful, with pink cheeks.

"And have you joined the Catholic Church?"

"Oh, yes!" She flushed with happiness, and told me all the steps she had gone through, and what a lay nun was, and that she hadn't taken vows and might not. But she said Daniel understood and even envied her.

I got us coffee, cream for her, the way she'd always taken it. She was pleased that I remembered, and gave me a searching glance. She played with the flimsy cream package.

"I should answer your question. I've thought about it now for years, of course. I'm not sure what to say."

"You don't have to, if you don't feel like it," I said in a rush, not meaning to. Of course she had to say. I had almost killed myself, but I was over it. What could she say now that would make a difference?

"Just tell me why you wouldn't take my calls. You could have explained. It's not like we weren't talking every day."

She waved one hand, laughed quick clean puffs. "I know, I know."

She seemed unable to go on. But something in her face told me I had to wait. I waited, wishing that I didn't need to know.

She did say something then. I know I heard it, saw her lips move and her eyes beseeching me. But seconds later I could not remember what it was. It may have been so vague my mind refused to take it in. Or maybe it was what I'd always thought, that, being married, she could no longer approve of me. Whatever she said, it might have held the secret of friendship.

But it was gone the moment she said it, and part of me began to keen, and shred its handkerchief, its plastic garbage sack. What did she say? It was as if no one was listening at all.

Celia seemed relieved, and talked with animation, asked questions about my life. I told her, leaving out the year with the psychiatrist, since it seemed rude to mention it. She talked about her children's choir, her husband's early midlife crisis, and how impatient she felt with it.

"He actually said lately that he doesn't know if he believes in God. As if he's twenty-two! The weekend he said it, we'd had this major breakthrough, too. I didn't think there were any more barriers we could overcome."

"What kind of breakthrough?" I said, not really following.

She flushed happily, began to shout.

"It was the most amazing thing. You know how, when you're fucking, and you feel the Holy Ghost descend? And your orgasm sends you up to a higher dimension?"

Around us, people froze. The same wait-nerd who'd been there every time appeared a few yards off, perforated ears opened wide.

I didn't pause. I shouted back.

"Your orgasm? The Holy Ghost shows up when you come? Do tell! How does it feel?"

I leaned back. I relaxed. At last I knew what was going on. I knew where we were headed to. Lifting my cup, I nodded encouragement, as Celia went on.

The Last Morning

The May morning I came to where
    I was not expected.
The May morning hazy with the mad
    swirl of maple seeds, where
you stood blocking the door.

"Where is Mom?" My voice lifted
    innocent as a child's balloon.
My face needy and vacant, the face
    you'd loved, or
someone had loved who stood now squarely
    blocking the door in overalls damp
    at the knees, in unbuckled rubber boots
    like strange growths of feet.

The May morning I came to where
    I was not invited and not wanted.
For always there is a May morning where
    we are not wished, and where
the Giant stands shrunken, and bitter.

"Where is Mom, is she inside?"—that May
morning, the last.

GEOFFREY G. O'BRIEN

In the Idle Style

It was discovered on an overcast day
that the eyes are two holes the sky passes,
that white lilies open without assistants
first to the roar of stretching space and then
the lion's loin of the sound, the dayflow,
and that there is no cure for this
except to think of a clear wreath in the air
to which everything alludes, the smell of flowers
shaken out of the smell of the earth
and the land again, young enough to know

Absence of the Archbishop

You meet at most four archbishops
in a lifetime. You have at most
one lifetime. You sing when in pain
and expect to be heard. You see the outline
of holy figures, their windows and blinds.
You want to kiss the gold of the coat and
you want it to come off on your lips.
You think of singing gold songs and are not
for a moment in pain. You see the sun not
as it is but as it will be without you,
cold gold with all the windows closed.
You expect to be heard singing in your house.

SHARON OLDS

Frontis Nulla Fides

Sometimes, now, I think of the back
of his head as a physiognomy,
blunt, rich with facial hair,
the elegant stone-wall shapes of the skull
like sensing features, as hard to read
as surfaces of the earth. He was
mysterious to me in his anterior depths,
occiput, lambdoid, but known like a loved
home outcrop of rock, and since words
can be lies, his silence had, for me,
a truthfulness, the preciousness of something
older than the human. I knew and did not
know his brain, and its woody mountain
casing, but the sheer familiarness
of his brow was like a kind of knowledge,
I had my favorite pores on its skin,
and the chaos, multiplicity, and
generousness of them was like
the massy stars over the desert.
And hair by hair the resolute shy
fiber creatures of his eyebrows—he hardly
frowned, he seemed serene, as if
above, or below, or alien
to anger. Now I can see that his eyes
were sometimes hopeless and furious,
but I saw them—and he seemed to feel them—
as lakes, one could sound them and receive no sense
of their bounds or beds. Something in
the paucity of his cheeks, the sunken
cheekbones, always touched me. Bold
ancient boner of the nose, wide
eloquent curve of the cupid's bow, its
quiver nearly empty, as if languagelessness

were a step up, in evolution,
from the chatter of consciousness. Now
that I travel the beloved land
of my husband's sealed mask of self
in memory, again, touching
his speechless contours—like the singing blind—
I feel that ignorant love gave me
a life. But from within my dream of him
I could not see him, or know him. I did not
have the art or there's no art
to find the mind's construction in the face:
he was a gentleman on whom I built
an absolute trust.

GREGORY ORR

Two Poems About Nothing

"I'll write a song about nothing at all…"
—Guillaume IX of Aquataine (1071–1127)

When I was young
I fell in love
with nothing.
Nothing had
my heart.
I was a moody
unpleasant youth;
even my mother
disliked me.
What are you
brooding about?
she'd ask.
                    Nothing
I'd answer.
For once, she
approved.
You're good
for nothing,
she said, and
nothing is good
enough for you.

*

When I was a child
nothing was everywhere.
It lay thick on leaves
and gathered in pools
under cedar trees.
Nothing filled
our barns
and grazed our pastures.

Nothing was so abundant
we never thought
to praise or prize it.
Those days are gone
forever. Now nothing
is scarce
and we lack for nothing.

Wild Heart

Where would I be if not for your wild heart?
I ask this not from love, but selfishly—
How could I live? How could I make my art?

Questions I wouldn't ask if I was smart.
Take the whole thing on faith. Blind eyes can see
where I would be if not for your wild heart.

Love or need—who can tell the two apart?
Nor does it matter much, since both agree
that I need you to live and make my art.

Are you the target; am I the bow and dart?
Are you the deer that doesn't want to flee
and turns to give the hunter her wild heart?

I bite the apple and the apple's tart
but that's the complex taste of destiny.
How could I live? How could I make my art

in some bland place like Eden, set apart
from the world's tumult and its agony?
Where would I be if not for your wild heart?
How could I live? How could I make my art?

JOYCE PESEROFF

Posthumous Birthday

A sad date, summer's end.
I rarely called but mailed
the basket of chocolates you loved,
and Mother monitored, *Oh, Roy!*
You were greedy for so little.
I'd send the few bad things
you cared for: candy, a humidor,
bitter, slender, black cigars.
Years ago I roused then wouldn't sleep
with a boy who smelled like you.
Now I hiss with effort the way you did,
fetching mail or pumping a bicycle tire.
Once my accusations made you cry.
I choked the same high snuffle at
my friend's funeral, but not for you,
a soldier who'd witnessed the ghastly
camps and dismissed everything after
with, *It's not the end of the world.*

Natural Light

That summer I saw you as a bird,

a whitethroat singing O Sweet
Canada Canada but a strange sooty color,

then as the dwarf peach that had never borne

ruddy with hanging fruit, actually bedecked
like a Christmas tree. Everything promised

transformation, day into night, stars

unrolling like an opera score for owls,
crickets, and skinny, long-legged frogs.

The orchard's been chewed to death by mice

the owls have fattened on.
This laptop's screen is meant for a cubicle,

not the porch with its natural light. You, gone

five years, used a Selectric. Your peonies open,
and your dog? Ash sifted on a bed of daffodils.

DONALD PLATT

Viva la Vida

Watermelon, not pomegranate, is the fruit of the dead.
        I eat it for breakfast
these hot midsummer days to feel my spellbound mouth

        crunch the cool flesh,
so many seeds to tease out with the tip of my tongue
        and spit onto my plate

with a small clatter. The dead thirst for such fruit. Their dry
        mouths water.
        You don't know
how good you've got it. Eat for us, whose one daily meal is

        rock salt and shadows.
The volts of juice jolt my tongue into speech. I glut myself for
        my grandfather
        and his bleeding ulcer, who sits forever

on the couch after dinner, worrying the last kernels of corn on the cob
        from his gold fillings
with a dark toothpick, sighs, and belches. I hack off another

        half-moon slice for Aunt Clara,
who let my wife, Dana, a small child shrieking with delight,
        throw the full

garbage bag every morning down the apartment's eight-story
        chute into
the incinerator, which burns all our years to a fine ash

        that will settle in dreams
on the ugly mahogany furniture, which we must then wipe
        clean. I eat

for Frida Kahlo, whose last painting is a great
                  watermelon split open
like a wound that won't heal. On one of the slices

              she has written
Viva la Vida. Come to the last entry in her journal, she pressed
    down hard
              and scrawled, "I hope the exit

is joyful, and I hope never to come back." Viva
              Frida,
anywhere out of this world. Viva the cut magnolia

              blossom swimming
in a bowl of water, whose wilted skin is the texture and hue of
    my grandmother's
              cheek after she applied

pancake makeup, but before she patted on her blush. Viva
              our first quick sex, the girl
in the Best Western motel, who holds a boy to her, plucks

              such music
from his lyre that the strings of his whole being tremble
              with the sound,

and makes him spill quicksilver seed into her mumbling
              mouth, full
of night and its dark, untold needs. Viva the new day

              that comes to our
blinded windows, rustles the aspen's leaves, and whispers,
    "Let me in," that old song
              whose only refrain is

"My burden is light." Viva Lucy, my younger daughter, who scoops out
              the chilled heart
of the watermelon with both small hands, crams it into her
    mouth, and tells me

her half-garbled story that begins,
"After God created food coloring, he put a little bit in the sky—
red and blue
for sunrise." It never ends.

LIAM RECTOR

Our Last Period Together

Lying in bed we feel soon
We'll do what's right and end
The wrong thing we've come to be,

I to you, and you to me.
Not all of us, as it turned out,
Was wrong. Years one and two,

For one...And perhaps remembering
That time again, we turn to make love
One more time, something we've

Mostly stopped wanting to do,
You to me, and me to you.
After you climax and I'm

Coming along, you lean back and soon
—No diaphragm, nothing—
You take all that sperm into you.

This much we give over to fate
In case we're wrong, in case
We shouldn't be separating, in case

We should stay. And as soon
As your period comes, two weeks later,
I go away.

Hope

There are nights I dream of goldfish
and in my dreams they sing to me in
fluted, piercing sopranos like the Vienna
Boys' Choir. Although in the daylight
they are mostly silent and ravenous—
the suction-cup grip of their mouths
on my fingertip like tiny rubber bathroom plungers when they rise to strike
at an offering of chopped green peas.
Sometimes a frenetic clicking of marbles
nosed and nudged across the aquarium
floor during scavenging sessions for food,
sounding like the rack and crack of a game
of pool. Such hunger. Such extravagance.

Their ovoid bodies are like Faberge eggs
filigreed with flakes of hammered gold,
a glittering armor of polished gill
plates, their dorsal fins elegant ribbed
silk fans that open when in motion,
and fold themselves shut in repose.
Clever pectoral fins maneuver and oscillate
like small propellers, and the circling
tails flare and twirl with the hypnotic
flourish of the toreador's cape. All
is endless metaphor here. All of it.

I once read the goldfish memory span
was three seconds, and does this mean
each moment is an astonishment
in a series of quick incarnations spiraling
outward the way water ripples away
from a disturbance, so that, in the end,

each brief flicker of awareness
is long enough to learn to simply *be,*
and isn't this really, after all, enough?

One morning I woke to find the red-capped
oranda in distress—fins clamped sadly
down, listless tail, gasping on the back
corner floor of the aquarium. I netted
her and put her in a glass bowl sugared
with a quarter cup of sea salt crystals—
the way my Japanese grandfather once
showed my mother, and the way my mother,
years later in America, once showed me.

And several hours later, the sheer veils
of tail and fin began to bloom, to resume
their arabesques and veronicas around
the sleek shimmer of her white satin body—
the scandal of her scarlet cap dipping
coquettishly, onyx beads of eyes swiveling
in their turquoise socket rings. She swam
around and around the clear glass bowl,
until my heart swung left and followed her
around and around from above the way
red-throated loons on the Island of Seto
circle and follow the fishing boats, tamed
by the fishermen, and calling out
with their strange and mournful cries.

Toothpick Warriors

Night sweats
to the rattle
and clink
of their armor—
marching grooves
around my bed,
pulling toothpicks
from tatami
to disembowel
each other,
or skewer
and roast
a beetle, fine
bone china
of their sake cups
rolling the sound
of marbles
when they drop them
on the hard-
wood floors at dawn.

You think
I'm making this up
but they never
liked you anyway
and you are less
than flesh,
more a ghost—
quick and sweet
as opium smoke,
indelible
as the curl of red
unfurling
into the syringe
before exploding

poppy-bright
into fire
and backdraft,
until everything
blazes gold
and heat,
like the memory
of Mishima's
golden pavilion
resurrected
into flame.

Stay and watch.
I can make them
afraid of me.
Here is the white
linen headband
I wrap around
your forehead.
Here is perfumed
cotton wool
I use to pack
your anus.
This is the dagger
I unwind from silk
to hand to you.
And here the sword
I'll use to cleave
delusion's head
clean off.

GIBBONS RUARK

Words to Accompany a Bunch of Cornflowers

Those beads of lapis, even the classical
Blues of dawn, are dimmed by comparison.
When I hand you this bunch of cornflowers
The only other color in the room
Illumines your eyes as you arrange them.

They are the blue reflection of whatever
Moves in you, serene as cool water tipped
Into crystal, oddly enough the willing bride
To a cloudy head of melancholy
So deeply blue it could prove musical.

This is the blue John Lee Hooker's gravelly
Voice in the sundown field was looking for.
This is the unrequited dream of an iris.
Ice blue, spruce blue, little periwinkle blue—
Nothing else that dies is exactly so blue.

Rainy Sunday

His beautiful daughter was attending church.
He sat with tea and limp tortilla chips
watching the rain. Not feeling left in the lurch
by things, but wondering at the odd ellipse.
Surely she wasn't enamored of the pale
Galilean on the shore; —apocalypse
yet further from her mind. She could inhale
the fumes of fellowship that would eclipse
the dailiness of things—it was their company
she liked.
        And he, tied by the helter-skelter
of distractions, imported beauty duty-free,
and by these guesses only now half-guessed,
turned from the rituals that once gave shelter,
from principle returned without the interest.

The Relic

All the way home, I kept thinking of the lost
finger of St. Teresa, displayed
in the gift shop of a convent where she spent
most of her life being thrown by the devil
down the stairs or gripping the handrail
after communion, so others wouldn't see
how it took all of her strength to keep
her body from flying away. A wild hen,
a fighting breed, she still broods over Avila,
as if she could hatch that penurious flock
into God's generosity. Now as then,
they grasp and peck, scraping—too poor to mock—
God's cold stone nest. For pilgrimage,
all they have left is her finger, a relic

of her body—often disputed,
buried elsewhere, periodically dug up
for proof of incorruptibility. It was said
for centuries, she refused decay,
though at each exhumation, a little less
of was left: a hand was taken for a monastery,
a splinter of sternum for the Empress,
and the peasants, well, took what they could get,
a woman bent to kiss her feet to bite
off a big toe. *"They go around crying
about the devil or longing for a sign,"*
she scolded, waving, perhaps, this finger,
though, probably, without this clot of green,
this emerald ring that makes one doubt

all vow of poverty. . . . Is the digit
even hers at all, or that of some fuck-me
lady, thought lovely enough to stand in

for a saint's? If godliness requires
beauty, then her finger of insult—flung
at God after a horse bucked her into a stream
you have so few friends because you treat them
so badly—has an afterlife of gem.
Life as a nun would be purgatory,
but better than an eternity in hell.
Yet it's her body that lingers in limbo.
A cloud of delicate mold—the halo
of God upon this earth, fine as an angel's hair—
clings to her finger, tries to call her home.

NEIL SHEPARD

Journey's End

Johnson, Vermont

Yet another metamorphic
swimming hole, waterfall
where language fails.

Gneiss, schist, slate.
You can hear nouns meta-
morphose to verbs, *gnarl, shiver, split,*

then strip down, tumble
in granitic kettle-holes
and camouflage themselves

in green water, green
because pines hang
above the fault-line

and shade language
from blue-blank sky where somebody's watching, listening

to the syllables of delight.
This is the place of pre-
delight, before the light

blinked on in our fore-
brains and pained us with fore-
knowing. No, this place

delivers a hiss, a wordless
rush through gray clefts,
the high chattering scream

of being submerged in momentary
cold so cold the body knows
undeniably, indelibly,

these are the high walls
of journey's end, of anaerobic
last-gasp, body-turning

blue. And tongues become
like limbs trying to climb
the high cliffs of death

to clutch a purchase
on exposed outcrops
where words can sink

their cleats, pitons,
grappling hooks, inventions
that turn humans pre-

human: moss-crawler, rock-clasper,
some thing attached to cold stone
that owns no language—

micaceous, gneiss-spark,
fissile schist, granite-fault—
that goes on climbing

as if it were stone dumb,
attached by its tongue
to the thing, the very thing.

Apollo on What the Boy Gave

Eyes the color of winter water,
eyes the winter of water where I

Quoits in the Spartan month
Hyacinthius, the game
joins us, pronounces
us god and boy: I toss him
the discus thinking *This is mine*
and the wind says *Not yet*

Memory with small hairs
pasted to pale wet skin
(the flower *hyacinthos,*
perhaps a fritillaria, not
the modern *Hyacinthus orientalis*)

After he smells of orange groves,
spreads white ass meat for me
him with a hole drilled in him I try
to fill: I ease my way into his orchard

(the ornamental Liliaceae
genera, including the spring
-flowering *Crocus* and *Hyacinthus,*
and the summer-flowering
Hemerocallis or day lily; also
Amaryllis, Hippeastrum, and *Narcissus*)

A blow struck by jealous Zephyrus, or
Boreas, by other accounts:
his skin annotated by the wound
that explicates his mortality

in red pencil, wind edits him down to
withering perennial, shriveled bulb

(perhaps a pre-Hellenic god, his
precise relationship to Apollo
still obscure, though clearly
a subordinate)

Him with a hole I keep trying
to make, dead meat of white
blooms in hand

(onion as well, garlic, leek,
chive, and asparagus)

And where he was
this leafless stalk (bluebell,
tulip, torch lily, trillium:
snowdrop, Solomon's
seal) I break to take for my own,
black at the core of blossoming

(a bell-shaped nodding flower,
usually solitary)

The Land

Preface & Dedication

Late last night, January of 2001, temperatures on this Vermont hill farm dropped below zero. Jeff was in the loft of our cabin, sleeping under two blankets and a down comforter, while downstairs in my pajamas and slippers, with a blanket draped over my head and around my shoulders, I stepped outside onto the deck. Immediately, the cold slipped under my bare heels, gripped them and sealed them over, like water freezing to black ice. The stars above me shone brighter than any dream or hope I could remember having—all but one. Ice in the nearby river popped and sighed; snow around me glowed. The moon seemed close enough to touch, but promised to be cold, so cold that my fingers might stick to it, as they would to a cube of ice, or to the inside of a freezer door.

I'm thirty years old. I turned twenty-eight and twenty-nine behind hospital white walls and blue glass windows on the eighth floor of a blood and bone marrow cancer ward. I watched through one weakly colored glass door as a nine-month-old baby was infused with enough chemo to kill a draft horse. I watched through another glass door as an engaged couple slipped rings on each other's fingers in the presence of a nurse and chaplain, and then the newlywed wife watched the newlywed husband die. He'd been in the ward since August, and he'd died the day after Christmas, and through those two seasons of disease he'd screamed one sentence only: I don't want to die in a hospital.

I didn't have cancer, but the man I am engaged to marry did. When Jeff was first diagnosed with leukemia, doctors told us we would be hospital-bound for a year and that Jeff's chances of survival were about fifty-fifty. When Jeff's cancer relapsed before that year was over, doctors told us that Jeff would need a bit more than another year, possibly two, of treatment and that his chances for survival had dropped ten times, to about five percent.

Sometimes after speaking such statistics, a doctor would sigh, or shake his head, gestures, I assumed, of sorrow, or at least sympathy. Always I would be on the hospital bed, stretched out alongside Jeff, who was often coherent but attached to so many IVs and electrical cords—hooked to chemotherapy, to morphine, to antibiotics, to saline, to heart monitors, and to this and that large black box blinking red and white lights—that he never could move much. Clear plastic cords carrying fluid into him and out of him would pass over my body, resting on my hip or arm, and I'd watch them as doctors spoke, examining them for air bubbles—cause for alarm.

"The chances are slim," doctors would say, "but you're young."

And then they would go, and I'd rest my head on Jeff's chest—carefully, so as not to disturb a wire or plastic tubing—and I would listen to and feel his heart thump on, despite the disease growing in his blood.

Seasons now have passed, and dear luck, dear God, dear medicine, dear two and a half years of treatments and sufferings, I dedicate this story to you. In the past, I cursed you, I doubted you, I even, at times, begged death to release me from you—but now, I pronounce a thousand blessings to you for January 7, 2000, when Jeffrey Scott Hale survived his second bone marrow transplant at New England Medical Center. Jeff's medical records are still stored there, in a file labeled "Patient #1," for he is the first to survive a variety of experimental procedures even most doctors cannot pronounce clearly.

From such a past, of course, we have horror and anger and bewilderment within us, at times overcoming us, but, too, our truth includes yesterday, when, eleven months away from our last overnight stay in the hospital, we hiked through blue sky and snow two thousand feet up to the top of Mt. Rochester. We could see across the entire Piedmont, from the snowy slopes of the Green Mountains all the way to the Connecticut River. To the east, New Hampshire's White Mountains shone white and bright, and Jeff and I stood in the wind gazing at them, red-faced, numb, but not yet willing to turn around, to go back down, and I thought of what now—come what may—is true: *We are here We are here We are here We are here We are here We are here We are here*

"It's back—" He came towards me from the front porch, arms outstretched. He had a short-sleeved T-shirt on, and his arms were pale, frail, like lines of light stretching from his body to mine. I stood by the car, across the dirt road, in the driveway. He was shaking his head, which was also pale, and bare of hair. He was crying. "I'm so, so sorry—" I didn't, immediately, know what he meant. I didn't move.

Jeff crossed the street. His face, I could see now, was wet and red. He was shaking, shaking his head.

"Baby, what—?"

Even at six p.m. the sun was still bright and warm. The whole world was green and gold with the lushness of an overripe summer. Vermont in August is always more generous than I can remember until the month arrives. I breathed in the season's smell—or sucked it in, really—a mixture of mown hay, pine trees, brook mist, and mulch.

Jeff took hold of my bare shoulders. He could barely speak, his lips and chin were quivering so wildly. "Is someone hurt?" I asked, as if a plane crash, car crash, explosion, or fire could save us from the news Jeff had to tell.

"Oh, Sarah—the leukemia—"

His fingertips trembled against my skin. Or was it me, trembling against his embrace?

"The leukemia has come back."

Instead of falling backwards, back against the car, its engine still tick-ticking behind me, I stood perfectly still, as if by not moving, I could deny time, and what I had just heard would be re-absorbed into the universe as an unspoken statement, a never-to-be-spoken statement. A lie. A ridiculous thought.

"Sarah—" Jeff put his face against my neck and sobbed. His tears were hot. I could feel his teeth against my skin. "Oh, Sarah—" Jeff squeezed me so tightly, all my bones seemed to fold into one thin line between his arms.

Still, my eyes remained dry and open. Over Jeff's head, which was pressed against my throat, I stared at the house that all summer we had called home, for we were renting a single room inside its two-hundred-year-old yellow frame, which drooped and sagged like an overripe sunflower. Birds nested in the eaves of its front porch, and I noticed one of them suddenly, a blue jay, swoop from the air into its shadows.

"Dr. Linn left a message on the phone. They saw it in the last blood test. I'm supposed to go back tomorrow."

I shook my head. Reality could not bend this way, it just could not, because if it did, it would be packed too tightly with tragedy, it would be too unbalanced between hard hits and grace, it would be devoid of design. It would have to explode, for no outline could contain it.

Jeff lifted his head and looked at me. I stared back at his red, ravaged face. All last year, we had lived in and out of a hospital, staying in a single room up to fifty days at a time, while Jeff suffered through ten-day-long chemotherapy infusions, over one hundred fifty blood transfusions, a bone marrow transplant, dozens of fevers and infections and weeks upon weeks of vomiting and boils that swelled red, then burst with the very poisons doctors pumped into him again and again...

"Let's go to the upper meadow," I said. "Mistakes happen in hospitals all the time. Let's go to the meadow and pray for a mistake."

Jeff lifted a hand from my shoulder to wipe his eyes. The meadow was where we wanted to marry, once Jeff's health returned. A quarter of a mile off the road behind our landlady's farmhouse, it was a concave scoop of land, at least twenty acres, south-facing, green and moist with seasonal springs. We called it our bowl of sun. Temperatures in the meadow were always ten degrees higher than anywhere else on our land. "I haven't seen our meadow for so long," Jeff said, his hand still at his eyes.

Only two years had passed since we first discovered the land in Vermont we now owned. Walking into the upper meadow that first time, neither of us had said a word. We spent the entire day there, rarely letting go of each other's hands. We lay on our backs and watched crows flap and hawks float; we hiked a couple miles into the surrounding woods swatting mosquitoes and stopping still each time a deer passed, a fox, a grouse. The land was a kingdom of hip-high ferns, blooming meadow sweet, maple trees, pine trees, birch, ash, spruce, so much greenery, all of it full to bursting with life, of such endless variety, and we yearned to be part of its design.

Six months passed before we were able to find financing—the land had been for sale since the early eighties—and then on January 28, 1998, we purchased titles to the meadow, plus one hundred more acres of forest surrounding it. We lived at first in a tent, then in a salvaged aluminum trailer, waiting for Vermont's harsh winter to pass so we could begin to build a more substantial wooden home. As soon as the snow melted and mud dried, we began to clear land and dig a foundation, and we hired a carpenter to help us carve out a traditional post-and-beam frame.

Jeff was first diagnosed with leukemia that September, just after he finished decking over the first floor of our cabin.

"Do you think you could walk all the way to the meadow?" I asked. This summer, in contrast to last year's, Jeff had been so weak after his bone marrow transplant that walking more than one hundred steps exhausted him. Climbing stairs made him gasp. We had thought the chemo used for the transplant was causing his fatigue.

"I have to," Jeff answered.

"I'll change quickly." I was still dressed for work in high heels and an ankle-length skirt, but when I tried to pull away from Jeff to cross the road, he held on to my shoulders. With one hand, he touched my face, smoothed a palm along my hair, which had grown long and blond over the summer. "You look beautiful," he said.

That was when I started to cry. I was twenty-nine years old and had never felt so happy, so full of energy, so healthy: *why* the downward tug back into the underworld? I pulled Jeff's hands down, off me, squeezing his wrists till I could feel blood passing through his veins and the thump of my own pulse in the tips of my thumbs and fingers. Leukemia, cancer of the blood, kills more than twenty thousand people a year. Was Jeff, really, one of this year's fatalities?

"Before the sun sets," Jeff said. "Come on."

We crossed the road together, towards the farmhouse, with Jeff's left arm wrapped around my shoulders and my right arm holding on to his waist. My vision filled with a view of us from behind, as if I were still standing next to the car. We looked so old, like grandparents who'd suffered hard lives, ungrateful children, negligent grandchildren, old people getting older whom the world had never treated kindly and was now completely defeating. Neither of us was steady enough on our feet to climb the three porch steps without help. We leaned upon each other, our knees rising slowly.

We climbed through the spruce forest to the upper meadow, never letting go of each other's hands. Every fifty yards or so, Jeff would stop, and we would wait until he could catch his breath. He was white as a moon, and his muscles trembled like leaves in a breeze. All summer, Jeff's blood counts had been less than one fifth to one tenth of what a normal man needs in order to breathe adequately, absorb enough food, and move his limbs. We'd thought time could heal him, though, time and love.

When we reached the upper meadow, the sun had already disappeared behind Braintree's western ridge of blue mountains. Their jagged outlines glowed gold, and above that arched a band of red. The remaining stretch of sky was a light blue festooned with orange and pink ribbons of temporal light, which multiplied every passing minute, until the whole world above us was a festival of warm colors.

Jeff and I stood in the meadow for a while, looking at the sky and not each other. Because the sunset splendor was in the west, we did not notice the moon—which in late summer rose in the southeast—until it was high in the sky. The moon swelled with brightness as the sky slowly darkened, as if the moon was sucking up all the day's light for its own nighttime glory.

Jeff sat down, then pulled me alongside him. He touched my eyes, my lips, my throat. In the brightness of the moon, I could see him clearly. He looked like something cut from stone. I leaned forward and placed my mouth against the side of his face: he was cold like stone, too. "Jeff," I breathed in his ear, but who would hear me, who would hear, if death swallowed away my witness?

Jeff began crying again, coughing out huge sobs, and I kissed the tears on his cheeks, his neck, I kissed his still-bald head, and then, suddenly, using both his hands, Jeff pulled my face in front of his own and placed his mouth on mine—hungrily, opening and closing his jaws, breathing in my breath, letting his own brief gasps escape into me. Instinctively, my hands moved to the back of Jeff's hairless head, and the sensation of our skin, our flesh finding its way into the old union of touching and being touched, after so long, made me shake and feel afraid. For five months we had not kissed or made love. Doctors had warned us about infections, bruising, internal bleeding—and I put my hand between us on Jeff's breastbone. A crazy pounding carried on beneath it, and again, I started to cry, this time for Jeff and for the life inside him that did not want to end.

"Don't—" Jeff pulled off my shirt, put his face against my bare chest. "Don't cry."

The sky was all darkness now, the moon high enough to seem small. I could feel my hair falling along my bare back, then the prickle of fledgling brambles under my bare legs. Jeff kneeled over me, smoothing his hands up and down my legs, up and down my waist and chest, up my neck and face, the tips of his fingers brushing me lightly, almost tickling me. The wind picked up and blew clouds in front of the moon, and with a strength I hadn't felt in Jeff since he first got sick, he lifted me up, set me down on my back, and moved over me, my hips in his hands, his lips on my throat. "Don't you go from me," I tried to say, but all my words were one long sound, then another.

Slowly Jeff moved into my body, deeply, so deeply, until I felt as if Jeff were inside every part of me, even my toes and my fingers, leaving no room inside me for sadness. I was filling up with Jeff, with the pleasure of him, and the ground underneath my back began to spin wildly, as if I were suddenly conscious of the earth's true speeds as it rotated on its axis. I imagined the moon from behind the clouds seeing Jeff and me, two tiny bodies making love on the gargantuan back of a spinning planet, and I wrapped my legs around Jeff's back, my arms around his neck, because there was no way, absolutely no way I was letting this man fly off the ground into the black space that surrounded us.

Too soon, the clouds were gone again, and in the moon's light, Jeff and I lay in a heap of limbs, like so many strands of golden, entwined straw. Jeff's bare head lay under my left hand; the fingers of my right interlaced with the fingers of his; our legs stretched out alongside each other, touching from hip to knee to ankle. Our sweat had cooled and dried around us like a protective shell, and—are bodies truly ephemeral? How could they be, these hot, mobile skin-pots of life? The light, the sounds of night, the wind, our exhausted and just about unified bodies—weren't these all eternal fixtures of earth's design? Who, or what, would dare bring death into this scene?

Eventually, Jeff and I pulled on our clothes and, shivering, stumbled down the hill, through the spruce forest and into the room we rented in the big yellow farmhouse. We showered in scalding hot water, soaping each other's faces, arms and backs, and then, bare-skinned and steaming, we slid under a heap of blankets on our bed and folded into each other like a fan.

"How do you feel?" I whispered against Jeff's lips.

"Better," Jeff answered, squeezing me, and we both spun wildly into sleep.

Vermont: the two syllables had been a mantra for us for what felt like half our lives, but really was only two years. Neither of us was born there or had ever lived there before we met each other. We'd grown up in cities on opposite coasts, then met at twenty-six and twenty-seven in Somerville, Massachusetts, a sidekick of a neighborhood across the river from Boston, often called "Slummerville," a place where tall, thin houses leaned and sagged like old, gray trees in an abandoned orchard, where the people were equally old, gray, and sagging, but, too, where a younger, transient, slightly grungy population was beginning to spring up like dandelions and yarrow. Self-employed artists, political progressives, writers, health-food advocates, poorly paid social workers, graduate students working for their second and third Ph.D.'s, substitute teachers—an assortment of colors and flavors were sauntering into the gray town's landlord-owned triple-deckers, renting out rooms for $150 to $250 a month, wearing ripped jeans and old leather jackets, talking art, talking hate, talking the system and what is the right way to live.

In 1993, with two friends, Jeff opened a coffee shop in Somerville called The Someday. It was right next to a community theater and movie house built in the 1920's, a place that used to sport vaudeville with a secret speakeasy underneath it. Now it hosted blues bands, folk rock guitarists, and classic stars like Taj Mahal, Merle Sanders, and Patty Larkin. The Someday first attracted theater customers and performers, and then all the growing younger crowd of Somerville. From seven a.m. to midnight, people talked over tall lattes and hot chocolate and starchy sweets, or they sat alone at tables sketching faces and poems into journals, or they stared through window glass to the silent rows of gray buildings outside, which leaned to the left, then to the right, depending on which way the wind blew.

For the transients of Somerville, Jeff's café was essential: it provided them with a sense of having community and even security, when they had not yet established these things for themselves. The Someday was actually more of a home for them than where they slept. It was where the family was always gathered, the coffee always hot, the air warm, the lights on, the music playing, and where there was always room for one more person on the couch. When people's heat got turned off because of an unpaid oil bill, they came to The Someday; when they broke up with their girl- or boyfriend, they came to The Someday; when they had a paper, proposal, or article to hand in and did not know how to begin, they came to The Someday. Jeff's café was the place where food and drink and single pretty people were in abundance, where ideas flew between lips and suddenly felt more real than previously private, unsaid yearnings, where people were able to say inside their heads, "I am not alone," and feel the truth of the words fill their bodies with each swallow of the hot coffee Jeff served them.

I didn't go to Jeff's café until two years after Jeff opened it, but the instant I walked in, I fell in love with him. A ridiculous statement, of course: I knew even as I felt it that I was crazy. Jeff was standing behind the bar, chatting with people as he made them their drinks, and I stood staring at him as if he had wings. He wore tan canvas shorts over black long underwear, hiking boots, a baseball cap, and purple T-shirt that said "One Less Car" inside the spokes of a bicycle wheel. His shoulders were broad, his smile as wide as the room. His laugh was loud and long—like a drum solo in a rock song.

I couldn't move, just watch and listen. Bob Marley sang about rivers and tears through two speakers over Jeff's head. A young mother held her two-year-old child's hands as it danced to the tunes on a couch. Jeff came from around the bar to hand her a glass mug full of coffee, and she smiled at him, and her child jumped up and down on the couch as if it were on a trampoline. "Who's next?" Jeff called out across the room, and, still in the doorway, I felt *so strange,* that after another thirty or sixty seconds, I turned around and ran back out to the street. "You are crazy," I said to myself, jogging to the subway, my backpack swinging, "absolutely crazy."

I was working long hours then, often leaving my apartment

before five a.m. and not returning until after nine at night. I felt as short on time as I did on money, and despite my feelings, it was many months before I walked to Jeff's café again.

He was there, of course, making drinks and serving them to customers, and, yet again, I stood as if stuck in the doorway of his café, feeling *so strange*, I thought I was going to have to leave just like last time—but, "Excuse me," someone said behind me, wanting in, and so I had to move forward, towards Jeff and the counter he stood behind, and, "Tea," I answered to Jeff's abrupt and unsettling question about what did I want, and then, "Whatever you recommend," when he asked what *kind* of tea did I want. I was so nervous I was sweating, but Jeff continued to talk to me— he mentioned green tea and black tea, sweet-flavored tea and smoky-flavored tea—and the whole time I was too shy to look at his face. I stared instead at his hands, which pressed down on the black Formica counter.

His hands were huge. Both of my hands could fit inside one of his. His knuckles were as big as the outside halves of walnut shells, richly patterned with wrinkles. His fingers were long and strong, as if he played guitar or basketball regularly. His nails were thick and broken off, and I imagined his work wore them down the way wild horses' hooves got trimmed when they galloped over rocks.

"Well?"

I looked up. Sun struck Jeff's face through the window, and the lenses of his round-rimmed glasses deepened to a dark purple. I couldn't see his eyes. "Surprise me," I said, shrugging, for I hadn't heard a specific word he'd said about tea.

Once I received my drink, I nearly ran into the back corner of the café, sat down, and watched this man who made me behave in such silly ways. My fingers were actually trembling around my teacup. "Crazy," I repeated to myself. "Twenty-six years old and crazy, you don't have time for cafés, you don't have time to date, he would never ask you out anyway, he's probably married, or celibate..."

Certainly, there is such a thing as falling in love at first sight, for the cliché would not exist otherwise, but why, for me, such insistent and instant adoration? Jeff was definitely handsome—particularly that jaw of his that was sharper than a knife blade, and his cheekbones, too, were sharp and defined, and those bare fore-arms, thick and muscled, with veins big as blue ropes twining around them—but lots of men were handsome, and I did my best to avoid them. I wanted to be single for a while; I had things I wanted to figure out about the world on my own.

And yet, there I was, sipping tea, staring at a man for an entire hour without blinking, wondering if he slept in T-shirts and box-ers or in nothing, wondering if he would go camping with me in the mountains if I asked him, wondering what he did, exactly, when he was not at the café, and could I do it with him.

What attracted me, I began to figure out, over time, as my visits to Jeff's café increased (despite my insistence that I had no time for tea and cafés), was Jeff's welcoming energy, his fortitude, a feeling that Jeff would last forever. He was a man who built things, even entire buildings, then stood behind them while other people enjoyed them—and in contrast, I felt insubstantial. I was a writer and teacher of stories, an occupation which too often felt fleeting, the mere studying and arranging of words on paper, some of which disappeared within a single year into the "no longer published" category. I watched Jeff as if he could teach me about what lasted, about what really mattered: how young I was, not to know flesh, strength, and even entire buildings might dis-solve, in a mere moment!

When Jeff and I finally started talking in 1996, "Slummerville" had begun transforming from a campy rental neighborhood to an up-and-coming urban center. The gray triple-deckers were being painted pastel colors, refloored, given new foundations and kitchen cabinets, and sold as condos for up to half a million dol-lars apiece. More restaurants and coffee shops opened up; dozens, then hundreds of more young people appeared, and these people wore high heels and blazers and caught the subway at eight a.m. for jobs in Cambridge and downtown. At first I was interested, then alarmed by the change—and when my monthly rent dou-bled with one month's notice, I decided it was time to get out. The hustle of the city had overtaken the slow, easy rhythm of what used to be a "ville," and I did not want to hustle. Not any-more.

As I began to wonder seriously about where I might move, Jeff and I began talking. I was at his café every morning by then, and every morning I asked, as he poured me my tea, "How are you?" Jeff always nodded at the question, then asked the person behind me for his or her order. Jeff's homey café had grown into a business, and he didn't have time to chat with his customers the way he used to.

One morning, though, no one was in line behind me. It was Monday, seven a.m., and raining. When I approached the bar, Jeff was leaning on the black Formica counter with both elbows, his head in one of the palms of his large hands.

"Good morning," I said.

Jeff frowned.

"How are you?"

Jeff shook his head at my question. "Not so good." He hardly moved his lips, so that it was hard, at first, to understand his words.

"Why not so good?" I was so surprised, I forgot to be shy. "Your business is booming, you're so successful."

Jeff straightened up and began to fix me my usual cup of tea. "Lapsang Souchong, right?"

I didn't know what to say other than "Everyone loves this place."

Jeff handed me my tea. "But I can't just work for other people all my life."

"Well—" I smiled. "Don't we all work for other people? I mean, isn't that the nature of... life?"

Jeff looked at me as if I were five years old. "That is a very narrow version of life, Sarah."

My jaw dropped practically onto my toes. I swear, my mouth was so wide, Jeff could have fit his entire head inside it. He knew my name! How? He must have been listening when I came to the café with friends. I felt as if I were on a bridge made of rope hanging over a bottomless ravine.

"Do you want to work for other people all your life?" Jeff continued, then bent down, lifted a cardboard box onto the counter, and began unloading scones into a glass display case.

"But—I don't really think anyone can work just for herself. You always have to answer to somebody—don't you?"

Jeff didn't stop working. "I like to believe there's more to work for than people."

I waited quietly. But Jeff seemed finished with talking. He emptied the box, collapsed it, put it back down on the floor. "Would you really leave your café?"

Jeff straightened up, wiped his hands on the front of his T-shirt, then placed one on the counter and leaned on it. His eyes were green, I noticed, with bits of gold and brown in them. "There's other things I want to do."

I placed my hands on the counter alongside his. I wanted to say, Can I come?, but instead asked, "Like what?"

We spoke for five hours that day, and for five hours every day that week. Conversation flowed like river water. I called work to say I was sick and would not be able to come in for an indefinite while, and Jeff told me he wanted land, he wanted to produce food rather than serve it, he missed sky and trees and free time. I told him about the two CSA farms I had begun working on during the weekends, about how much food each farm was able to produce per acre. He told me what herbs he wanted to grow to make medicinal teas for his café. We discussed the warmth of North Carolina, the expanses of Montana, good land deals in Eastern Washington State. I told him I'd lived in India, Israel, about my commitments as a teacher and as a writer. Jeff explained to me about yurts, geodesic domes, timber-framed cabins—ways of building houses for less than fifteen thousand dollars. He lent me *The Book of Tea;* I gave him *The Gift* by Lewis Hyde.

Five days of talking, and then it was Saturday. The café on weekends was always as crowded as a dance club, and when I arrived, Jeff was racing around. He looked vexed. The back of his T-shirt was wet with sweat. He noticed me right away, though, standing in the doorway. "Are you ready for the mountains?" he called out to me over people's heads.

I smiled like a bride. Was he joking? Didn't he know I owned a car and would hop in it with him, forever?

Someone called his name, and he turned around and began refilling coffee containers behind the bar. I backed out of the café—it was too crowded, and Jeff was too busy to talk to me—but oh, outside on the sidewalk, I felt like a shook-up can of soda about to bust. I was thrumming with such a buzz of energy—light and air were zinging their way along all my dark and locked-up insides. That evening, I couldn't help it, I returned to the café and left for Jeff an envelope containing seven cow beans.

Cow beans are beautiful beans—a deep maroon red with bright white spots speckled over them, colorful and remarkable enough to seem special, even magical, like Jack-and-the-beanstalk beans. With them I enclosed a note: "Yes, I'm ready for the mountains."

The next morning, Sunday, Jeff was waiting for me. "Beans, you gave me beans! No one's ever given me beans before!" He came around from behind the bar and, for the first time, touched me, placing his large hands on my shoulders. I looked down at our four feet. "When are we going?" Jeff said to the hair on my head.

I licked my lips, then looked up. "Now?"

Two months later, after a month more of talking, then another month of kissing and lovemaking, Jeff and I were on the road in my car scouting out land deals in nearby rural areas. Over the next sixteen months, we explored lots and old farms in West Virginia, North Carolina, Maryland, Maine, New Hampshire, Vermont, Washington, Idaho, Montana, and Wyoming. We wanted cheap land with water, a place where we could create expansive gardens of exotic edibles, and, too, I was finding that I wanted time and quiet so I could write down the stories that had always spun through me but which I never had time enough to write down with poetical precision.

Finally, one day in mid-August, 1997, we were driving in Vermont, after cruising through Maine and New Hampshire just the day before, bumping along Thayer Brook Road looking for the old Albright farm. I was making a sandwich out of cheese and bread on my lap, and Jeff was holding a map in his left hand, steering with his right.

"We're looking for two trailers on our left, one silver, one blue," Jeff said.

I looked up, holding my sandwich with both hands. "Some nice houses along this road," I said, seeing a white sprawling Victorian and barn, then a little while later a yellow one of similar design and age.

"Not too close together, too—about a quarter of a mile between."

"You don't want it farther than that, in case you have an emergency."

"I want to be able to walk naked from bedroom to garden without anyone seeing."

"I want you doing that, too."

Jeff smiled, then—"Hey, there they are." He swung the car up onto a muddy mound of driveway and cut the engine. "Where's the plot lines?"

Still holding on to my sandwich, I looked around the floor of the car. "Somewhere," I said. "I'm so hungry. Can't we just get out and eat?"

Jeff let a bit of a sigh sneak out of him, but agreed. I put my sandwich back in the bag of food we'd brought along, told Jeff to grab the gallon jug of water, and we hiked up to the trailers.

It took me only about a third of a second to wake up from my malaise. Behind the two dilapidated trailers, the land was spectacular, no less stunning than Emerald City would be if it were countryside rather than kingdom. The grass was hip-high, a sweet green that became gold each time the wind changed direction, which it did every few seconds, a shifting, soft breeze, like the grass that brushed along our bare thighs. Thirty acres of meadow stretched up and over a hill, only a few sapling birches shaking leaves and whispering in its expanse. On the right side of the hill, forty acres of dense spruce forest stood quiet and dark, a place that springs, deer, fox, and even moose, we'd soon learn, trailed through, depending on the season. There were no sounds—not a car, not a saw, not even a bird. The day was Sunday, the time was noon, the temperature over ninety degrees, and it felt as if the whole world were sleeping in the shade, except for us, standing here, sunned, dazzled, and, finally, home.

The owners of the property allowed us to camp out on the land every weekend until we were ready and able to hand them the required check. By the end of January 1998, the land was officially ours, and by March, we stood upon it in boots, coats, scarves, and hats, my car far behind us full of cleaning supplies, construction tools, coolers of food, and—a surprise from Jeff—three dozen roses.

The initial plan was this: fix up one of the two trailers to live in, tear down the other, build a timber-frame cabin before next winter's snow started to fall.

Both trailers were built in 1948 and looked it. We focused on salvaging the smaller one, spending days pulling trash out of it and scrubbing it down with orange-scented disinfectant. That March, the days' temperatures ranged from ten to twenty degrees. Whatever water we used—which came from gallon jugs we filled up at a hole in the brook—froze within half a minute. So we scraped and scrubbed off the ice as well as the dirt and used up probably a thousand paper towels. We filled two dumpsters with trash. After working, I'd be wet with sweat, then so cold, I'd shake as if riding a wooden cart down a rock-strewn road.

Jeff made bonfires of trash to warm me, and we put rocks in the coals, which later we'd pull out and huddle over with blankets over our heads to catch in the heat.

"I love this," Jeff said the first night we did the hot rock experiment. The air was so full of snow, I inhaled at least three tablespoons of ice with every breath.

"You're a nut." I was still cold, despite the smoke and flames.

Progress continued, though. The air warmed and the ground began to thaw. In the shelter of the spruce forest, we dug a hole four feet deep (that task took us two days) and lay two pieces of lumber across it for an open-air outhouse. Our shower was an old apple tree from which we hung a five-gallon black plastic container full of river water, with a pine-board pallet as a floor. We also salvaged a tin tub, which we balanced on cement cinder-blocks. Occasionally, we'd run a hose from a spring on the land to fill it, then build a fire underneath it and soak.

As we grew more resourceful, our trailer became more of a home. Jeff tacked purple carpeting on its floors and installed an ice-fishing stove in the kitchen. That tiny stove could raise the temperature from zero degrees to sixty in less than half an hour. We also paid a propane company to hook up a salvaged gas stove inside the trailer, and even though only two of its four burners worked, it allowed us to stay inside while heating up water for tea and cans of chili for dinner—as opposed to us huddling over an open fire outside at night, even if it were snowing or raining. Progress, progress.

It was late April by the time we decided to tear down the second trailer. It was a monstrosity, stretching over fifty feet long, reeking of spilled beer, leaking oil, and nasty old men. Bullet holes scarred its entire outside. Everything inside of value, we'd taken, used, sold. It looked like the ghost of a landfill risen to wreak havoc upon all of wasteful mankind.

"This is going to take all summer," I groaned to Jeff. The day was beautiful, full of blue air and tiny specks of gold. The snow was gone. Insects burst from the sodden ground; so did green weeds. The air filled up with a million smells—of wet earth, rotting vegetation, and of something being born.

"And our options are…?"

"I'm sure there's, you know, professionals who could just…"

"Say abracadabra?"

"For a few dollars, maybe."

Jeff lifted his crowbar up between our faces: "Herein lies our magic—and the protector of our dollar bills—which you'd rather spend." Jeff moved closer to the trailer. "If you hear anything louder than crashing and banging, make sure I'm not dead."

With that crowbar and a redheaded axe, Jeff actually brought that trailer down. First, he wrenched off the aluminum siding with the crowbar, which we saved in pieces for the dump. That took two weeks. Then Jeff began smashing down the walls with the axe. He could only work four or five hours a day, the work was so brutal. My job, while he rested, was to drag all trash to the dumpsters and also to roll up and bag the exposed insulation.

Fiberglass insulation is nasty stuff, especially after it's sat inside a wall for fifty years. Despite the growing warmth, I had to wear two layers of clothes, for the glass filaments moved like fleas through clothing and skin to itch a body to death. I wore a wool knit hat over my hair and tied an old shirt around my mouth. A neighbor had warned me that breathing in the old fiberglass dust could ruin my lungs forever.

In a strange way, I enjoyed those hours. It felt good to accomplish something. I was anxious—at times, desperate—to keep progressing. I really, really did not want to be living in the other trailer for another winter.

I also enjoyed the work because it was surprisingly interesting: an entire ecosystem was thriving inside that insulation. I found mouse turds in there, gray paper bits of wasp nests, and bunches of dried leaves that must have been some creature's nest. When I found a two-foot long snakeskin, I called out to Jeff: "Hey, come look what I found. Maybe there's more! This stuff is supposed to be good luck!"

Jeff came up just as I was reaching above my head to pull down a thick fold of insulation. Instantly, something huge and heavy came whirling down towards me—black and hissing. I screamed, leapt back against Jeff, and kept on screaming and screaming. Jeff pulled me back farther.

In front of us, a black snake mottled with brown splotches coiled up and hissed, its mouth opened wide. It had teeth. It was fat as a bicycle tire.

After ten seconds of stunned staring, Jeff let go of my shoulders (I whimpered) and threw a stick. In an instant, the snake was gone, tall grass rippling ever so slightly, marking its path.

For a full minute, neither of us said a word.

"I'm going to get my boots," Jeff said.

"I don't feel like doing this anymore today," I said, and followed Jeff into the other trailer.

Like almost every American, I believe in will. I believe in humans' undying ability to act negatively or positively upon their own lives and upon others' lives, too. But the return of Jeff's disease had pushed him and me into all that lies beyond will and self-directed action. There really are times when the circumstances around people—and in Jeff's case, within them—cannot be affected by human intention. Hurricanes, wars, falling in love, disease—there is so much that sweeps people into what they did not create individually and therefore cannot control individually.

But how does a person stay *human* inside such events? For to be human—Americans are told—is to affect things, to act upon them with their own ideas. If all people can do is *experience* what life lays down upon them—or throws down upon them—then what are they? Animals? Slaves? Fodder to fate?

Jeff and I tried so hard to avert a story of death. Not only did Jeff agree to the most harsh and intense Western medicine methods of fighting cancer, he also tried every alternative method as well. Throughout the first year and a half of his disease, he met with an Eastern acupuncturist, a Western herbalist and nutritionist, a hands-on healer, different massage therapists, and he prayed. Every day he prayed for God to show him what He wanted, and Jeff vowed to follow any set of orders. All he wanted was more time to walk on Earth. Jeff was willing to give up everything but time.

Despite all the effort, money, mental energy, and time we both put into Jeff's healing, his cancer came back anyway. And again, Jeff chose to fight it. There we were, back inside the hospital, for another year. His odds of surviving the second transplant were about as good as those of New England suffering an earthquake within the next ten years.

We knew we weren't exceptional. Over the last year in the cancer ward, we'd met many, many people—parents and grandparents and people younger than us—who were trying to live despite their disease, and the disease would not let them. Absolutely unaffected by the faith, hope, and goodwill those people demonstrated, their cancer returned, and they died. Such inexplicable punishment terrified me, bewildered me, and at times, I did not feel sane. If Jeff died, I began to believe that I also would have to die. I had been engaged to Jeff for two years, and for one and a half of those two years, Jeff had had cancer. I had spent over three hundred eight-hour days in his hospital and spent over fifty nights in a cot beside his bed. My skin had become as pale as the hospital walls; purple half-moons opened up underneath my eyes and stayed there. When Jeff was not living at the hospital, we still had to go there for day-long clinic visits two to three times a week, and often we had to monitor IV infusions of antibiotics or chemo throughout the night. I had quit three teaching jobs on three separate occasions in order to care for Jeff and had supplemented our shrinking income by stocking groceries in an all-night supermarket. Between hospital stays, I had moved us seven times, saving rent by housesitting and staying with friends while our half-built cabin in Vermont wasted away under blue tarps for two winters in a row.

I tried to take breaks by walking outside the hospital, hoping to relieve myself from the pain I witnessed and seemed, even, to absorb from Jeff, but the air of the city stunk worse than burning trash. Sleet and freezing rain had become a daily reality, and the noises of trucks, buses, and bulldozers were a constant grinding in my ears. My walks usually ended with me leaning against a brick building, or sitting on a guardrail of a parking lot, putting a hand over my eyes, and crying, as one hundred people per minute passed me by. I cried for Jeff, horrified by such ghastly destruction of a body that had seemed to me more divine than human, and I mourned the loss of our life in Vermont, our abandoned home, the woods we walked, the job I loved, the few spaces and positions we had been creating and arranging into a shared life.

And more than anything, I cried because I wanted our love back. I was starved for our love, for the physical and reciprocal cycles and sensations of it, and yet I did not believe, *could* not believe that chemotherapy and radiation were anything other than agents of war and horror, and why did *they* get to have our last days?

Three times in January 2000 I wheeled Jeff into the hospital basement for twenty minutes of total body irradiation (TBI). He was thin as an eleven-year-old boy by then and so easily folded into the 4′ x 4′ box the two nurses led him to. The box was tilted on its side, and so sitting in it, Jeff's knees pressed against his chin. The nurses strapped plastic bags filled with rice on whatever parts of his body touched other parts of his body—in the hollows of his knees, between his stomach and his thighs, inside his elbows. "Want boiled rice for lunch?" one of the nurses joked.

Then they leveled the radiation machine at him. It looked big as the nose of an airplane. They tested it: a thin blue line beamed straight at Jeff. I felt I was watching a video game in an arcade: Can you hit the tied-up cancer patient in the 4′ x 4′ box?

Then we left. We closed a door that was twelve inches thick behind us and watched Jeff on a miniature black-and-white TV screen.

"Are you afraid of getting cancer, working down here?" I asked, turning away from the screen. I felt green and was struggling not to vomit.

Both nurses shook their heads. One pulled up her sweater and showed me a radiation meter attached to her belt. "I'm four months' pregnant," she said. "I wouldn't be here if I didn't feel totally safe. This thing never gets beyond normal levels."

"I'd be more scared of chemo than this stuff," the other nurse said. "This stuff is way less harsh than those bags."

Who could say which was worse? Radiation and chemo tore their way through Jeff, sores opened up all over his body, inside his mouth, and even along the inside of his throat and intestines. Migraines made him scream, fevers made him sweat so that I had to change the bed sheets every other hour. He could not eat, could not even swallow water, and had to be fed and hydrated through IV tubing. His liver and kidneys began to fail, and his eyes, his palms, then all his body developed a sickly yellow color. He also began to react against antibiotics (he was on three): his hands and feet became swollen and broke out in a bright red rash that burned like an infection from poison ivy.

Meanwhile, I cried in a chair beside him, wearing a hospital mask and rubber gloves. Occasionally I rubbed his head with a gloved hand, but then he would whisper, "Enough," and could say no more because of the sores in his mouth.

Before reentering the hospital for his second transplant, Jeff and I had discussed forgoing more treatment. In August, after his leukemia was rediagnosed, we spent one, then two full days in Vermont. Our last afternoon, we spent resting on a beach of small stones by the river that cut through the northwest corner of our land. My head lay on Jeff's chest. His heart was still running hard, even though we'd been still for fifteen minutes.

Jeff picked up one of my hands and brought it to his lips. I watched his lips pucker; I listened to the river run over stones.

"Jeff, why are you still ill?"

Jeff didn't answer. When we'd first moved to the land in 1998, he'd moved rocks half the size of me into a wall, planning out the gardens, patios, and paths of our first home. He'd hand-tilled a quarter of an acre for our first garden—a circle garden—with a spiral path winding around inside it. He'd ridden his bike up three different mountains. Now, he couldn't even push his bike across the driveway.

"I had a lot of bad stuff pumped into me at the hospital, Sarah," he finally said, "and so has the earth. There's just a lot of poison out there."

"Are you thinking—of not going back? To the hospital?"

Jeff picked up strands of my hair and let them fall. "Of course." He wasn't crying; he just sounded exhausted, so exhausted, like he hadn't slept in a hundred years, like he was a spirit and not a man and had witnessed just too damn much of mankind's folly. "Two days," Jeff said. "I wouldn't last two days, if I were to lie here and not go back. I'd suffocate from lack of blood. The leukemia's growing. I can feel it."

"I don't know of what I'm more scared—the hospital, or—" I stopped. My hand found one of Jeff's hands and squeezed. "I can't imagine it."

Jeff was quiet again. Then, finally, "I can't, either. I've asked, 'Am I supposed to die by this river?' but Sarah, I know the answer's no." Jeff grabbed a handful of stones from the ground beside him and poured them slowly into a small mound beside us. "I have to go back, to the hospital. I have to try again."

Tears slid out of me silently, one after the other. I imagined them pooling around Jeff and me, then under us—and yet where could a river of them carry us, so we could be free of disease?

"I just don't feel ready to die yet," Jeff continued, then lifted his head, kissed my hair. His arms held me to him tightly. Those arms! Arms of a man who built things, then stood behind them as others enjoyed them, arms of a man who I thought would last forever—

"You swear?" My voice was shaking. "You swear you're not going to?"

"I swear." Jeff rolled on his side so my head was on sand looking up at him. His eyes were gold, green, brown: oh, the love inside them seemed too big for a human head to hold. "I swear, Sarah. Stay by me, and you'll see."

Syros, 1989

No woman knows the power she holds at fifteen until it's gone.
Long, loose *S* of the lower back. Inchoate cheekbone,
bracelet of wrist. Soap-soft, uncertain fingertip. Dumb
curve of the bottom lip, stunned to mute by its own prettiness.

I wore a shell-pink dress with a boat neck collar, my long hair
back and up. Limbs dark from days spent propped beside
an ocean blue as eyes of boys we planned to meet.
My best friend Arianne read magazines out loud about

what men want most and whether toothpaste helps bad skin
while we sipped gin and tonics pilfered from the house
her parents kept for weekends out of Athens, though
they never came. We claimed their bougainvillea-splattered deck

with pasta feasts for twenty-five of Arianne's close friends
and left the dishes in a sauce-encrusted sink to go out dancing.
Outside the ocean glowed, air dissolved like sugar grains
and even widows sleeping in their black nightgowns dreamed

of the boy with bedspring curls whose first kiss felt like drowning.
That summer everyone was young. In the afternoons I'd wander
down the hill to buy a peach, ro*tha*kino, the word I memorized
to ask for fruit so huge and ripe each peach I've eaten since

has rushed that summer back. The mythically wrinkled man
who sold them in his hut liked to repeat, Ro*tha*kino?
to see me blush. Up at the house we halved the pink-gold flesh
and pondered ways to live our lives like movie plots.

Winona Ryder's latest apple-cheeked display of angst
had, in a rage against her mother, drunk too much

and in her mother's makeup teetered up the steeple steps
where yes, the boy with devastating patience was just waiting

to complete her. The church bell, stars, and haloed lantern
he had lit seemed so exactly right that nothing ever need
come after. So when a charmer named Alexandros held out
a lime-tipped gin and tonic at the discotheque and told me

I was beautiful, I smiled mute assent and three nights later
heard myself explain I would go all the way.
No poem could invent the naked woman I watched wade
into the moon-marked water when I made this necessary claim

until I couldn't see her anymore. Even in her bone-white flesh
as firm as bark he'd leaned me up against "to talk" I knew
she wasn't real to anyone but me. And that the pebble-trail
of moonlight she was trying to apprehend would steadily

elude her. It hurt, the way a hip might hit a table in an unlit room:
one quick sharp pain spread slow through the rest of the body.
Then it was over. Mosquito netting swept around the bed,
and just beyond the widened windowsill that sometimes Arianne

slept on, the ocean stayed completely still. (The next night
I would glimpse a hand-sized scorpion on that sill, and watch it
slip into the wall just seconds from her neck's blithe contact
with the sheet.) When Ari's older brothers stumbled in to ask

would I please join them for a drink, Alexandros's mouth above me
yanked into a smile as if connected by a chain to the boys' laughs.
They must have left me there to dress, though all I recollect
is how the tiles shone on every countertop and square of floor

after I cleaned that filthy house for hours. Until the sun came up.
Alexandros returned, to offer dinner and protection rights
he thought he'd earned. The boys and Ari watched while I refused,
and heard the offer quickly turn to some excuse about a girl in Athens

he had left behind. I didn't mind. I don't remember what I said,
or how I felt beyond relief, or why I made the bet with Arianne
that in our last remaining days of summer break I could seduce
every man named Alexandros on the island. Or what the stakes were.

This is a story about a story. In two weeks I would be sixteen.
This was always a story. I lived each moment of that August
just to tell it, though I never told. The scorpion's quick flight,
the moonlit girl, and how I didn't sleep all night were facts

I stored as IOUs, to be exchanged for Life, that locked-up jewel,
much later on. They were my planned escape, before I knew
that time lets fall from trapdoors more than anyone would wish.
Or that a story's as true as anything. For every fact there is a sly

infinitude of truths, no less for how they contradict. I've left
so many versions out simply to say the word for *peach*,
and that my hair was long. For instance: Alexandros was deaf.
He read my lips, and clipped the edges off of adjectives

he whispered in my ear. Or this: the year that followed Syros
I would sleep with men whose names I didn't know. A story's
true as anything. Fifteen years old. The body still belongs to you.
Not yet a currency with which you pay your way down streets,

and after years will give up like a coat for warmth, or restlessness,
or what small muscle love becomes. You want to tell the ones
that ask for more, I'd give that too if it were mine. Maybe it never was.
Maybe I lost only those afternoons of peaches and dry heat.

But stories have no stakes, so I don't know. And those slow,
sweet-skinned months when I assumed the moments
I'd accrued would all add up somehow to gloriously cohere,
have disappeared to one dim memory of a room

I never entered. Shadow of a boy's face on the pillow.
Of stone-smooth hips and blindly perfect breasts I watched
with gentle, distant awe, as if my own, and not some
stranger's gaze, were separate from, and longing to come back.

LOUIS SIMPSON

The Willies

I asked Johan why he left home
and came to America.

How sad it can be in winter
listening to the wind...
No wonder that in the dawn
in the mist, one by one
figures appear among the trees,
making their way to the sea.

This is the day when the pack-boat leaves.
Better a voyage with storm and ice
than to sit in a creaking house
with a dog and old man for company.
Better a strange, hostile land,
people who do not speak your tongue,
than to listen in winter to the wind,
and look at snow on the trees.

At night when you go outside
to chop wood, you see the Willies,
those dead girls, giggling
and running. It's no dance
they mean when they crook a finger.

"You have never been to Skon," he said.
If you had, you'd understand.
If you heard the wind against the house,
and the voices: "Come out, we are so lonely!"

It's no life they have in mind for you
in a house with wife and child,
but wedding with the wind and snow.

Kinfolk

I read somewhere
that in Kentucky
they had to pass a law
forbidding a man
from marrying his
grandmother. It's the
damnedest thing,
but I don't doubt it.

I have a cousin there
who lives in farm country
where the most handsome man
is the mortician. Every night
Becky prays for a beautiful death
so that finally
she'll have that man's hands
all over her naked body.

BRUCE SMITH

Airless

The viola sounded like a buzz saw and looked like the sun
on methamphetamine. It was necessary, no not necessary,
(which was the quid pro quo of mom and pop on Long Island)
but amusing, to have something European
be dragged through Louisiana in the rain. Our geography
was indoors, in the exclamation and point below the navel.
Our memory was like the symptoms of arousal, desolately
beautiful, then forgotten as the faces in the cattle car
or the stumps of white pine rotting in the understory
when you were experimental. The one note of your dulled
unpeopled self was the repetitiously compelled
hours of a little bondage, a little discipline, enough
exquisite emptiness and pressure around the throat to get off.

W. D. SNODGRASS

Night Voices

Clear out here
you don't hear screams, shots, chants
of mobs raging, ambulances
   or fire sirens;
maybe some rabbit a fox caught,
some young bird squirming in a cat's
   jaws or the clenched claws
of an owl. Otherwise,
the outstretched countryside lies
   still. Until
here in my bedroom's wall-
absorbing darkness, one small
   cheep insists that sleep
is inappropriate for anyone
whose lifelong insomnia will be done
   too soon—
my discarded wristwatches' thin
alarms whose instructions have been
   lost, yet unexhausted
batteries lurking where they're buried
in my drawer of outworn underwear
   survive to drive
them wide awake again
like closed networks in the brain:
   these memories
of some that you once loved who'd never care
to hear from you, of questions you'd scarce dare
   hear, of what fear
underlay those days you used all wrong
or didn't use. Just how long
   can shrieks turned so weak
still carry on? We'll learn, no doubt,
which of us can longest last this out.

ELIZABETH SPIRES

Ghazal

My name in the black air, called out in the early morning.
A premonition dreamed: waking, I beheld a future of mourning.

Our partings were rehearsals for the final scene: you and I
in a desert, saying goodbye on a white September morning.

The call came. West, I flew west again. Impossible, but the sun
didn't move. I stepped off the plane and it was still morning.

I've always worn black. Now a blank whiteness outlines
everything. What shall I put on this loneliest of mornings?

You've left an envelope. Inside, your black pearl earrings
and a note: *Your grandmother's. Good.* In ink the color of mourning.

I remember the songs you used to sing. Blue morning glories on the vine.
An owl in the tree of heaven. All of my childhood's sacred mornings.

Your mother before you. Her mother before her. I, before my daughter.
It's simple, I hear you explain. *We are all daughters in mourning.*

I was your namesake, a firstborn *Elizabeth* entering
the world on a May morning. I cannot go back to that morning.

Glass House

Drink your cod-liver oil or the moon will eat you, my grandmother used to say. Well, I didn't drink my cod-liver oil and the moon didn't eat me. But one night I refused to drink my milk when I was visiting my grandmother, who lived in a white-frame farmhouse on the outskirts of Bloomington, and my bed, my teddy bear, and the tinker toys I'd spilled over the quilt were all whirled away in a tornado. Neighbors found the headboard caught in a barbed-wire fence down the road, along with the bodies of thirteen sheep.

I wasn't in the bed, thank God. I was huddling down in a corner of the cellar with my grandmother, who had pulled an old mattress over our heads. But nothing was ever the same for me after that. I've never fallen asleep with any feeling of security since that time. Who knows where a bed might fly to in the night?

My grandmother's house was flattened. By dawn they'd pulled us out of the rubble, shaken but unharmed. I followed my grandmother around, admiring her courage. She didn't cry or complain as she contemplated the wreck of her house. The men from town, bleary-eyed and no doubt thinking about their own damaged roofs or blown-out windows, offered her coffee from their thermoses, and they collected as many of her possessions as they could find and fitted a tarpaulin over them. But everything was broken—the dining-room table split in two, chairs reduced to kindling, dishes and glasses scattered in shining chips. Even some of the grass had been torn up by the force of the tornado, and the big elms that shaded the front porch were uprooted, two of them carried clear across the sheep pasture.

After the tornado, I was sent back to Peoria, and my grandmother bought a tract house in town, and lived there with her youngest daughter, my aunt Florence, who moved home to work in the admissions office of the hospital. My grandmother died five years later. By then Bloomington was booming. The quarries were shutting down, farms were going bankrupt, but a plant that manufactured television sets opened up, and was followed by another plant manufacturing microwaves.

My mother was delighted when I was admitted to the university in Bloomington.

"You can have Sunday dinners with Flo," she said.

So one evening in September, a week after classes had started, I found myself on the plaid couch in Aunt Flo's rancher. She brought out a bowl of cheese curls, poured me some iced tea, and sat across from me in a matching plaid rocking recliner.

There was a picture of my grandmother in a silver frame on the maple coffee table. I picked it up. My grandmother was wearing overalls, and she had a cane fishing pole in one hand, and a big fish she'd just caught in the other. She was grinning widely.

"She was a tough old lady," Flo said. "She lost everything in that tornado, but she kept her spirits up."

I'd told Flo over her fried chicken and mashed potato dinner that I was looking for a part-time job, and she said she'd ask around the hospital. A week later she called. A woman with a broken ankle, whose professor husband was off in Europe, needed someone to come over to cook her dinners.

"But I can't cook," I said. "All I ever did at home was make the salad and set the table."

"Doesn't matter. She'll tell you what to do. She's on crutches and is having trouble getting around her kitchen."

"Well, in that case," I said. "Great. Thanks so much, Aunt Flo."

The directions I got over the phone took me into the best neighborhood in Bloomington, a neighborhood called Windermere that was the equivalent of River View Drive in Peoria, where my father took us on Sunday drives to admire castles and mansions. But this neighborhood was so well-hidden, though close to campus, that I hadn't known it existed. I walked down a winding road, lined with trees, excited by glimpses of big mansions built on the hillsides.

The house where Mrs. Berglund lived was a breathtaking contemporary glass house that dominated a sloped landscaped yard, fringed with forest and expansive gardens. I walked slowly up the long drive to the enormous, carved double-front doors, savoring the experience.

Chimes sounded somewhere deep inside when I pushed the bell button. One half of the door opened. A tall woman on crutches smiled at me. She was wearing a pink, shirred nylon blouse, and a long, silvery skirt.

"Hi," she said. "You must be Edie. I'm Sandra Berglund."

Her graying blond hair was pulled back into a ponytail. Her skin was pale, faintly lined, but shining as if she'd just rubbed it with lotion. She had a cast on one foot, partly covered by the silvery skirt, and a pair of crutches stuck awkwardly under her arms.

She moved back, and I followed her into a large, bright marble hallway. Before me was a glass-walled atrium where a fountain, surrounded by holly bushes, was jetting water into the air. The water fell back into a marble basin.

"Oh, it's beautiful," I exclaimed.

She smiled. "Come around this way."

Mrs. Berglund hobbled around the atrium, the wooden tips of the crutches making a pocking sound on the marble floor of the hall, which surrounded the glass atrium on three sides. The fourth side of the atrium created an inner wall for the living room. Across an expanse of white carpet was the outer wall of glass, stretching from the floor up to the nine-foot ceiling, so that the room seemed to extend out into the gardens beyond—a terrace with a wrought-iron table, a sweep of grass still bright green and leafless even though it was October, and terraced hillsides set with chrysanthemums of every imaginable shade, from purple to mauve to gold to red to brown.

"I just made some coffee," Mrs. Berglund said. "It's in the kitchen, through there, if you'd like to bring us both a cup. I'll just settle here."

She sat down on a piece of a white sectional sofa that I only noticed for the first time as she spoke to me. I forced myself to gaze away from the enchanting out-of-doors. I glanced quickly around the living room as I crossed it to the kitchen. It was all shades of white and beige and gold.

The kitchen had its own wall of glass, and sliding doors out to the terrace. Everything was built-in with an island in the middle, where a cook could stir a pot and still look out at the chrysanthemums.

A fancy coffee machine, called a Bunn-O-Matic, stood on the counter. The glass pot was full of fresh coffee, and I poured it into the two china cups sitting on a silver tray next to it. The tray already contained a plate of little spade-shaped cookies.

I carried the tray back to the living room and placed it carefully on the glass coffee table. Then I handed one of the china cups to Mrs. Berglund. She motioned for me to sit near her, but on another section of the sofa.

"Please help yourself to the madeleines," she said, gesturing to the cookies. "A friend just sent them from France."

Suddenly a flash of shadow crossed my face. I glanced up. There were glass skylights in the ceiling. Clouds crossed the blue sky.

"Your house is mostly glass," I said.

"Yes, it's a glass house. My husband loves it. He's a volcanologist, and he says the views are restful. But it's not a house for someone living alone."

"What's a volcanologist?"

"He studies volcanoes—he's off on an expedition in Italy right now. He'll be gone several months. I was about to join him when I tripped on some broken sidewalk."

She had a gray pearl ring hanging on a gold chain around her neck. She began to roll it idly back and forth between her fingers.

The cloud crossed the skylight again. "Do you have a basement?" I asked.

"Just a crawl space," she said. "Why?"

"Tornadoes."

She shrugged. "Don't they usually hit out in the countryside where it's flat? Anyway, what are the odds?"

I didn't say anything, so she reached out for one of her crutches. "Are you hungry? How about a nice omelette for supper? Let's go out to the kitchen. I'll sit on a stool and order you around." She laughed.

I followed her out to the kitchen, glad she had changed the subject. I found it almost impossible to talk about the tornado that had destroyed my grandmother's house, even though I'd gone through therapy when I was a teenager after my mother had found me cowering in the basement during a thunderstorm. The therapist had explained that I was traumatized because no one had encouraged me to talk about my fears when it first happened.

"Tell me about the tornado," he'd said. He was a big man with a shock of graying hair, and square hands that he kept folded on the desk in front of him. "Did it sound like a freight train?"

I shook my head.

"What did it sound like?"

I shrugged, and shifted uncomfortably in the armchair that faced his desk. It wasn't true that I'd put the tornado into a little room inside my head, and kept the door closed, which is what he'd told me I did. Actually the tornado had the run of my head. I never felt safe. Even sitting around the Christmas tree with my brothers and sisters, opening presents while snow fell outside the picture window, I was aware that at any moment a tornado could blow down the walls of our house—not at that exact moment, perhaps, but in a few months it would be March again, when the sky could darken any afternoon, so how could I allow myself to be happy and carefree when our cheerful living room might not exist next Christmas, and some or all of us might be dead?

"Close your eyes, Edie," I remember him saying. "Tell me what it sounded like."

I sighed. I closed my eyes. I wanted to get the consultation over with so I could go home.

"It sounded like shrieking," I said. "Shrieking and weeping."

He frowned, and leaned forward. He looked concerned. "You mean, like people shrieking and weeping."

I was going to tell him the truth, that yes, the tornado had sounded like many people shrieking and weeping as they were whirled around inside the funnel. Afterwards it had seemed to me that I could even pull out some individual cries from the strand of noise, but I wasn't sure if that was my imagination or not. But something about the therapist's attentiveness made me wary. So I only said: "No, like the wind shrieking and weeping."

He sat back in his chair, reassured, pressing his fingertips together.

So four afternoons a week for the next few months, even after the cast came off her foot, and except for the three weeks when I went home to Peoria for Christmas, and Mrs. Berglund flew to Italy to visit her husband, I went over to the glass house at four o'clock and either cooked a simple dinner myself, or helped Mrs.

Berglund to cook something more complicated. Part of the arrangement was that I ate the dinner with her, for she was lonely and hated eating by herself. We always sat in the dining room with the doors open to the atrium, where the holly trees were strung with tiny white lights, and the fountain glittered. It was like eating in fairyland, for there were tall silver candles on the table as well, and snowy white linen. Mrs. Berglund would drink one single glass of white wine, and we both had crystal goblets filled with fizzing mineral water that came from France. She'd tell me all about the wonderful places in the world where she'd traveled. She described a glacier called the Sea of Glass, and the butterflies at Iguassu Falls.

And of course I was delighted to get out of eating dorm food—increasingly hard to face on the nights when Mrs. Berglund went out to dinner, or had professional caterers over to cook elaborate meals for friends. Occasionally I had a Sunday dinner with Aunt Flo in her eat-in kitchen, and tried to focus on her cheerful kindness, rather than let myself feel depressed by her salt-shaker collection, her ruffled pink café curtains, her plastic placemats printed with photographs of lighthouses (she always asked me to choose the lighthouse I liked best), and her tuna noodle casserole or meatloaf.

Then one day in early March, a warm front moved in from the Gulf, and the air turned sultry. But a cold front was heading down from Canada, and even though the weathermen were only talking about a chance of thunderstorms, I knew it was tornado weather.

I usually set off for Mrs. Berglund's house around three o'clock, after my biology class, but that day I was tempted to call her up and tell her I wasn't feeling well. But then what would I do? Cower in the dorm basement under the steam pipes when I could be listening to tales of the Great Barrier Reef or the fjords in Norway while dining by candlelight?

Mrs. Berglund always drove me back to the dorm after dinner in her Mercedes. The storm might not hit until late in the evening, so I decided to risk going to her house as usual, and try to act like a normal student, like all the other thousands of normal, carefree students crossing the warm, windy campus at that moment, glad to be free of winter coats, heading for classes or the library or jobs in flimsy fast-food restaurants.

The warm south wind was soughing through the bare treetops. The raked winter lawns of Windermere already had a faint green sheen, and the maple buds seemed to be reddening the branches. My hair tangled behind my shoulders, and I unzipped my jacket as I walked up the hill.

Mrs. Berglund had slid open one of the sliding doors to the backyard, and gusty air blew through the house. She was wearing a filmy sleeveless dress that fluttered around her ankles.

"Doesn't it smell wonderful," she said. "Spring at last."

"Tornado weather," I said.

"Oh, Edie. You worry about everything. Let's just enjoy it. I'd love to eat outside, but the wind would blow everything off the table."

We started to make a quiche and a salad. I tried not to jump at the sound of branches knocking against the roof. Then a whirlwind of dead leaves blew noisily across the yard, and I dropped the lettuce spinner.

"You're like that doe I saw this morning," Mrs. Berglund said. "When I pulled back the curtains, she was in the yard, looking right at me. But her whole body was quivering with fear, and when I moved, she turned so fast I only glimpsed her white tail disappearing."

While I rolled out the dough for the quiche, Mrs. Berglund went into the study to catch the nightly news on the TV. She came back in a few minutes.

"There's a tornado watch," she said. "But it's just a watch. Conditions are favorable."

"I know that," I said. "It's getting dark out there."

"That's just twilight coming on."

"Aren't you afraid of anything?" I asked.

She laughed. "I'm afraid of being by myself. What else is there to be afraid of? Death? That's nothing." She held out the gray pearl ring that she always wore on the chain around her neck, sometimes loose, sometimes tucked into her clothes. "Here. Give this a rub. It's my magic ring. It belonged to Carl's great-great-great-grandmother."

She let the ring fall into my palm. It was a twisted band of gold, designed to look like a vine, set with a single, grayish-blue pearl.

"It's beautiful. Why don't you wear it like a ring?"

"Look at my knuckles. Arthritis, that's why."

I rubbed the top of the pearl. "Weren't you afraid when you climbed the volcano at Christmas?"

"Well," she said, tucking the chain with the ring back inside her neckline. "Once a big, red hot boulder shot out from the rim and started rolling toward us. Naturally I was scared, and I turned around to run. But Carl and the other scientists stopped me. They said we had to face it, because we had to see which way it was rolling, and step aside. If we'd turned to run, it might have caught up with us."

"You can't do that with a tornado," I said.

She laughed. "Have you ever actually seen one, Edie?" She took the rolling pin out of my hand and dipped it into the flour. The dough had gotten sticky on me, and I was starting to make a mess.

I took a deep breath, facing away from her. I could see the kitchen reflected now on the glass sliding doors. The figures of two women wavered dimly, as if underwater. The wind was picking up outside. "Yes," I said finally. "I was in a house that was destroyed by a tornado about five miles from here."

"Oh, God. I didn't know that. No wonder you're scared." Mrs. Berglund came around and gave me a quick hug, leaving floury prints on my shoulder. "And you're worried because this house doesn't have a basement? Well, it has something better than a basement, believe it or not."

"What?" I asked.

"A bomb shelter. An old-fashioned 1950's-style bomb shelter. Carl insisted on having one dug when we bought this house. We lived in Geneva once, and all the houses in Switzerland have bomb shelters."

Just then the lights flickered.

"Shit," Mrs. Berglund said. "This quiche may never get baked."

The wind screamed, and I thought I heard wailing. "Listen," I said. I ran over to the glass door and slid it open a crack. Over the howl of the wind I could hear the wavering pitch of a tornado siren.

The lights went out. I sucked in my breath and slammed the door shut, but in a second Mrs. Berglund had a flashlight in her hand and was illuminating the kitchen.

"Grab the salad, Edie, and those plates and forks over there. Okay, this way, the door's just down the hall."

My hands were shaking, but I followed her calm orders. I saw her shadowy figure reach into the refrigerator for a bottle of wine, then we were heading down the hall. She opened a door, and to my great relief I saw a stairway in the dancing glow of her flashlight. She made me go first, and kept the stairs bright so I could see my way down.

The room was a small, carpeted cube, completely empty except for a few cardboard boxes. Mrs. Berglund set the flashlight on top of one of the boxes. I placed the salad and plates on the floor.

"I'll go back for wineglasses," she said.

"No, don't!" My voice sounded strained even to my own ears.

"And we need the radio down here. What's the good of a bomb shelter without a radio and wineglasses?"

I could hear her groping her way back up the stairs in the dark.

I huddled against the wall, folding my arms tightly against my chest to try to stop my trembling. I remembered the soapy smell of my grandmother's skin as she held me under the mattress all those years ago, telling me to keep my head in her lap in case the shelves of canned goods in their glass jars got knocked down. Then the shrieking began. It seemed to me that the tornado had already been full of cows and sheep and children and grandmothers, all swirling around in the black funnel and crying for help as it bore down on our house, but maybe what I heard was only the sound of our own shrieks of terror, my grandmother holding my face tight against her as the glass jars broke in counterpoint to the crash of the walls above us exploding outward.

A light flashed at the head of the stairs. Mrs. Berglund came back down with a second flashlight tucked under her arm, two wineglasses, a loaf of French bread, and a small radio.

"It's wild out there," she said cheerfully. "You need a glass of wine, Edie. You look like a ghost."

She handed me a glass of white wine. I never drank alcohol, so the first mouthful seemed to run through my veins like electricity.

Mrs. Berglund settled against the wall next to me and switched on the radio. The campus station had interrupted programming, and the announcer was talking about a tornado that had touched down in Ellettsville. But the sighting hadn't been confirmed by the sheriff's office. Nevertheless a warning was in effect until eight p.m.

"Let's switch it off until eight, then," Mrs. Berglund said. "Is that doing you any good?"

"Yes," I said. I'd finished my glass quickly. She poured me another, but she was still sipping her usual single glass. I did feel calmer. I looked at her more closely. "You've never told me where you and Carl met. Did you fall in love right away?"

"We fell in love at first sight. You see, he saved my life. I fell off a slippery pier on a lake in Italy on a stormy day, and Carl, who was in line for the ferry, too, jumped in and rescued me. It turned out that he was going to be doing research in the U.S. the next year, so it was easy to get together again. Losing him is the only thing I really fear—but I'm not a scientist, so I can't follow him around everywhere he goes, though sometimes I try. I know he's smart and careful." She sighed. She took out her ring and began to turn it over in her fingers. "Actually, dear, I'm terrified that a volcano will erupt while he's up there. But there's nothing I can do about it."

We ate our salads with the flashlights focused on our plates, our heads in shadow. Mrs. Berglund tore off a piece of bread from the long loaf, then handed it to me. "What is this wine?" I said dreamily. I had never been drunk before in my whole life, and I felt as if I were hovering a little ways above my body, watching myself from a distance.

"Lacrimae Christi—the grapes are grown on the slopes of Vesuvius. It's Carl's favorite. A great-great-great-grandfather of his once climbed Vesuvius in the nineteenth-century, and did some sketches." She lifted her ring. "This was the wedding ring he had made—it looks like a pearl, but it's really polished lava."

"There's a sketch of a volcano on your living-room wall," I said.

"That's one of his sketches. We used to have several, but Carl's son took the others."

"He has a son?"

"From an earlier marriage. A fussy little asshole. I can't stand him."

The recessed lighting overhead flashed in our eyes. We both blinked and looked around like startled rabbits. Mrs. Berglund switched on the radio. Even the tornado watch had been canceled for our area. The cold front had moved through much more quickly than expected.

We went upstairs. I looked out the sliding glass door again. It was windy, and ragged clouds raced across the sky. Mrs. Berglund cut me a piece of cake, made us coffee, then drove me back to the dorm, where I lay down with a spinning head and dry mouth to suffer the first, though not the last, hangover of my life.

Mrs. Berglund could hardly speak when she called me two months later to tell me that she'd just had some terrible news. Carl had been killed in a car accident in Italy.

I was standing at a bank of phones just off the main lounge of the dorm, and all around me girls were talking to their boyfriends or gossiping with other girls about boys they wanted for boyfriends. I kept saying, "Oh, no, oh, no," and "That's terrible, that's terrible," so it wasn't long before the girls on the other phones were glancing at me with pity, and hastily ending their own phone calls.

Mrs. Berglund was leaving for the airport that evening. She wanted to see me briefly before she left. She must have been watching for me, for the door opened before I'd even pushed the bell button. I'd never seen her in anything but long flowing skirts and dresses, so it was almost a shock to see her in a short green suit, wearing nylons and high heels, her knees and calves and ankles visible, as if she were an ordinary human being. Her face seemed to have crumpled in on itself, and the skin below her eyes was red and swollen.

We hugged each other. "I must have turned my back on that boulder," she said, her voice rough. "Because I didn't see this coming."

"How could you," I said.

"I worried about lava the way you worry about tornadoes. I realize that now. But I should have worried about speeding."

"Was he speeding?"

"Somebody's always speeding." She sighed, reaching into her suit pocket. "Anyway, I wanted to give this to you. I want to make sure that fussy little asshole of a son of his never gets his hands on it, not even after I'm dead."

She handed me the antique lava ring. "Here, Edie. If I had a daughter, I would give it to her. So you wear this, and whenever you're afraid, just rub the stone."

I looked at the ring in my palm. "Oh, it's so beautiful. But I couldn't take something this valuable."

"Who knows whether it's valuable or not? It would only be valuable if you sold it. If you wear it, then it's just a gift from a friend." She closed my palm over the ring. "Please," she said.

"But what if you're afraid of something, and miss it?" I asked.

"There's nothing left for me to be afraid of," she said.

I nodded. I slid the ring onto my finger.

"My taxi will be here any minute. Let me get my purse and lock up."

She disappeared into her bedroom. I stood looking out the glass wall at a small flowering pear tree. The grass was bright chartreuse, and birds were flying back and forth. Tulips of every shade and shape, from red to deep purple to yellow, some ruffled and doubled like roses, glowed around the edge of the terrace. One chair was pulled out from the wrought-iron table, as if someone had been sitting there enjoying the sunshine and had just that minute gotten up to go inside and answer the phone.

I wasn't inside the house in Windermere again for twenty years. But last year when I accepted a job in the geology department of the university in Bloomington, I drove around with a real estate agent looking at houses.

Nothing pleased me. The old houses close to campus had wet basements and no yards to speak of, and the seventies houses farther away had low ceilings and few windows. The newer houses in the far suburbs had lofted ceilings, but the doors were made of plastic.

"There's an interesting house in Windermere," the real estate agent said. "It's been on the market for a while."

I recognized the glass house from the bottom of the curving driveway, and drew my breath in sharply. The grass in front was long and weedy, and the bushes looked half-dead.

Karen, my agent, got the key from the lockbox. We went inside.

It was cold. The heat wasn't turned on, and an April chill had invaded the empty rooms. The fountain was missing from the atrium, and the holly bushes looked like they needed watering.

The glass wall to the terrace was spotted with rain and bird shit. The white living-room rug was stained, and someone with bad taste had laid bright shag carpeting in the dining room.

"This house is always changing hands," Karen said, brushing back her blond bangs from her blue eyes as she shrewdly noted the look of dismay on my face. "It's all electric, and costs a fortune to heat."

I looked out at the weedy terrace. I had never seen Mrs. Berglund again after I waved to her in the taxi that day. She never wrote to me, and in the fall, when I came back to school, the first thing I did was walk to Windermere. But the house was for sale. I knocked, but no one answered. The geology department in which Carl taught when he wasn't doing fieldwork gave me an address in Rome, so I wrote to Mrs. Berglund again. Still no answer. And gradually I threw myself into my classes, and learned to tolerate the bland food dished up on thick cafeteria china. When the clatter of plates and forks, the taunts of football players horsing around, and the blare of the banked TV sets overhead got too much for me, I'd look at my ring and remember another world.

MAURA STANTON

Milk of Human Kindness

Tastes like the melted centers of toasted marshmallows. Tastes like tears of nectar squeezed out of clover blossoms. Tastes like sips from rivers running through lands of milk and honey. Remember those wax bottles filled with colored liquids, how as a child you bit off the top and sucked out the sweet purple, or red, or orange? You opened waxed cartons in the lunchroom, stuck in your straw, bubbled and gurgled. You loved chocolate best. So did your friends. And there was always enough to drink, more than you could finish. But now your mouth is dry. The milk of human kindness tastes like a punch in the nose. It tastes like phlegm, like snot. Tastes metallic like coins you don't give to homeless teenagers panhandling downtown, tastes like your blood-pressure medicine, tastes like a dry martini, tastes like the ring of soured froth in the cat's unwashed bowl, still sitting in the sink. She's meowing at the refrigerator door. She knows where you keep it.

GERALD STERN

Salt

I was sitting at a picnic table at
one of the godforsaken places peeling
an egg as if in this act I could recover
what there was of gentleness and I
was alone unless you counted the two forms of life,
one sea and one land, that fought over the eggshells
and stole pieces of bread from each other
with total disregard for the proprieties,
and I abused some rot and pulled out a screw
that hardly held itself in place, I could have
rocked the table with my hands, such was
the purchase; and the woods were birch, cattails
down below, a train sliding slowly
past the stone station, up above me;
and what I missed was salt, for I had wine
and even a tomato, I should have taken
one of the beautiful cellars from my shelf
and put it in my pocket or wrapped it in foil
and packed it in the bag, it would have made
the animals happier, it would have blessed our supper.

MARK STRAND

The Great Siberian Rose

The movie about the great Siberian rose,
Brought back to life by the doctor who killed her,
Was playing a block away at the Lane. The usher
Was dressed like a nurse, and scowled, and told us
Not to make noise. I wish we had
For as soon as the movie began, a tomblike room
Appeared. And against the far wall
On a pillow-strewn bed, the great Siberian rose,
Thorns flashing, leaned back to receive our stares.
Thunder broke, lights flickered, and a huge machine
Was wheeled into view. We sank deep in our chairs,
And even deeper when a door creaked open,
Revealing a hooded figure, up to his knees
In mist, who said in a voice no one could place:
"The Golden Age of dust will now begin."

BRIAN SWANN

Tamias Striatus Poetics

"The poem is a sort of animal."
—Ted Hughes

I give him words to tell me who he is.
  He gives them back, begins a visual discourse
on invisibility, gunning by me a film in snippets &

  jump-shots, starring him. Light flashes everywhere.
But you can still make out frames that form a sequence,
  though there are deep lacunae only he can leap

as a kind of semiotic stuntman—I guess it's him, though
  it could be a series of doubles (impossible to know).
There—in that shot he's signifying a signified, so

  in what follows he's multiple as the seeds he collects
like mnemonics. There, off he goes again, but now in a
  series of silent sequences subtitled: "The Vital Nothing,"

"The Plump Filling," "The Cake of Soap," "The Full Stop,"
  &, dramatically, "Tamias Striatus Meets Pale Ramon."
He's starting to blur like a piece of stained air, or

  something identical. But to what? Himself? He cuts a
dashing solipsism, so comparisons are useless. Now he's
  riding a fast vehicle. He *is* a vehicle. But of what?

Himself? Here we go again ... I'm about to call him accident
  & let it go at that, but suddenly a small yet purposeful charge
goes off & something claps shut after itself, closing me out.

  All I can hear is a series of finger-snaps, fragments of old songs,
theatrical effects that burrow into worlds & then pop up again,
  now here, now there, more believable the more you believe.

Clearly, he's an idea whose time has come & gone almost
   in the same instant, an ironic reading that can't quite
cancel itself out. So this reader's response is to have him stay

   just as he is, whatever that is, in that moment when I can say
He's there, because as soon as I say he isn't he jumps out
   of my head, skitters off fingertips, skirrs just behind my heels,

& off we go again. He's turning me inside out, in circles, stripping
   my defenses. He's—*Wait! There he is! He's there!* What you see is
what you get. But what have I seen? Sometimes you can think

   too much. I give in. He knocks me out.

DEBORAH TALL

Your Absence Has Already Begun

Say a calling
knocks you out of sleep,
draws blood,
is accessible only by water.

Say you believe you
own your life
but you have looked away
and your absence has already begun.

You struggle out
patched together by medication
and makeup

scaling the broken cadence,
the frost-heaved lanes,
walking papers clenched to your chest.

It's late in the day.
You forget the thing
that made you thirsty,

Icarus still tumbling
through the stunned stars,
his fingerprints
all over your heart.

SUSAN TERRIS

Shadow of a Falling Bird

The shadow of a falling bird against a building
is more real than the bird.
Shadow of a glioblastoma on an MRI
is not real at all.

It will be short and brutal, the doctor says.

She sees the shadow of her head
on his shirt, sees a framed photo of
the shadow of a biplane across foothills
in the Valley of the Queens.

An approximation of truth,
only one measure of reality. She hears
the doctor's voice in the hard sanity
of morning, in the gray uncertainty of morning.

The Lie of the Ordinary Life

A muster of white peacocks preens
by the inverted lake pooling the ceiling.
The peacocks are mute.

He is not quite mute. An inattention.
Letters answered in such haste, he fails
to answer. Words overlaid,
commas sliding out of line—a riff
of lost eyelashes punctuating nothing.

In this hungry place, there is a bed and a sign
noting the danger of temporary tattoos.

"I think," he tells her when they've fed one another
raspberries and champagne grapes,
"you may find me too ordinary."

An ivory plume breezes down, not yet knifed
into pen or dipped into black-squid ink.

His gift to her: a silver arrow lancing
an amber heart. And, of course,
the dense sweetness of his soap, his skin
on the pewter of her silky burnout gown.
Her gift to him: a magic stone left behind.

Then the peacocks screech.
Gravity arrested, the plume begins to fall up
toward the mirage. Lake. Sky. A void.

Cabin

Slate gray lake. Willows in a rough wind. On the far island, where
the shoreline is tattered with fallen trees, it is not yet spring.
The waves won't allow it. Won't allow anyone to land there, let
alone to leave. Not today; maybe not for a long time to come.
The bramble takes care of that, shadows and old leaves covering
the snow, a quilt and a cradle,
the bramble carefully knitted so you must take the one path
through the place, or grow wings.
Or grow to about the size of a groundhog, for all the larger
animals have starved or left no offspring, or fell through the
thin ice trying to get back.

I never imagined such happiness could fit into two days out of
the month. It is morning and I don't get up—
how easy. The shutters in need of painting. The tall grass, stunted
all winter, already too tall to mow.

ELLEN BRYANT VOIGT

Autumn in the Yard We Planted

Whoever said that I should count on mind?
Think it through, think it up—now that I know so much,
what's left to think is the unthinkable.

And the will has grown too tired to stamp its foot.
It sings a vapid song, it dithers and mopes,
it takes its basket to the marketplace,
like a schoolgirl in her best dress, and watches
others ask outright for what they want—
how do they know what they want?—and haul it away,
the sweet, the dull, the useless, and the dear.

A maudlin, whimpering song: in which I lament
my own children, scything their separate paths
into the field, one with steady strokes,
one in a rage. We taught them that. And,
not to look back: at the apple tree, first
to shatter its petals onto the clipped grass,
or the blowsy heads of the russet peonies,

or even that late-to-arrive pastel, all stalk
with a few staggered blossoms, meadow rue—
though surely they could see it from where they are.

REBECCA WEE

How Was It Sudden Your Long Death

how was it sudden your long death
shock fixed black

parking lots ramps the bright art
in the hallways flagrant flowers a fish tank
in the white places

one latex glove
like petals spilled on the way
to or from some room with a horror in it

glass coffin rice flour your skin
taking on radiation burn your heart's
new gallop your eyes without you
behind them

the toxic pills
soldiers in small paper cups

each day the walk
past hibiscus blossoms
each day's sunny traffic peculiar trees
with white thorns in the bark

each day with white thorns

your grip on the bedrail the acid you
vomit the shiny cards you will not have
pinned to the wall the bloodstains

then

exile of such physical scope
my tongue torn from its place
incisions in every lungful of air
every day more frantic

for tokens strands an old letter
words in your hand some evidence
that you *were* here it was not

fabrication chimera conceit
not like anything else our language
your touch

water in the Mojave left off the maps

wild mustard in the bluffs
in the cornfields a soft wind

when you died the sky opened it
does not close

In Memoriam
Michael Hudson, 1961–1998

Before This Day There Were Many Days

They heard their mother yell their father's name, and came from their beds barefoot and squinting. Jeff Driver was in the kitchen. He was crying, and he told them that the bridge on Cascom Mountain Road had washed out. He looked at Kate's mother and said her name, "Carey." Then he looked at Kate and David, and no one spoke. The floor was tracked with water and cold under Kate's feet. The front door was open, and it was raining hard.

"Down to Lorde's place," Jeff said. "The truck just went over. Swept off."

Their mother lifted her arms as if she didn't dare touch herself, or close up and only find emptiness. Her hair was dripping.

Kate pressed against David's arm. Then David hit Jeff, swung out and punched him in the shoulder, and Jeff hung his head, and put his hand on the spot where David had struck him. Their mother said to stop, and there was the water drumming and pouring from the gutters, and suddenly it all went still, like that, and Kate heard the words as if they were said right next to her ear: "He's dead."

Before their mother yelled *Lendel* into the night, they'd been in their rooms, and Kate had been asleep. Before that, she was awake. It wasn't raining then. It was hot, sticky. She searched for the cool spots with her feet, and every now and then she snapped the top sheet up like a parachute and let it fall slowly and coolly back on her body. The crickets trilled in the field, and far down in the valley she heard the brook. The noise of the brook was constant, a muffled roar, a rushing sound, but louder than usual. It was overflowing, full of all the rain of the past few weeks. She and David had been down there. Fast water tore up the banks and dragged down bushes and little trees, and there was foam and swirling pools, all that water in such a hurry. It was remarkable to think the rain had done this. The sound was so loud that you had to shout to be heard, so she and David hadn't said much. They stood and watched, then ran along the bank upstream. There was a big rock they knew of that rose above a pool. It was a broad expanse of granite that stretched across the brook like the smooth back of a whale. You could fit your body into its potholes and worn spots. It felt soft, almost. Now the rock was completely underwater, and you wouldn't know it was there except for a dip in the surface where a rill folded backwards. And also how the water streaming over the top took the rock's shape, only glassy and moving. The beaver lodge was gone, washed away. The beaver dam, too, completely knocked out, but there were still some of their felled trees caught up on the side, the ends chewed into sharp points.

From her bed she could forget it was the sound of the brook just as you forget the hum of a refrigerator until it clicks off. The grown-ups were on the front porch. There was her mother and father and Jeff Driver. They were drinking cool drinks; she could hear ice cubes in the glasses.

Sometimes the grown-ups stayed out there a long time, and Kate would fall asleep hearing them, but not hearing the words, just the lull of their voices. There was her mother's tone, like she was singing, though she wasn't. It was her way of speaking with airy notes that seemed to hook one word to the next. Her voice moved over and around some of the men's tones, or broke through, and the men would stop to listen.

Jeff Driver's sound came in little bursts and stutters, and sometimes if there were more grown-ups, like the Lordes from down the road, if they were also there, Jeff's sounds would be very easy to pick out because he was nervous around groups. He had a stopping sound he made, like he couldn't get around a ball in his mouth.

Her father's timbre was smoother, and she heard him less because he was a quiet man who took his time in saying things, and only said what was necessary. Though sometimes he could be very silly and make everyone laugh. It took you a little off-guard, and it gave you a happy feeling.

The grown-ups laughed, and chairs moved. The loose spring on the screen door jingled, and Kate listened, but the door didn't close all the way. The spring was broken. It would be Jeff Driver coming in. It would be him because if it were her mother or father they would pull the door to, and then there'd be a clunk, but there was none this time. Jeff was inside using the bathroom, and her parents were quiet outside on the porch. This was before Jeff Driver and her father went down to Leah Flats for a game of poker.

Before this, before they went to bed, she and David had joined the grown-ups on the porch. They'd had cool drinks, too, lemonade. Moths fluttered against the outside lamp, and the air was thick, and they knew it would start raining again. More rain was coming, but it was nice to have this little break, and sit outside in the still air. There was no breeze at all.

Kate sat next to her father. He smelled of kerosene from washing his hands in it, trying to clean the stain off. Earlier in the day he'd stained the table in the back room. It was a picnic table he'd built with long benches attached. It looked funny in the back room, but soon it would be put outside in the yard.

He wore jeans with a hole in one knee, and Kate stuck her finger in the hole to tickle him. He let her do that for a while, pretending it didn't tickle, but she knew it did because the pitch in his voice rose just a little, and she ran her fingernail lightly over the soft skin just below his kneecap, and then he grabbed her hand like it was a little mouse, or a spider, and brought it to his mouth like he was going to eat it. She shrieked and pulled her hand away, and there was some of his spit on her fingers because he'd put them in his mouth. She wiped her hand on his leg and said, "Yuck."

Jeff Driver laughed, *guff guff,* and Kate's mother smiled, and they all sat back and listened to the sounds of the night and the thundering brook down in the valley. David sat in the rocker, and there was also that noise of the runners clacking on the wood floor and one of his heels scraping back and forth. David didn't laugh because he was always a little annoyed with Jeff for no reason—maybe this time because of Jeff's laugh. David didn't laugh, but Kate could see his eyes were bright and he was happy to be there.

It was just an evening on the porch. Soft light spread across the worn floorboards, dropped to the stone steps. The light waned on the walk, and surrendered to the blackness out there in the yard. But up on the porch they were in a cove of light. And the light draped over their arms and outstretched legs, and made elongated shadows that flowed from the bottoms of their chairs. Kate looked at the faces of her mother and father and brother and Jeff. There was an ease in her mother's face, but also a weariness around her eyes. People always said she had her mother's eyes. Kate gazed at her mother's face, and it was as if she could see down through the years to when she'd become a woman, a wife, a mother. There would always be pleasure in warm evenings on a porch, these quiet gatherings of people, family. And there would always be a sadness in it. There's always a sadness in happy, content moments.

Before they adjourned to the porch—*Shall we adjourn to the porch?* her father said with a pretend haughtiness, as if he were addressing important people, royal people—before they went out to the porch, they'd eaten supper. There was venison and macaroni, and the spirals of green fiddleheads that her mother had harvested from the woods. The smells of garlic and rosemary rose from the oven, and when they ate they tasted those things, too.

Before supper there had been the day. Kate and David watched the brook, and then they'd crossed the field, and four deer grazed there. The deer caught their scent, jumped and fled, though one stopped at the edge of the woods and looked back with shining eyes. Then it leapt, and they watched its high white rump bob until it disappeared between the trees.

David said, "Remember that story Dad was telling us about the woman who was a deer?" It was a bedtime story, and they hadn't heard it in a long time because they read books now, but it was good to remember the story, and it made Kate want to follow the deer that had hesitated; maybe it was asking them to follow. Kate was ten years old, but she still liked to believe in things. She liked to believe that animals could talk to you with their minds; that beavers had elaborate mansions inside their stick huts; that there were fairies living in the poplar trees. She knew that those things weren't real, yet there was something about being able to pretend, allowing herself to pretend, that felt like doors opening in her heart. Being ten was a very good age, she had decided. She was happy, and she wished that when she died she would be ten in heaven, no matter what else happened to her in her life, or how pleased she might be at other ages, she must remember that ten was the best, and that she should be ten in heaven, if there was such a place.

They left the field and crossed over the brook on the bridge the loggers had built, so it was stronger than most, and could hold huge trucks loaded with hardwoods. When they came up the hill to the cabin they saw their father hiking down. He was coming from his writing shack next to the cabin. He'd built the shack so he could have quiet while he was writing, and he went there in the mornings and closed himself in. Sometimes Kate stood on tiptoe and peered through the tiny window. He sat in his chair and typed on the typewriter. Then he'd lean back and smoke, and stare at the wall. There was a little sill where a two-by-four crossed, and on the sill he kept things: the skull of a raccoon he'd found picked clean, a piece of black mica, a dried polypore as big as a dinner plate, a dog she had made out of clay, and an old silver belt buckle. Then he'd turn back and type some more. If she giggled, he'd unlatch the door and talk to her for a few minutes, but only a few because he had to get back to work.

Now he was coming down the hill, and they ran to him. He had brown stain on his fingers. He said, "How's the brook looking?" And he wanted to go see it. It was exciting to go with their father, to show the brook to him as if they'd discovered it. They told him they'd seen four deer in the field, and he nodded, proud of them for knowing that seeing deer was a special thing. Kate knew the things he loved, and so she wanted to love those things, too. Like spotting deer, or the bear-claw marks on the apple tree, or moose track. Or the brook swelled and running out of control. A porcupine asleep and curled into the crotch of a tree like a huge bird's nest. The rain sweeping down the mountain and across the valley in a sheet until it rattled over the cabin roof. The smell of the woods just before rain, and after rain. The sun when it sank behind Cascom Mountain, and mostly that moment when the last ray wavered and held at the ridge, then went down, like it had been swallowed. Fireflies blinking above the field like stars going on and off.

The three of them watched the brook, and they showed him how the big rock was completely submerged, and you'd never know it was there except for that dip in the water just below it. He said, "We used to swim here, your mother and I, before you were born."

The deer were gone, and no more came.

They went on up the logging road, away from the brook, and the sound of the water diminished. Their voices sounded brighter in the quiet woods. They went up the old road, past where any regular cars could travel, where it got steep and muddy and the grass grew like the hair on a Mohawk right down the middle. They climbed up to the top where there was a view and they could see the cabin below with its shed roof and windows like eyes. Kate thought about her mother inside and that she was making supper for them, and also for Jeff Driver, who would be coming from his job in the fire tower. Jeff usually came on Saturdays before he and her father went to Leah Flats to play poker with some other men.

In the clearing at the top of the ridge they stopped to look at the marker where they'd buried their beagle a few years earlier. The beagle had been shot by someone, no one knew who, and it was sad to remember what a good dog he was, and also it was sad to remember that even in this sunny opening in the woods with the yellow grass, and mica glinting in the outcroppings of granite, there was someone out there who could shoot a dog.

They looked at the marker, then went on up the ridge to the old cellar hole where Zach Bean's great-grandfather had built the first farm on Mount Cascom, when the land was mostly fields and not so grown up with trees. Zach had sold these acres at eight dollars and thirty cents each, so now her father owned this land, and all the way across the field and over the brook and up the hill to the cabin. Bushes grew at the rim of the cellar hole next to lopsided stone steps that led up to nothing. Saplings had taken hold down inside the foundation and grown taller than the hole was deep. Branches reached above the crumbling walls, and some of the rocks had tumbled down into piles. It was from this place that her father and mother had hauled a long piece of cut granite for the mantel above the fireplace in their cabin. Her father had chiseled the words *Len and Carey Built This House 1954 AD* in the stone.

They sat and dangled their feet into the cellar hole. Kate was in the middle between her father and her brother. Her father sat close, and his legs went down, longer than hers, and David's, too, and she felt small next to them. There was some dirt turned up in a pile and shovel markings down there where people had been looking for artifacts.

David had found some china fragments in the ground a few yards away, and one time he'd been very lucky and discovered the silver belt buckle. But most of the cellar holes around the mountain had already been excavated by people who stayed at the lodge across the valley, and there wasn't anything left to find.

Kate leaned forward. The base of the old chimney still stood, and orange daylilies grew in a tuft at its base. Once there was a kitchen and a stove, where Zach Bean's great-grandmother set a kettle to boil. And there were rooms where children slept and whispered to each other, and then fell quiet, listening to the comfortable murmur of adult voices. A family had lived here and ate and slept, and much more than that. It was strange to sit here and imagine people walking around and moving through invisible rooms. What if they glanced up and saw Kate and David and her father looking in?

Kate leaned out. There was a rusty barrel down there for some reason. She stretched to see more, and then she was falling headfirst into the hole. Someone clutched her shirt and yanked her back. Her collar came up tight on her neck, and it hurt, also it hurt where the hands grabbed her. David's fingers dug into her arm. Her father's hand went into her stomach. Her father gasped and said, "Oh," in a way that sounded like he was falling himself, just catching himself from falling. It hurt how they seized her, and for a moment she felt angry. But her father had made the noise, and now she saw how she'd scared him. She knew he would not want her to fall or be injured. He'd made that noise, and she felt his arms around her, squeezing her, pulling her back onto the bristly grass away from the edge. He let out his breath.

"Be careful, Katy," David said, annoyed, and in a way that was nothing like the sound, the "oh," her father had made, and how she'd said that same word, *oh*, at the same time he had, as if they were one person falling when it had only been her.

Then her father said, "We should head back."

Before this day there were many days, like the day Jeff Driver found the beagle lying dead on the trail, and how he wrapped the dog in a blue blanket, carried it to them like a baby. Or when Peter Lorde drove his big truck through the little poplar trees to make a road, and how they popped as they broke and flattened under the tires. Or when her mother and father held each other and circled the living room to the beat of a scratchy blues record, and how he lifted her and stood her on the table and held her hand so they danced like that, with him below, reaching up to her. And those nights when headlights came down the road flashing through the trees. And a kiss on the forehead and the sweet dream of a deer that could turn into a woman. Of believing in whatever you chose.

Though there were some things you would never want to imagine. Things you didn't want to believe could happen. Things that made the world never the same again, changing the last moments of before and before and before because they were the last hours, the last minutes, the last sigh and breath.

JONAH WINTER

Season's Greetings!

Well, another year has passed!
And, while it hasn't been a perfect one,
we have survived. Oh, first there was
the house burning down—everything ruined:
furniture, original artworks, priceless family heirlooms lost
because of some sort of electrical short
according to the arson squad
who, incidentally, interrogated us for 3 months,
making damaging allegations to our insurance company,
causing them to cancel our policy
before, alas, we could collect.
During that difficult period, Edith and I
both lost our jobs—just another case of
"corporate downsizing," I guess!
Fortunately, we did get a couple of rather
hefty severance packages which, unfortunately,
had to go almost entirely towards a deposit
on our new 2-bedroom apartment. You see, the landlord
asked that we pay 14 months in advance,
seeing as how we were both out of work
and had 3 kids to feed.
Two of our gang, Jason and Rebecca, I'm sad to say,
were taken away from us
by the Department of Human Services.
They said we were, quote,
"unable to provide a stable home environment or
adequate health care"
(our health insurance was canceled, too).
Jason, as many of you know,
has acute agoraphobia—fear of open spaces,
fear of the world, basically—
and so he apparently hasn't been outside
of his foster home for 4 months.

He receives his food through a slot
in his bedroom door.
The little guy only comes out late at night
to bathe and use the toilet.
We've discussed this problem with Jan and Bob,
his foster parents, and they've come to the conclusion
that Jason will change when he's ready.
In the meantime, his 18th birthday
is coming right up, and we're planning a BIG party
to which all of you are invited!
It promises to be a gala event!
Hopefully, Rebecca will be out of rehab
by then. She just turned 15
and, as fate would have it,
fell in with the wrong crowd.
When we saw her turning tricks
on Harry Hines, we knew it was
time to have a heart-to-heart.
We found out that our little Rebecca
has developed a bit of a drug habit—heroin—
and felt she had to turn to prostitution
in order to pay for it. Her pimp,
Mickey, threatened to kill all of us
for taking her away from him.
We offered to pay Mickey recompense
for his financial loss, and he responded
by stealing our car
and driving it off a cliff.
Because we also lost our car insurance,
Mickey's estranged wife, a transsexual
named Jill St. Jacques, is suing us
for every last penny, because, she says, legally
we are responsible for Mickey's death.
We can't afford a lawyer,
and so we do face a high possibility
of life imprisonment.
And, we have no way to get to our new jobs
out in the country,
on the chicken farm.

So, we've had to tighten the old belt
a few notches, dining nightly on cat food
and uncooked potatoes (all our utilities
have been shut off).
The adjustment to such a life has not been easy,
especially since our various medications ran out—
my high blood pressure pills, and Edith's,
well, Valium!
Frankly, we've been a mess.
I'm afraid it hasn't been much of a cakewalk
for poor Barney, our youngest.
He's developed a whole range of obsessive-compulsive ticks
as a coping mechanism, we think.
Right now, as I type this,
little Barney is bouncing his head
against the floor—in multiples of three.
What usually happens now is our downstairs neighbors
crank their stereo really loud
until about 3 or 4 in the morning.
That's okay, though—we're being evicted
and must vacate by noon tomorrow.
So, don't bother sending any Christmas cards
this year. But do
have a very merry Christmas!

Nostalgia II

January, moth month,
                    crisp frost-flank and fluttering,
Verona,
Piazza Bra in the cut-light,
                    late afternoon, midwinter,
1959,
Roman arena in close-up tonsured and monk robed
After the snowfall.

Behind my back, down via Mazzini, the bookstore
And long wooden table in whose drawer
Harold will show me, in a month or so,
                    the small books
From Vanni Scheiwiller, *All'insegna del pesce d'oro,*
That will change my life,
Facsimiles, *A Lume Spento,* and *Thrones,* full-blown, in boards.

Made in Verona. Stamperia Valdonega.
That's how it all began, in my case,
                    Harold and I
Ghosting the bookstores and bars,
Looking for language and a place to stand that fit us,
The future, like Dostoyevsky, poised
To read us the riot act.
                    And it did. And it's been okay.

Promises to Keep

After graduating from Amherst College in 1963, I lived in Manhattan for the summer and worked at *Redbook*, of all places. At night, I pounded out Kafkaesque short stories, which I promptly sent to *The New Yorker* and which were promptly rejected. In the fall, I headed for Cambridge. I had been granted a Woodrow Wilson Fellowship to the Ph.D. program in English at Harvard.

I found a furnished room near Harvard Yard; the on-premises landlord, a man close to my age dressed in a white dashiki, liked my "spiritual vibes." Apparently he had chosen the other nineteen roomers by similar means. Each side of the double-entry building shared a half-kitchen, a pay phone, a foyer mail table, and two bathrooms, accommodations reminiscent of a coed fraternity house. The owner had recently converted to the teachings of a stateside maharishi. He spoke of Nirvana and the spiritual path.

I signed into courses in Nineteenth-Century American Literature, Seventeenth-Century English Prose, and Sidney and the Sonnet Tradition (where we read the entire *Arcadia*). During lunch each day I reread *Anna Karenina* for relief, feeling that this was my best substitute for life, while the rigors of scholarship otherwise preoccupied me. Graduate students at Harvard had no contact with each other and were treated coldly. The pressure grew so depersonalizing that I felt I understood when a fellow graduate student committed suicide in Inman Square by throwing himself between the wheels of a tractor-trailer, bouncing off, then trying twice again.

In late October I drove back to Amherst to hear John F. Kennedy dedicate the newly completed Robert Frost Library—an appearance, it turned out, just weeks before his assassination. He arrived late, by helicopter, then swept into our indoor track and field area in the gymnasium, where perhaps fifteen hundred folding chairs held guests, including me, and mounted the stage. A leather rocking chair had been placed there to ease his back, and the presidential seal had been attached to the front of the podium. He spoke of writing as a national resource. "The nation that disdains the mission of art," he said, "invites the fate of Robert Frost's hired man, who had nothing to look backward to with pride and nothing to look forward to with hope." In Amherst terms, he sounded like an English major.

Back in my second-floor room, I stole hours from the reading and writing of papers for my literature classes, in order to write stories that emerged as forced imitations of the Transcendentalists. Finally, come spring, I was convinced that my only way to leave Harvard and to write without being drafted—at twenty-three, I was being closely monitored by my draft board—was to apply to the Writers' Workshop at Iowa. Accepted, I took a leave from Harvard and was granted continued deferment for graduate study at Iowa.

With the blessing of my doubtful parents, I drove on to Iowa City, where I continued to live in furnished rooms—this time in an attic, in a single-family house, with the owners a young couple living downstairs with a three-year-old and a wailing infant. Two other roomers shared the attic, both Taiwanese, as were three roomers in the basement, where we all shared a bathroom and a kitchen. When the roomers' phone rang, someone would call out, *"Yang-a-wa!"* One night, late, however, the phone turned out to be for me, Richard Yates calling.

I had read and admired Yates's 1961 novel, *Revolutionary Road,* at Amherst, been surprised at Iowa to recognize his name among the fiction workshop teachers, and had signed up for his section. Later, we had met to discuss my stories, and he had persuaded me to get on with new work. Now, having just gone over a story set in my family's candy factory, he was calling to congratulate me on this as "the real thing" and to find out more about me. This had to be a novel, he told me.

With his encouragement, for the next year I lost myself in creative fervor, completing eighty pages. I was celibate, antisocial, living, dreaming, and waking fiction, while also teaching freshman rhetoric at seven a.m., and taking Advanced Latin and Medieval Literature to continue progress on my Harvard degree. I even stayed in Iowa that hot summer, and was dismayed to learn that Yates had taken a leave to write a film in Hollywood, and that come fall, when I had been given a research fellowship, thanks to him, I would switch to his replacement, Nelson Algren. Unlike Yates, Algren disdained my work, saw me as an Ivy League snob, and advised me to drop out and join the Peace Corps. My progress on the novel stopped. I switched to Vance Bourjaily, but still couldn't write.

I became aware of the Vietnam War as an issue. Iowa students held draft card burnings. Drugs appeared as commonplace. Hairstyles went to no styles. The birth control pill was made widely available. My first year at Iowa I had no real contact with anybody but Yates. The second, I sought out social life from the undergraduates, not from workshop writers, most of whom I viewed as pretenders.

Meanwhile my parents back on Philadelphia's Main Line had moved from the house where I had grown up to a new "retirement" house in nearby Villanova. If I couldn't write, if I were only wasting precious time—career time—up the river, then I'd better go back East. At least the scholarly work was something I knew I could do.

I was readmitted to Harvard for fall, wrote the Cambridge landlord and got his best room, and with my savings from Iowa (where the cost of living was half of what it was in the East), I bought a new, not a used, car at home that summer. Settling back in Cambridge, I worked with Reuben Brower, a critic whose prose about literature was as clear as Hemingway's about life, and who had taught at Amherst. I felt challenged and impassioned again.

Having reached my twenty-sixth birthday, I could still be drafted, but the possibility was remote.

I was more a baffled witness to the public events of these years than an active participant. Intellectually, I was progressing slowly on my candy factory novel. I taught my first fiction writing class to Harvard upperclassmen in fall 1968. I was reading books about books to prepare for my orals, which I passed in November 1968, and then for two more years, while also teaching, I was researching and writing my dissertation on *Romeo and Juliet*.

The standout student in my fiction writing class was Kip Crosby, a twenty-two-year-old Harvard senior, who also became my

friend and my self-appointed guide to a Cambridge underground, including folk rebels, druggies, nymphets, bikers, and
hippie communeers, all of whom he saw as fallen geniuses.

He was crippled from birth by cerebral palsy, and would say of
his girlfriend, Hilary, who was from a wealthy Jewish family on
Long Island, "She thinks she is a freak; I really am one."

I had a poet friend, Bruce Bennett, whom I had met during my
first year at Harvard, and who had been away from Cambridge
since, having finished his degree and then gotten a job at Oberlin
College, where he shared in founding a poetry magazine, *Field*.
Now, from the summer of 1969, he'd quit teaching and moved
back to Cambridge, to concentrate on his poetry. He organized a
writers group, which met in members' apartments; I was invited,
and later I invited Crosby, and Crosby, in turn, introduced me to
a woman from Madrid, my age or older, Leonore Aparicio Hush-
far. Leonore had befriended Kip's girl, Hilary, in a class at BU and
thought her remarkable, and was aspiring to lead a literary salon
herself; she also wanted to write poetry, and claimed to have been
a disciple of Jorge Luis Borges during his residence at Harvard,
and to have read Robert Frost out loud to him every morning.
She, too, joined Bruce's group, and later she had parties.

My student/folk revolution/commune circle now overlapped
with the Harvard grad student and local writer circles. I saw this
as a wayfaring from knowing no one to having choices.

Kip and Hilary passed on Hilary's Central Square apartment to
me, while the two of them moved into a commune together. A
woman I met at a Harvard party and dated led me to Peter O'Malley and the Plough and Stars pub, which had been recently re-
habbed from a seamy taproom, where postal workers would drink,
to a stylish recreation of an Irish literary pub, or to something like
Dylan Thomas's White Horse Bar in New York. The Plough was on
a corner just down the block from me. O'Malley, a tall, black-
haired, hearty Irishman from Dublin, was the bartender. The
woman and he had dated, and now he was planning an expedition
to sail a trimaran to Rio de Janeiro, and she was tempted to join in,
along with her four-year-old son. In addition to sailing, O'Malley's
passion was music, in which he was taking a degree, and he would
play the classical music station in the pub and give a pint to anybody who could name that tune. He seemed to share my curiosity

about people and my pleasure in commotion as forms of relief from serious, creative ambitions underneath.

Teaching had started for me again, meanwhile, and my thesis work had grown difficult. The woman and I soon stopped dating.

I was smitten, pretty much at first sight, by Connie Sherbill, whom I met in Leonore's apartment in the fall of 1970. Leonore had been taking a class at BU with Kip's girl, Hilary, and had also befriended an even younger BU student, who was Connie's roommate in a Brookline apartment.

Kip, Hilary, and I were at Leonore's for brunch. Leonore hung crisscrossed chains on the window in place of curtains, had painted a slashing black and silver diagonal across the walls, had a tapestry hanging, and floors bare except for straw mats; also she had an expensive stereo system, exotic cappuccino to serve us, and a piano in one corner. At the time, a rock band was playing in Harvard Square, on the common nearby, its noise echoing in the street so loudly that we had to shout to understand each other.

The doorbell rang, then a knock at the door, Leonore went to answer, gave some excited greeting, and in came a short, plump girl, whom Hilary knew, hello, hello, and this other really beautiful girl, Connie. They had come over for the rock concert and then decided to drop by. They liked that kind of music, yes, of course! Didn't I? Connie was shy, but attentive and witty. Neither girl said much. She wore tight jeans and boots, and a vest; she was fresh and young, with full breasts, nice hips, shoulder-length brown hair, and eyes that sloped down, suggesting melancholy. I didn't ask her out, but I was driving back to my Central Square apartment and offered the plump girl and her a lift, dropping them off on the Cambridge side of the BU Bridge—stalwart, self-reliant, no-nonsense girls, I thought. I did ask Leonore about Connie later, suggesting interest. But I was involved with another girl, whom I found glamorous, and whom I'd met in one of Cambridge's continental cafés.

Then Leonore had a party, supposedly a birthday party for herself; lots of new people, lots to drink, dancing. And Connie Sherbill was there because Leonore had remembered that I'd liked her before. Connie and I started dancing. A boy her age was trying to interest her, but I kept dancing with her, and when we sat down, I put my hand on a bare part of her back, and she didn't flinch. She was flushed and into the party. And in the salacious spirit of the night, I said: "How about going to another party in town? One special guy, Max, I want you to meet, is supposed to meet me there. How about it?" She said sure.

So feeling physical—did I kiss her in the car?—we found our way in town. When we got to the party it had wound down; people were stoned and dancing, but Max had been there and left, and I knew no one else. So we danced a while—I was trying to impress her with the dangerous, streetwise world I inhabited—and then I asked her back to my place, and kissing me now, flushed and excited in the car, she said yes.

Perhaps on our third, or fourth date, at my apartment, Connie got a phone call from her sister in Waltham that their father had just died.

Nearly every girl I had been serious about, from my first love in high school on, had lost her father; I seemed to respond to that, and they seemed to respond to my responding. Certainly I had the conviction that family tragedy made people more real.

Now I felt Connie's loss and wasn't afraid of it. With other women, people I really didn't love, anything this serious would be something to avoid. I also liked the sense of family in Connie's Jewishness, that family for her was at the heart of what mattered, which, in different ways, was my parents' creed, too.

Now, here, unexpectedly, after only two or three dates, I was facing her family grief and driving her out Mt. Auburn towards Waltham, where I had never been, out a winding, complicated main street I had never followed before, counting, and wincing as I counted, one funeral home after another, some seventeen in all (since then, I've realized that these were ethnic neighborhoods, Irish, Italian, Armenian, each with their own burial traditions, parishes, churches). Following her tearful directions, we found Brandeis, and across the street, the modern apartment complex where her older sister, Lonne, and brother-in-law, Larry, lived with their new baby. Connie ran sobbing into her sister's arms. Connie's date, a stranger to them, I was greeted with embarrassed politeness.

Next evening I went back with her, as the whole family gathered to sit shiva. Her mother, Hazel, and youngest brother, Ray, had flown up from Miami; her oldest brother, Danny, a rabbinical student, had come from New York. Her sister's in-laws, Mr. and

Mrs. Weinstein, arrived from Newton, along with their grown children. We went outside later, at Danny's urging, to stand in the chill fall night and view the northern lights, which dimly shimmered, thanks to a trick in the atmosphere.

Connie had been born and raised in Miami. Her parents had been divorced only a year before, she said, "after twenty-four years and many attempts to patch things up." Her father, Joe, had been a truck farmer at one point, growing vegetables. Another time, which had involved their living in Panama, he had dealt in used cars. "He intimidated us," she told me, "but loved us dearly." They had had money at some point, but then had lost it. Generally, I gathered that he'd been luckless and intent on get-rich-quick deals. After the divorce, he had been alone, drinking, and financially destitute. Given that Connie loved him and was his favorite, she would torment herself now for not being there for him at the end. Deep in her own mind, he had needed her, and she had refused to see him when she could have; and she was to blame for deserting him and for his dying alone in a hotel room.

Hazel had had to rally first as a single parent after the divorce, and now as a widow. Having worked for her husband and having had to juggle an unpredictable income for years, she now made her living as a certified public accountant, while harboring passions for art, music, writing, and literature. She had put Lonne through college and seen her married to Larry in Boston. She had seen Danny, who had been a state debating champion in high school, through BU. Then Connie; then Ray still to follow. Connie's education had been financed partly by a student loan, which Connie would be paying off for years to come.

Connie, I felt, knew life in her guts. She believed in my ambition to write, and was ready to share in sacrificing for that ambition. She had majored in art history at BU, and her own ambition was to develop as a visual artist, and to teach young children.

By January 1971, she had moved in with me, and I would from our first sleeping together date no one else.

I need to credit now, as I did not then, the effort for her I must have posed, given my age, background, and the momentum of my life. The space we shared was mine: my furniture, my address, my phone, my record player, my records, my décor, my habits; my desk and typewriter dominating the living room, where as I worked, she would study in the bedroom. My father might call, one of his random maintenance calls, and Connie would answer, and we'd say that she was over visiting, or over for dinner. We were always lying for appearances to the official world, which included Mom and Dad, and the landlord, at least.

By then my Shakespeare thesis had been accepted, and I would have my Ph.D., officially, come June; meanwhile I still taught fiction writing and freshman composition at Harvard and worked on the novel. Having spent a total of eight years rather than the usual four completing my degree, instead of having my pick of assistant professor jobs from a bulging placement file in the English department, I found the file nearly empty. My application letters for the few jobs that seemed appropriate failed to generate an interview. Even my most influential professors had no advice or leads. An oversupply of baby-boomers receiving Ph.D.'s and declining undergraduate enrollments had combined to bring on the unforeseen: an academic depression in the Humanities, which would last, in effect, for the next ten years.

Kip and Hilary were married that Memorial Day.

When I turned thirty in June, I commented in my notebook: "I can't get a job. I can't have the things that normal people my age enjoy. I can't afford a family. When I was twenty-five, that was clearly a matter of choice. I was trying to be an artist, and I could always give up that ambition and still succeed by worldly standards. But here I am skilled, educated, and living alone on $4,000 where any stiff can make $10,000."

Connie graduated from BU and began working at a Head Start classroom in the basement of an Allston-Brighton church. Her BU roommates were breaking up. She took a room in Cambridge for appearances, but hardly ever slept there. Then in August, Mom and Dad visited Cambridge, and Dad assured me gruffly: "Don't worry about jobs. Persevere. You'll make it." For this visit, incidentally, Connie had had to hide her things and move back to her room, where we'd pick her up to take her for dinner or an outing, then drop her back off.

The bar down the street from my apartment, the Plough and Stars, had put a sign in the window in the spring of 1970 asking

for poems and stories for a broadsheet, and I had left a chapter
from my novel there, shortly after I'd met the bartender, Peter
O'Malley (whose sailing expedition to Rio had fallen through). As
I stopped back months later, early in 1971, O'Malley told me that
he liked the chapter and wanted to use it for the broadsheet, but
the actual printing of the broadsheet had been stalled, because
once they'd seen how much good work they'd gotten, they'd wondered whether they shouldn't be starting a magazine. Would I be
interested in working on something like that? he asked. I
answered sure, having edited the *Amherst Literary Magazine* for
three years; we shook on it, and arranged to meet in the pub later
with the owner, some poets, and other literary "blokes" to talk
about it more.

Through the spring, in the midst of everything else, we met at
the Plough and Stars, in my apartment, or in O'Malley's apartment on Green Street. The founding group included my own
friends, Bruce Bennett and Kip Crosby, myself, O'Malley, and
O'Malley's friends or regulars from the Plough, Aram Saroyan
(son of William, who claimed that his father had already done
everything worth doing with fiction), George Kimball (a Hunter
Thompson fan, who had studied at Iowa, run unsuccessfully for
Sheriff of Kansas City, lived in the Bowery, then come to Cambridge to write for Cambridge's underground weekly, the
Phoenix), Bill Corbett (a poet with ties to the Temple Bar and
Grolier bookstores and locally prominent writers who gathered
around them, as similarly tribal writers gathered around City
Lights in San Francisco or the 8th Street Bookstore in Manhattan), David Gullette (an actor and poet who taught at Simmons
College), and Norman Klein (a poet who had also studied at
Iowa, knew Andre Dubus, and taught at Simmons). We settled on
the name *Ploughshares,* thinking mainly of ourselves as a collec-
tive emanating from the bar, and one whose members would otherwise be fighting ("Realism is dead," "That's not poetry,"
"Robert Lowell is a fossilized fool"), but who, in creating a magazine, were turning their rivalry to the purpose of finding an audience and building a literary community. We agreed on having a
different member of the editorial board serve as "coordinating
editor" for each issue, with me being the first. As our streetwise
entrepreneur—and partner of the six or so Irish-American inves-

tors who owned the bar—Peter would take care of the business matters, printing, the paying of bills, distribution, and advertising.

Some of us—not me, thank you—were dedicated subterraneans, cultural mutineers (as Ronald Sukenick would later write) who had friends, counterparts, and heroes in the Bowery, in the Village, and in Berkeley. O'Malley boasted that the Plough was a place to meet others "whose failures are more glamorous than your own." Our motives were mixed, but none, give or take some notion of O'Malley's concerning publicity for the bar, were materialistic. I saw us as primarily refugees from other places where writing had mattered: in my case, Amherst and the Iowa Workshop. I had kept alive my own sense of vocation, somewhat, despite the rigor of Ph.D. work, in Bruce's writing group and in my teaching, and for me editing and producing a literary magazine was a still wider exercise of that vocation. Another excerpt from my novel had been chosen for the issue, and this would be my first publication since college; I was eager to share my best work, especially among other writers. I also felt the need to network and to publish as part of searching for a teaching job—and this was the motive I emphasized in long-distance calls with Dad at the time (he was skeptical, and made me vow never to put money of my own into such a venture; fine, so long as *it doesn't cost you anything*).

Over the summer of 1971, Peter and I met with Joe Wilmott, a friend and former student of Bill Corbett's at Emerson College. After dropping out of Emerson, Wilmott had gone to work for a South Boston printer, and having been granted after-hours run of the shop, had joined with poet Thomas Lux in starting The Barn Dream Press, a small press devoted to poetry. Barn Dream (named for what cows might think at day's end), in turn, had been inspired by a professor at Emerson, Jim Randall, who had been Lux's mentor, and who was bringing out Lux's first collection of poems from his own well-established small press, Pym-Randall. Lux was a serious poet that Bruce Bennett had come to admire while cofounding and editing *Field* at Oberlin. Peter O'Malley and I, in any case, concluded that Wilmott was sensitive to poetry, altruistic, and otherwise sympathetic to our publishing goals, and would work with us in trying to keep down costs. Part of our deal involved Wilmott's contracting the typesetting, but then using my volunteer labor in the production process: proofreading, pasting up phototype for camera-ready single pages, and, later, opaquing and stripping the negatives for offset plates. We used an old issue of *Transatlantic Review* for our first dummy, imitating its format and pasting proofs over actual pages in the issue. All of this, of course, appealed to my teenaged hobby of letterpress printing, and, as I commuted by subway to and from the print shop that humid summer, and worked whole days in the shop's airless and un-air-conditioned darkroom, the old romance of trade engaged me, as well as the chance to learn offset printing, which seemed to demand more knowledge of darkroom photography than of operating presses.

I threw myself into all of this, in the face of ignominy, my struggle with my novel, and joblessness; I thought of my effort as one of personal rehabilitation, a way to use and prove my worth, regardless of whether established "society" wanted and was willing to pay for me. Connie, meanwhile, trusted and admired my commitment and supported its supporting dreams, as well as the long-term rationale with which I tried to explain it to my father.

In September 1971, the first issue of *Ploughshares* appeared, one thousand copies costing $2,000, a bill that Peter somehow settled with Wilmott's boss. Other than giving away copies to family and friends, we hadn't considered publicizing or distributing the magazine yet, but we printed a cover price both in dollars and pounds, to allow for Peter taking copies to Ireland. Kimball drove to Manhattan with a box and left some on consignment at the 8th Street and Gotham Bookmart. Peter and I left five copies here, ten there, at the various bookstores around Harvard Square. We tried selling a stack in the bar. Corbett knew a friendly bookstore in San Francisco and got them to order. We had a publication party in the bar, where a public broadcaster friend of Peter's interviewed us and then aired the interview on WGBH radio. Later the same friend got us to appear on a community affairs TV show, *Catch 44*. Thanks to Kimball and the *Phoenix* editors who drank at the Plough, a full-length review of the issue appeared in the *Phoenix;* the reviewer was the Emerson professor, Jim Randall, who quipped that "*Ploughshares* is as much a happening as a literary event," questioned the compromises of our editing by committee, regarded the fiction as competent but unoriginal, yet ended by confessing "to liking both the magazine and its promise."

From the first, *Ploughshares* lent me social identity as a writer. Through that first issue and the sample of my fiction in it—about which Dick Yates wrote me, "Perfect, don't change a word"—I was taken seriously by writers my age who had themselves managed to publish books and land teaching jobs, among them Andre Dubus, Carter Wilson, Geoffrey Clark, Sidney Goldfarb, John Bart Gerald, and Fanny Howe.

For fall 1971, I managed to continue teaching a section of expository writing at Harvard; I also was hired to teach remedial composition as a part-timer at Simmons College. The following academic year, however, I was unemployed, though I did keep applying for jobs, and in spring 1972, had turned down one offer to teach composition at Roger Williams College, in Rhode Island, where another student of Dick Yates's, Geoffrey Clark, had found full-time work fresh out of Iowa; and another at Wichita State in Kansas. Both schools seemed academically dismal; neither seemed worth relocating and giving up the promise of Boston for. Out in the cold—no income, no health benefits—I continued my volunteer work on *Ploughshares* and worked on my book, while I lived off of savings and Connie's meager salary from her daycare job. *Ploughshares* and its mission became so consuming that after forcing myself to canvas Harvard Square typewriter shops, bookstores, restaurants, bars, and clothiers in search of advertising, I would walk past new cars like an anarchist, angry at the unnecessary and indifferent wealth everywhere around me. *Ploughshares* became my social focus, extending to my conviction that there should be some average bracket of material need for each citizen, no more, no less, my version of socialism.

I had gone into partnership with Peter O'Malley in publishing *Ploughshares,* offering as capital my time and brains. In some way, too, I saw Peter and myself as an odd couple, complementing each other's strengths. Where business was concerned, Peter was the icebreaker, the commotion-maker, the fast-talker; then I was to do the follow-up and make the blarney real, as it were. Peter supposedly knew the ways of the world; I knew writing, editing, and scholarship.

From the first, however, I was committed to the magazine and its cause for keeps. And that would mean, before long—in addition to editing, pasting up in the print shop, distributing to bookstores, and selling and designing ads—having to take over most of the so-called business and legal details as well.

We opened a bank account under the name of *Ploughshares,* with Peter and me co-signers on all checks. We discovered grants. Bill Corbett knew Russell Banks, editor of *Lillabulero,* who was serving on the board of the Coordinating Council of Literary Magazines in New York, which sub-granted funds from the National Endowment for the Arts. Peter put in an application, friends lobbied friends, and we came up with our first $2,000 grant, which paid for Kimball's issue, but then, surprise, we had to show proof that we had matched this amount or pay it all back. At this point, I put in $800 of savings (despite my promise to Dad), and together with a supposed list of donors from the bar and our meager revenues, Peter managed to raise the rest.

Next, Connie heard about the Massachusetts Council on the Arts in connection with some Head Start project and urged us to look into it; Peter asked around and played his Irish political card—the Plough partners knew some powers at the State House—and we went into Beacon Hill and met with a very supportive Irish-American administrator at the Council, applied for and got another $2,000. Suddenly, between annual CCLM and Massachusetts Council grants, *Ploughshares* seemed possible after all, though we were now required to incorporate as not-for-profit and to apply for tax-exempt status from the IRS. Peter and a lawyer friend finally did the state incorporation, copying passages from a law book for our bylaws, which Peter regarded mainly as paper; properly bold and authentic spirits went ahead and parked in no-parking zones or lived on barter-and-cash rather than taxable income: up the system. The idea was to make the legal gestures and then do pretty much what you liked. He continued to view the magazine as a partnership between we two "directors," only instead of owning stock, we would accrue salaries on our financial statements, towards some eventual sale. The pro-bono accountant who recommended this was also accountant to the bar. From this point on, however, the future of the magazine would depend on "getting civilized." I insisted on taking over the checkbook. I did the grant writing and reporting. I dealt with the accountant. I learned nonprofit law.

In my singles life, before Connie, I had taken pride in making one small room an everywhere. In clothes, in food, in furniture, in cars, apartments, in everything but books, I lived proudly at the poverty line—proudly because this was my choice, it had its ideology, and because like a mendicant monk, my eyes were not fixed on worldly matters. But as life went on, and as that became a life that I was asking Connie to share, my confidence in two sources of my eventual rescue from genteel poverty, in tickets back, as it were, namely a full-time teaching job and family money, wore thin, if not out. And outside of "the system," I was learning, you lived one day at a time, trading on your youth and chance.

Throughout this time I was, or felt myself to be to Connie, what I dreamed myself to be: the writer about to be recognized; the spiritual and sexual seeker settled down; the schooled scholar, critic, teacher, and editor, also about to be recognized and given cultural stability with a livelihood and a good job; the provider, family man, and father of children yet unborn, which had been put off only briefly until my promise was achieved; the branch of good Wasp stock, socially entrenched and better off than her own family, hence an upward opportunity in assimilated America.

We didn't rush into marriage. We talked about love, but never marriage. We were always mutually elective, a balance of powers; neither of us was without choices. Marriage was only necessary for children, and children were only possible with a Real Job and income, and a Real Job could only be had, seemingly, either by compromising my dreams and accepting an offer like Roger Williams's, or by finishing and publishing my book.

Together with dreams, however, for Connie, there was always the uncertainty. "Do you love me?" she would ask over and over, never satisfied with the answer; if you had to choose between your writing and me, would you choose me? Unfair question, I would answer. If she had to choose between having children and me, or between her religion and me, what would *she* choose? It was the same kind of unnecessary, extreme question that you couldn't answer until you were faced with it as a real choice and either did or did not. She must have lived with the double prospects of my success and failure, even as she got up at dawn every day and took the bus to her Head Start job, which was bringing in our only income for the time being. What if some publisher, as Dick Yates expected, on the basis of the half of my novel that was finished, believed in its prospect of being finished, and offered a contract? What if the book was published, as my students' books—Nick Gargarin's and Kip Crosby's—had been, as Andre Dubus's, as Bart Gerald's, as Fanny Howe's, as Russell Banks's? If the dreams were achieved, then what would the next dreams be? Would I still love her, would I ever commit myself to the part of me that craved the completion of children and family, or would I only give parts of myself, like a tribute or toll, that I could afford to give? Would I, once I had some public recognition, look again to glamorous, pleasure-seeking women, women who had no imagination or desire to live risks with or about me, but only to enjoy the apparent benefits?

On the other hand, what if the book was never finished, what if even I had to admit its flaws? Or what if it kept taking years and years, and then when it was finished, it wasn't published? What if all the doubters and naysayers were right? (And who, she must also have asked herself, who was she to question, given the years alone of this man, the complexities and experiences untold, the years of graduate school and teaching? And yet she was offering her life, and questioning was her right.) What if, indeed, realism was dead and even Dick Yates had no audience? What if there was some streak of self-defeat in Dee (as Connie called me), afraid of real success or adulthood? What if time or love ran out?

George Kimball was supposed to have been coordinating editor of the second *Ploughshares* issue, which we only managed to publish after delays and mishaps in June 1972; in fact, after the initial editorial meetings, George had vanished—rumor had it he was being sought for questioning by the FBI or CIA—leaving it to me to finish editing in his persona.

If the rotating editorship was going to work, we needed outside help—Kip Crosby, having married Hilary, had published his novel, and started acting as if his career had moved beyond the likes of us. Peter and I asked Jim Randall, since he'd reviewed us, if he would edit the third issue. Agreed. I also applied to Randall for a job teaching writing at Emerson, but he turned me down, in favor of Fanny Howe, "who had books." We started having editorial meetings in Randall's Harvard Street apartment, out of which he and his wife, Joanne, operated the Pym-Randall Press. Corbett and Gullette continued from the earlier group, joined now by the Poet-in-Residence at Emerson, Paul Hannigan, and a friend and former student of Bruce's, Katha Pollitt. Randall remained skeptical about my allegiance to realist fiction and my Harvard background, and I often felt the outsider among his circle. He had guest-edited an issue of *Sumac* and his Pym-Randall list was impressive, including Kenneth Rexroth, Robert Kelly, Allen Grossman, Basil Bunting, and Ford Madox Ford ("our only dead poet, because he is a personal favorite and his poetry has been neglected," he wrote), and he appeared to have made numerous literary acquaintances and friends over his past twenty years in the area. Given his creative writing program at Emerson and his literary convictions and friendships, he was the unofficial pope of Cambridge literary life, excluding Harvard; he himself had graduated from BU. His literary court, other than his apartment, was the Toga Lounge across from Harvard Yard, and his way station was the Grolier Book Shop. He brought a new level of credibility and of contacts to the magazine.

We agreed that I would do an interview with Richard Yates for his issue. Geoffrey Clark, who had had a story in the Kimball issue, had invited Yates for a reading at Roger Williams College in April, at which time I drove down, and Clark and I questioned him together. I later transcribed the tape and patched together a draft, sent it to Yates in Wichita, where he was teaching; Yates rewrote, cut, and added; I then offered extra questions by mail as well as a draft of a concluding statement about neglect and fame that I thought he should make—in all of this I was inspired by a cover interview that James Alan McPherson had recently published in the *Atlantic* with Ralph Ellison. Randall was happy with the result.

About this same time, Peter asked me if I knew anything about Richard Wilbur, and I said sure, that together with Robert Lowell, I thought he was the best poet since Frost. Peter took that in, then explained that he'd been seeing Wilbur's daughter, Ellen, here in

Cambridge, that she was a writer, and would I mind looking at some of her stories and poems sometime. Before long they were engaged. Connie and I were invited to meet Charlee and Richard Wilbur in Ellen's apartment in one of the Harvard houses, where we stayed up most of the night drinking, telling stories, and singing along to her brother's guitar. I was dazzled. Peter as a quantity seemed to challenge them much as he challenged me; Ellen, with all her natural elegance, heart, and intellect, had somehow set out to redeem and direct Peter's raw energy (his "daemonism," as I described it to Yates), and to help him foster his talent as a composer. As a gifted writer from a writer's family, she also believed in the magazine and added to Peter's commitment to it. They were married that summer, and Connie and I stopped by their big wedding in the Berkshires, then drove on down to Philadelphia to visit my parents, where Connie argued heatedly with my father about McGovern and ending the war, and we visited my grandmother in her nursing home, as well as my second oldest brother and his family in New Jersey, and went through all our family photographs.

Nixon was reelected. A cease-fire was called in Vietnam with the New Year. The early Watergate hearings began. By March 1973, the draft had ended and U.S. forces were leaving Vietnam. Spring, I worked with Thomas Lux in editing the fourth *Ploughshares*. Also my writing was getting attention.

Finally, Randall hired me as Emerson's Prose-Writer-in-Residence from July 1973 to 1974. The pay was $4,000 to teach two workshops, and at the time it seemed like a rescue and an affirmation. A job in the world lent force to my faith, not only to continue with *Ploughshares*, but to marry Connie.

REFLECTIONS

Fall 2001

To commemorate our thirtieth anniversary, we invited former editors to contribute anecdotes about their beginnings as writers, their experiences editing issues of the magazine, the early years of *Ploughshares* and other literary ventures, and the scene in Cambridge and elsewhere:

ANN BEATTIE

When I think about my beginnings as a writer, I think of the floor. I suppose I could think about burning desire, or tenuous talent, but really I have to say that without the particular place where I sat on the floor, I might never have become a writer. Because it was cold in New England, and I lived in a house where everybody else was conscious of conserving energy (read: too cheap to pay the heat bill), I set up my workshop in the living room by propping a pillow behind my back and placing my typewriter between my bent knees, its cord trailing off to an outlet across the room. In those days I also grew plants under lights: such things as columnea and hypocerta and various other things I got from the compost pile at the local greenhouse and dipped in rooting powder before placing in a mixture of sterilized soil and perlite, sometimes adding a plastic bag to increase humidity. Now, I struggle to do the simplest yoga stretches, sit in a grown-up leather chair at a desk (well: it is the former dining-room table), and live in a place where some of the tiny plants I struggled to grow years ago now grow as hedges (lantana; lipstick plant). I am warm enough, and those times I'm not, I crank up the heat. If I sit on the floor, it's because at times it's easier to deal with the avalanche of mail that way. But I still improvise: in the summer, in Maine, I carry my computer out to the back porch and write at the picnic table; I sometimes put my computer on the kitchen island and feel that I most certainly am not obliged to prepare food when I'm typing. Ah, but those days of easy flexibility, that time of minimal self-consciousness, with no conviction

I'd really have a career . . . that time before faxes spewing and computers crashing and the telephone answering machine screening calls . . . I had a good time down there on the floor, and some days I think the inherent humility of being down there might be the best antidote to being the grown-up writer I don't want to be, taking myself seriously.

ANNE BERNAYS

Growing Up Rich was my fifth novel. It was published in 1975 by Little, Brown. Up until then, my novels had surfaced briefly and were immediately forgotten. I don't know how he came across it, but James Randall, who was one of *Ploughshares*'s several editors way back then, decided he liked my novel and wrote quite a nice review of it, one phrase of which I can't, immodestly, help repeating here. He wrote: "one reads Anne Bernays's prose so effortlessly and with such speed that he is inclined to think it is his own accomplishment and not the author's. But the art is there." I had grown into writing convinced that clarity is next to godliness, and he appreciated that as much as anything in the novel. Jim Randall gave my confidence a big bump; he was the first "literary" person to take my work seriously. He was devoted to good writing and was extremely generous to those practicing it. I think he had what's known as a "falling-out" with some of the other editors on the magazine and quit it to run an antiquarian book business. I have never stopped being grateful to both Jim and *Ploughshares*.

ROSELLEN BROWN

I harbor a painful memory of a day and an evening in the life of *Ploughshares* in its early days.

It was early afternoon on October 6, 1979, a Saturday, and I was living in New Hampshire at the time. DeWitt Henry, the founding editor, had invited me to introduce the Irish writer Mary Lavin, whose work I loved, in a benefit for the magazine, a double bill in which she would read with Elizabeth Bishop at Sanders Theatre in that old Victorian Memorial Hall on the Harvard campus.

I remember very clearly that I was in my garden—I'd have envisioned this as summer if I hadn't just checked the date. What I might have been doing there in October eludes me—cleaning up after the summer's bounty, perhaps, or checking out the lingering crops that would winter over: Brussels sprouts, parsnips. My husband called me in to the phone: DeWitt was on the line, and he had terrible news: Elizabeth Bishop, beloved by Cambridge, where she had taught for many years, had died that morning. "Of course you'll call off the reading," I ventured, but the situation was more complicated than mere good taste and a moment for sorrow would allow. Mary Lavin, who would not fly, was aboard the QE II and could not be stopped en route, and how in the world, DeWitt asked, could they simply tell her the event was canceled and her many weeks of travel, here and back, were for naught? The evening would proceed: she would read, and the projected Bishop appearance would become a memorial instead.

Bishop had been a much-revered teacher at Harvard, modest, astute, and private; she had many friends and was a fixture of the poetry community, though she was (allegedly; I didn't know her) as unassuming as certain others were flamboyant. And many, perhaps most, of the people who came to see her that evening had not yet heard the news. When they arrived at the doors to the auditorium, there were signs announcing the awful news, and—it is always terrible to watch others receive a shock, like witnessing an ambush—I remember the gasps and the tears.

My task, still ahead, was one of the most uncomfortable evenings of my life. I hardly remember Lavin. I only recall that, introducing her, I felt a vivid sense of what I can only call betrayal: the living writer, a stranger, seemed by her very presence to have triumphed, however inadvertently, over the dead one. I almost expected to be booed off the stage as I read my admiring little essay, whose sudden irrelevance was palpable. Had the audience come so provisioned, I would not have been surprised had I been pelted by ripe tomatoes. What Lavin felt, I have no idea.

But of course her listeners were polite—the awkwardness was not her fault. And when she had done, a series of impassioned speakers came forward to honor Bishop, that neighborhood friend. In the end, it turned out to be a very good thing that the grief-stricken friends and ex-students and admirers of the poet could be together, like family at a wake, to mourn her loss. *Ploughshares* had accidentally—but also by its emerging centrality to the community—provided a hearth around which they could gather and absorb the news. It was an odd, welcome, and unrepeatable step in the making of the magazine into an institution.

MADELINE DEFREES

Excerpts from a co-editor's journal and from letters to Tess Gallagher:

Letter, April 25, 1986: I've been reading until I'm nearly cross-eyed, so I'm taking a break to walk to the mailbox, having followed your wise suggestion and bought my very own postal scale—weighs up to five pounds—on sale at Arvey's. At the moment, it looks to me as if we should try to get together as early as possible after my return from the May 8 reading in Eugene. Since I'm planning to drive, I probably won't be home until May 10. How would May 12 sound as a target date for our meeting?

Journal, May 19: A month since I last wrote in this journal. During that time and a little before, I've had houseguests five times in six weeks and have driven nearly seven hundred miles for a reading at the University of Oregon. Tess Gallagher was here two nights just after I came back from Eugene. The car she was driving had been hit by a truck scarcely three hundred feet from the exit to my house. And she was driving Ray's Mercedes, so we spent most of the next two days dealing with that before we went to work on the manuscripts.

Letter, May 22: I'd like to put the issue together with your help, and although activity is stepping up, I'm in a good part of my energy cycle right now.

Letter, July 13: My procrastination comes from a kind of panic that seized me when I received in the mail twenty-eight books and full-length manuscripts for the Washington Arts Commission contest. I had agreed to be a reader when assured that there were only nineteen entries last time around. The twenty-eight, I was told, are *half* of the entries, and our meeting was originally set for June 16. I called the chairperson and said it wasn't difficult, it was IMPOSSIBLE to read all that by June 16. Now the deadline has been extended to August 20.

Letter, July 16: I'm hoping to wrap up the balance of my *Ploughshares* correspondence today, have run out of blank stationery a second time, and have one more set of poems to send you with this letter.

Letter, July 23: I've been up since 4:20 a.m. working on *Ploughshares,* and there are so many things I need answers on that I'm going to explain them…and include a checklist for your reply to be sure we cover everything and to save you some time. Enclosed you will find a recalculation of the pages, which I've checked with the adjustments, some of them not yet confirmed with you. You'll also find a Table of Contents for the order. Last night I read about half the mss., and this morning I finished up and made a few shifts in position, but I think it's a good arrangement, and I made notes as I went along to help me write an Intro, which I hope to start after a trip to Sears to see about a security door and a storm-screen door for the back of the house.

Journal, August 4: I took the weekend off from *Ploughshares,* and Tess will be climbing the walls, but I have to take charge of my life.

Journal, August 6: Finally got notes for the *Ploughshares* Intro and a bunch of manuscripts off to Tess yesterday.

Journal, August 20: Already pressing: the task of preparing the final manuscript and Table of Contents for *Ploughshares.*

Letter, August 27: Yesterday I mailed off the *Ploughshares* material to Jennifer Rose, along with a revised version of the Table of Contents. I'm enclosing a Xerox of the letter for you. Hope I didn't leave anyone off this time. I checked it against the manuscript, so I hope that it's right.

Letter, September 2: You did a great job on the pay schedule, and I've done as you recommended, sending one copy to DeWitt and keeping one. I also liked the way you added and expanded the introduction, except for one blockbuster paragraph with a mouthful of polysyllables. "Tess must have been tired," I said, sympathizing totally with the way your time has been broken up with all this company. I don't know how you keep track of everything because I do exactly the same thing about sweeping things into drawers or onto shelves or into folders when someone comes to stay, and I have a horrible time sorting it all out again.

LORRIE GOLDENSOHN

When I edited my issue so many years ago, featuring Amherst poets, I knew I wanted to have Saint Emily preside over our doings. So I got Jerry Liebling, then teaching at Hampshire, and a very distinguished photographer with many awards and shows at places like the Guggenheim in New York, to agree to take a photograph of Dickinson's white dress. VERY reluctantly the official keepers of the dress allowed us to make an appointment with it, first trying to fob us off with a suggestion that we photograph their blurry little postcard of the dress, the postcard they stack on a little table in the hall. But finally the day came when we all trooped upstairs to the famous southwest corner bedroom to see the dress in person. We went to its closet. Solemnly they opened the door; but refused to take the dress out of its plastic sheath, or off the hanger that held it inside the sheath—indeed, refused even to take the hanger off the wooden closet shelf, suspending the untouched relic in front of us. So Jerry focused, clicked, and the lovely, spooky, moony, glimmery photograph that resulted, with a black wire hook coming out of its neck, twelve mother-of-pearl buttons down its front, became the cover of *Ploughshares*. Quite successfully, I think.

DAVID GULLETTE

DeWitt Henry (without whom there would be no *Ploughshares*) running the magazine out of his Brookline Street, Cambridge, apartment, a book-crammed fifth-floor walkup, and later from a storefront next to a pizza shop on Waverley Avenue, Watertown: DeWitt, who kept the faith and wrote the grant proposals and answered the mail and talked endlessly of his heroes: Richard Yates, Dan Wakefield, Ray Carver: DeWitt, who brought *Ploughshares* to Emerson, tough, persistent, indomitable, like his own fictional anti-self, Anna Maye Potts.

Peter O'Malley, whose "share" of the till of "The Plough" (and Stars) supplied both the name and the seed money we needed to get the magazine up and running: Peter, the world's greatest schmoozer, who, like Stephen Dedalus, had been beaten by the Jesuits at Clongowes Wood, telling a rapt audience at a famous Cambridge New Year's party how he had come over from Ireland to America "looking for a rich widow with a bad cough," confronted by a (slightly drunk) Harvard professor: "You must get a lot of mileage out of that cute Irish accent," so that punches were thrown, glass broken, tables overturned, and we had to drag the two of them apart and spirit them away in separate cars.

The Long Lunch Editorial Meetings for Vol. 2/3 held in my living room: DeWitt, Norman Klein, and I (we were all teaching at Simmons then), and Peter O'Malley, George Starbuck, and Lloyd Schwartz: we had a complicated numerical rating system, with one *fiat* per editor, and the noisy brilliant debates over individual poems and stories stretched sometimes all afternoon and into the early dusk amid disordered piles of manuscripts, dirty plates, and empty beer bottles: 2/3, the breakthrough issue, the first one with "big names"—Kenneth Rexroth, Peter's father-in-law, Richard Wilbur, Ray Carver, Octavio Paz, interviews with Simic and Strand.

Out on the Cape my wife and I had met Octavio Paz and his wife, who had lamented the unavailability of cilantro in Boston: they invited us to dinner (with Mark Strand) at their Harvard Street apartment; I was actually experimenting with growing cilantro at the time, but I detested the taste—this was long before my life was transformed by Latin American culture—so I dug up my "entire crop" and put it in a clay pot as a gift to Señora Paz. To this day I blush remembering the look on her face when she opened the door and saw the four or five droopy anemic stalks held out to her. But that was the dinner at which Octavio agreed to let me translate passages from *El Mono Gramático* for Vol. 2/3, so all was not lost.

FANNY HOWE

Ploughshares Vol. 2/1—the issue that I edited—was published twenty-seven years ago. Contained in its pages are the markings of a very specific period in Boston, including a line drawing of Peter O'Malley sitting in the Plough and Stars, cap pulled low, newspaper raised, and notices for the Grateful Union Bookstore, Guinness stout, and Emerson College's workshops with a staff consisting of James Randall, DeWitt Henry, William Matthews, and William Corbett. Inside the pages are writings by two former nuns, by Eilean Ni Chiulleanain, Calvin Forbes, Mahmoud Darwish (translated by Carl Senna), Bobbie Louise Hawkins, Susan Howe, Russell Banks, and Paul Hannigan. Paul's phenomenal story, "Slot People," is the centerpiece—hopefully not forgotten by the few who are still alive and able to remember that deep and skeptical tale.

The assassinations were over. And most of us involved in that issue were young parents, living in broken zones in the midst of reconstruction. When I look at the contributors, I see many of the people who influenced years of my life, and the kind of aesthetic we shared, which was Lowell-based in some cases, and Olson-based in others, with echoes of Creeley, Oppen, Levertov, Plath, and O'Hara in others. Some would not continue writing poetry, others would change their line lengths as they changed their minds over the years, and a couple would become famous. But at the time, wedged as we were into our situation and our condition, it was all very Boston, white and bricked in, with people competing and being mean, with weak power being brandished as big gain, and powerlessness instantly politicized.

We drank a lot and drove wildly up to Gloucester, we tossed bananas over our shoulders into the back seats for the children to eat when they fussed (no safety belts), we smoked, and we marched. We were desperate for work. Those who had jobs grew pinched, shirking the glow of envy that followed them. Harvard and *The Atlantic Monthly* threw huge shadows over the readings we held in church basements and coffee shops. People who couldn't leave often became embittered, drunk, afraid to travel farther than New York or Dublin. I think of Boston as eternally ringed by a luminous but hard halo. It was never a city that protected its own but had a kind of provincial arrogance that generated repressive attitudes towards poetry and the arts generally. Yet many wanted to stay inside that circle, and many of us had to leave.

MAXINE KUMIN

By then—1947—I had gone back to Harvard to earn my master's degree in comparative literature and quickly completed the required credits. Hugely pregnant with my first child, I flunked the Latin exam, for which I was underprepared (the French exam was easy). Harry Levin, who had been my tutor during my senior year, interceded for me on grounds of impending motherhood, and the committee agreed to award the degree so long as I was not planning to go on for a Ph.D. Levin was a wonderfully generous mentor. He oversaw my undergraduate honors thesis, grandiloquently titled "Amorality and the Protagonist in the Novels of Stendhal and Dostoyevsky," and never flinched at its pretentiousness, gently steering me to various critical texts he thought I should read. Some ten years later, that M.A. enabled John Holmes to secure for me a profoundly underpaid and overworked adjunct teaching job at Tufts, my first venture into academia.

That halcyon year in graduate school I had another mentor, Albert Guerard, Jr., who had, along with Mark Shorer and Otto Schoen-René, team-taught English I, a survey of English lit course I took as a freshman. Guerard conducted the most exciting graduate seminar of my brief academic career, a course John Simon, who went on to fame as a theater critic, was also enrolled in. I was high on Conrad, John on Gide, and all ten or twelve of us in the seminar were in Guerard's thrall, meeting ahead of time in the old Hayes Bickford cafeteria on Brattle Street to try out our literary theories and repairing there after class to continue the dialogue.

It didn't occur to me to take note of the total absence of women faculty at Harvard. How myopic I was to complete four years as an undergrad, a fifth in grad school, blissfully unaware of their exclusion!

DON LEE

When I think of those early years, I think of hard labor in brutal conditions—ridiculous, I know, patently false and nostalgic, as if we were working in a gulag, an outpost in the literary tundra. I first volunteered to read manuscripts for *Ploughshares* in 1986, then began working part-time as an assistant editor in 1987, then, in 1989, became the journal's sole full-time employee for the next twelve years—variously called the managing editor, fiction editor, director, and editor.

I don't think people knew what to make of me—this cocky Korean-American kid from California. Later, there were some who thought I had usurped the founding editor DeWitt Henry's position, and quietly resented me for it. But the majority welcomed me from the start, and I carried on with all the energy and compulsion of youth, working mostly solo for the first year in the Watertown office (see Joyce Peseroff's piece for a description; I'll just add that during the winter, the desk with our lone computer was far enough from our lone space heater that I had to wear half-fingered gloves to type).

This is what would happen when a new issue of *Ploughshares* arrived from the printer: I would unload and wheel in about forty boxes—each weighing over fifty pounds—from the truck, and stack them in the office. Then I would stamp fifteen hundred Jiffy

#1 mailing bags with two impressions: the return address on the left, the bulk-mailing permit on the right. I would stuff each envelope with a copy of the issue and close the flap with three staples (required by the post office). I would then stick on subscriber address labels and sort the envelopes into bundles according to zip code—all five digits, the first three digits, the same state. These bundles had to be rubber-banded by length and girth (required by the post office), then crammed into canvas sacks according to districts. Then I would rent a van and load, transport, and unload the forty or so sacks at the post office in Central Square—usually something like twelve hundred total pounds.

Thankfully things began to change in late 1989, when Emerson College became our institutional sponsor. I no longer had to defer my salary in order to pay bills, and, with health benefits, I could go to a doctor for the first time in three years. We moved to Emerson's campus, and all of a sudden we had windows, running hot water in the bathroom, and other amenities that were heretofore considered extravagant. The following year, we received the first of three large grants from the Lila Wallace–Reader's Digest Fund, and thereafter came rapid growth, state-of-the-art computers, a new design, procedures and office manuals for every conceivable task, aggressive marketing campaigns, and what's aptly called "fulfillment"—the printer shipping copies directly to subscribers.

Throughout, we kept renting the old Watertown office to store back issues, but the arrangement made less and less sense. We could shelve boxes in a warehouse with a speed-racking system for a fraction of the cost. So three summers ago, DeWitt—who still lives in Watertown—and I spent a succession of Friday afternoons inventorying stacks of issues in the office basement. We were going to keep two hundred fifty boxes, but we were being forced to get rid of another two hundred fifty, somewhere around *sixteen thousand copies.* We wanted to cry. It confounded us that these issues of *Ploughshares* weren't of use, of value, to *someone* out there.

We spray-painted Day-Glo orange *x*'s on the overstock, hired a removal company to haul them out, then stuck labels with bar codes on the remaining issues. A storage company came and went with those boxes, then the removal company returned for the final clear-out, using shovels and sledgehammers, smashing up anything that was too large or inconvenient to carry through the door.

I don't know how DeWitt felt—DeWitt, who, with Peter O'Malley, had given birth to *Ploughshares,* who'd spent so many more years than I had building the magazine's reputation—but I looked at the bare floors and walls of the office, and I felt cowed. Bereft. Everything had been so much simpler in the old days. We did the best we could, and no one expected anything more from us, given our paltry resources, our lack of money, our shithole of an office. But, lo and behold, over the years, we'd become a bona fide *organization,* more than tripling the circulation and budget. This was what we'd wanted, wasn't it? We were now adequately funded, staffed, and housed. Everything was in its place, compartmentalized and digitized. Yet, for all the magazine's professionalism, it seemed more impersonal, even bureaucratic. Didn't we used to have more *fun,* wasn't there more of a sense of camaraderie, weren't we happier operating on passion alone? Probably not.

Anyway, nostalgia be damned. For me, for all of us at *Ploughshares*—David, Gregg, Maryanne, Susan, and our many readers and interns—it's still a labor of love.

PHILIP LEVINE

I have one powerful reflection regarding the issue I edited of *Ploughshares.* A friend, a former student, a poet, an ally in the battle against the Vietnam War, a wiry little Irishman with a great sense of humor, phoned me about that time and asked if I were busy; he was in town and wanted to see me. I said the only thing I was doing was editing *Ploughshares.* "'Ploughshares,'" he said. "What's that?" I said, "A literary magazine." A Westerner who'd been out of the literary scene for fifteen years or more, he'd never heard of it; he still thought *Kayak* was "the" poetry magazine. "What a title," he said. "They should change it to *Uzis,* turn your ploughshares into Uzis." I told him to come over and bring his boxing gloves.

JAY NEUGEBOREN

Twenty years ago when I guest-edited a fiction issue of *Ploughshares,* I wrote in my introduction about a scoreboard I had been keeping for the previous seventeen years: a sheet of paper I kept tacked to the wall beside my desk upon which I listed various items out in the world (stories, novels, scripts, essays)—where they were, the dates they were sent out—and upon which I posted, for each item, odds. At the bottom of the scoreboard I listed a Best Bet, Long Shot, Hopeful, Sleeper, and a Daily Double, and I kept a running score, "THEM" vs. "US." The odds on film rights to an unsold novel on my very first scoreboard (1963) were 989,989 to 1; the odds (after a dozen rejections) on a novel I sold the year I guest-edited *Ploughshares* were 500 to 1. Before my first acceptance ever (a short story, in 1962) I had accumulated, by count, 576 rejections; before I sold my first novel (and ninth book) in 1965, at the age of twenty-seven, I had accumulated more than 2,000 rejections.

An anniversary update, then: In the twenty years since I wrote of the scoreboard in these pages, I've racked up 1,387 additional rejections while selling nine books, a few dozen stories and essays, and several scripts. Based on information from a usually reliable tout, the odds on a new short story collection (*News from the New American Diaspora*), opening at 5,000 to 1, dropped suddenly just before Thanksgiving this past year to 50 to 1, at which odds it came in a winner. Previous to that, the Best Bet for three years running, at odds ranging from 500 to 1, to 25,000 to 1, was *Imagining Robert*, which, after forty-one rejections, sold in 1997, and has since then, among other payoffs for shrewd and faithful bettors, come out in paperback, been optioned for a feature film, and gone into production for a PBS documentary.

For those open to chance, the current scoreboard features attractive odds on several items: the early line on film rights to my first novel, *Big Man*, recently reissued, are 10,000 to 1; a new novel, rejected sixteen times (mourning line?), are 5,000 to 1.

For players who like to handicap the field themselves before placing their bets, stats and data are available; I have retained all scoreboards from the past thirty-seven years—and all rejections, personal and form. My own read on the field, after four decades of making book: few sure things, but lots of surprises, and, now and again, a sweet victory that washes away the memory of despair and loss.

JOYCE PESEROFF

I remember the office on Waverley Avenue in Watertown and the karate studio next door; periodically the floor would vibrate and the walls would thump with energy I like to think we reciprocated. On my first day as managing editor, I remember sorting through hundreds of three-by-five index cards with names of subscribers, none of whom had ever been sent a renewal notice. I remember Ruth Henry, twenty-four months, peeling shrinkwrap from Seamus Heaney's international issue as the rest of the family stuffed copies into Jiffy bags.

I remember driving to Cambridge to get the mail, the treasure trove, and sorting envelopes—submissions, orders, subscriptions, ads, checks—while ripping them open with greed and joy. I remember fresh typescripts from Allen Grossman, Maxine Kumin, Robin Becker, Howard Norman, Robert Bly. I remember the visceral process of reading submissions into the night, after a day's cares, seeking the jolt of poetry: its ability to name the unspeakable, needle the mind, astonish sensibility, and beguile the ear, crying, "Sleeper, awake!"

I remember galleys and review copies—first on my block to read the new; first to know, while handling permissions, who'd be publishing a book next season. I remember editors and local writers sharing pizza or subs while debating this novel, that poem; art and gossip, gibes and jokes. I remember rivalry—a *Ploughshares* author beating *The New Yorker*'s for a Sunday *Times* profile. One day Richard Yates came looking for a typewriter, and DeWitt Henry gave him the manual Adler I'd donated to the office, my college graduation gift. I remember DeWitt matching color samples for our covers—Mike Mazur's gorgeous lilies, Ralph Hamilton's spooky portraits, George Schneeman's Coca-Cola collage.

I remember Sam Cornish, director of the Mass. Council on the Arts' Literature Panel, annoyed by police as he walked from the bus stop in Waverley Square. Later I edited Cornish's memoir, *1935*, the first *Ploughshares* book, and heard it reviewed on *All Things Considered*. I remember ambition, ferocity, eloquence, independence, contrariness, and a gas heater that made us headachy by day's end. I remember my years as an editor with disbelief that two decades have passed, and that *Ploughshares* remains, fundamentally, unchanged and ever-changing.

JAMES RANDALL

During the early years of *Ploughshares,* from about 1971 to 1974, a group of us, an informal literary board, met at Joanne's and my living room on Harvard Street in Cambridge. The people I remember were David Gullette of Simmons, the poet Paul Hannigan, Katha Pollitt, George Kimball of the *Phoenix,* Peter O'Malley, one of the founders, later Tim O'Brien, and, throughout, the reliable mainstay and cofounder DeWitt Henry. We made suggestions, read manuscripts, talked about design, and did whatever else we could to forward *Ploughshares.* Some of these people only met with us a few times, and in the magazine our published writers were mainly local.

In the early years, I edited four *Ploughshares,* the first of which was provincial. For the next three issues, I used the format of an interview with the featured writer, some poems by him, a portrait of the writer on the cover (very well done by the artist Michael Mazur), and perhaps a critical article on the poet. The three I chose were Michael Harper, Bill Knott, and Seamus Heaney, a distinguished trio and quite different from one another as was *Ploughshares*'s wont.

Later, I was involved in bringing DeWitt Henry and the magazine to Emerson College, to the benefit of all three. I am proud of my contributions to *Ploughshares,* but they are essentially minor. DeWitt Henry did almost all of the irksome tasks for the magazine and made almost all of the creative decisions. He kept the magazine alive from its modest beginnings to its later triumphs. He is a man of extraordinary perseverance and extraordinary perspicacity. My tributes are to him.

LLOYD SCHWARTZ

Excerpted from his article "Ploughshares: Breaking New Ground in Literary Magazines," which was published on January 19, 1982, in The Boston Phoenix:

My first contact with *Ploughshares* came in 1974 with Vol. 2/3. The coordinating editor was David Gullette, director of drama at Simmons College and one of the charter members of *Ploughshares.* Gullette was a powerful actor whose presence was much sought-after on the Boston-Cambridge theater circuit. I had performed with him once, and he knew I was interested in poetry. New blood was being more actively solicited at the magazine, and Gullette invited me to be on the editorial board for his issue with Norman Klein, also from Simmons and another founding member, and George Starbuck, who at the time was the best-known poet to become involved with *Ploughshares*. Editorial meetings, as Gullette accurately described them in his reflective apologia, were fun but not particularly harmonious. "New blood" meant lots of new opinions and prejudices. As Robert Bly once wrote about the Vietnam problem, "no one agreed." Each board member controlled a certain number of pages and had the power to choose something no one else on the board could stomach. The coordinating editor was more of a juggler than an arbiter. I'd like to think it was the liveliest if least coherent issue up to that point—the *Ploughshares* goal of variety and continuity acting itself out with a vengeance within the covers of a single issue. It was the last time that happened—the last poetry issue put together by committee.

This change was Frank Bidart's doing. Even before his first book, *Golden State,* he was becoming widely respected for his absolute standards of judgment and profound, helpful criticism. Robert Lowell had already come to depend upon his poetic advice (Lowell's *History* is dedicated to Bidart, who is now Lowell's literary executor). Bidart was not elected by a board but invited by *Ploughshares* directors Henry and O'Malley to edit his own issue (Vol. 2/4); he accepted with the proviso that he could do anything he wanted, including change the design of the magazine. Robert Pinsky and I were "associate editors," but every decision was, finally, Bidart's. For nine months we worked with printers Pat Botacchi and Joe Wilmot of the Barn Dreams Press, driving them crazy with questions about typefaces and breathing down their necks with demands about layout. The "new look" was suggested by the old *Kenyon Review* (where Robert Lowell had published his first poem)—larger print, elegant running heads, more white space, more breathing space. Ralph Hamilton designed a new logo (not used since) and was commissioned to provide artwork that would help define the new look. He came up with a series of nine black-and-white cut-paper collages, *The Awning at the Ritz*—each image identical in outline but with different details visible, and utterly different in atmosphere. Each introduced a section of writing (Lowell compared them to the large-letter pages of an illuminated manuscript). For the first time in *Ploughshares,* art was integrated into the texture of the book. For me it's still the most beautiful single issue of a contemporary magazine.

Bidart knew in advance what he wanted to print; he was not interested in unsolicited manuscripts, so for the first time the issue was officially closed. Robert Lowell, James Merrill, Richard Howard, Mark Strand, Helen Vendler, John Malcolm Brinnin, and Octavio Paz were among the more notable writers responding to Bidart's invitation for new work. Elizabeth Bishop translated the poem by Paz and revised a group of Brazilian "Sambas" that had originally appeared in her article about Rio de Janeiro in the Sunday *Times* magazine section. There were essays on Lowell, Bishop, Allen Ginsberg, and George Herbert, and pages devoted to quotations about writing and art that were touchstones for the editors. Lowell later revised his three *Ploughshares* contributions for his last book, *Day by Day;* the best of these, however, is one of his few poems not improved by revision. The definitive version of "In the Ward," one of the greatest and most moving poems of Lowell's last years, is in Frank Bidart's issue of *Ploughshares.* (When the pages were finally printed, the last page of "In the Ward" didn't look right and an uncaught typo was discovered. At his own expense, Bidart had the page reset, which required tearing apart and rebinding copies already finished and a rushed drive to the bindery in New Hampshire with the new pages. The *Ploughshares* directors have never—until now—been informed of this episode.)

FRED VIEBAHN

I didn't exactly grow up on them—not like the way my teenage years were permeated with the music of Josh White, Lightnin' Hopkins, Bob Dylan, and the Beatles. The Rolling Stones grew on me later, late in the sixties when I was in my early twenties and my subconscious was searching for some kind of ersatz for the real thing, psycho-intoxicants to replace the poorly defined revolution we had toyed with, the '68 turmoil we tossed flowers into before turning our coats and renouncing sit-ins for a more "sensible" strategy: the long march through the institutions. In 1969, in the wake of my first novel's modest success, I began to pen articles and reviews about the "beat" business, as rock was called in Germany then. But never on the Stones. By the early seventies, however, I dropped out of the pop and rock scene, keeping not much more than a dust-garnering record collection and my long hair as souvenirs while turning to more serious matters: I entered the holy grail of highbrow culture, making a living by covering the theater scene for papers and radio.

In the dead of a clear September night in 1973, I was rushing home from a cultural reporting assignment. The autobahn was nearly empty, and I whooshed past the occasional truck at well over a hundred miles an hour; north of Frankfurt, my bladder forced me to slow down and pull into the next rest area.

Just two cars were parked at the lavatory cabin, both late-model Rolls Royces with British license plates. I pulled alongside and got out, my silver-metallic Ford coupe dwarfed by their sleek excessiveness. The interior lights flickered dimly through tinted glass; there was some commotion inside. I didn't know what to think—drug lords, perhaps?

As I stepped up to a urinal, two gaunt guys with long hair (although not as long as mine) were shaking off the last drops while chatting in English faster than I could comprehend. I glanced sideways, and the one closest to me grinned back. It was Bill Wyman, and next to him Keith Richards was zipping up his fly. I feigned coolness while trying to control my palpitations—hey, nothing to it, most ordinary thing in the world—who cares about the spurious personality worship of the day, cranked-up celebrity cults; after all, it's art that counts, the great masters nobody would recognize in the streets... Frowning as if deeply committed to my business at hand, I pretended not to recognize my piss pals while part of my brain frantically sent marching orders to my muscles in a desperate attempt to loosen my vocal cords.

I left the loo and hit the night air to find Charlie Watts leaning against an open car door, smoking who knows what. A couple of sturdy fellows dressed in black were milling about. As I stopped to unlock my car, those unmistakable lips pouted from the half-drawn curtains in a rear window. I nodded to no one in particular and clambered behind the steering wheel, revved the engine, and pulled out of the rest area, cursing myself for my timidity. I don't remember if my tires actually screeched, but it certainly would have fit the sound in my head.

DAN WAKEFIELD

After two and a half years in Hollywood, I came back home to Boston in 1980 feeling like the cartoon man in a barrel. After making the most money I'd made in my life, from writing a TV series I created called *James at 15,* I was (amazingly) broke. In addition to being out of money, I had also lost the woman I'd lived with for seven years, the only house I owned, and my health, sporting a resting pulse of 120, which was twice the normal rate for a human being and more like what a horse should have after running the Kentucky Derby. I had also lost the sense of a literary community I'd enjoyed in Boston, and the fear that maybe I'd lost the literary—and maybe even literate—part of my brain. Accustomed to churning out TV scripts, it had been several years since I'd written sentences that went clear across the page.

Word that I'd returned got around to my friends and colleagues, and before long I was contacted by DeWitt Henry, who not only welcomed me back but asked me to be the guest editor of an issue of *Ploughshares.* I don't know if tears of gratitude came to my eyes, but I felt the relieved emotion of reconnecting to a part of my life that had been temporarily out of commission. I think the payment was somewhere in the mid-three figures, which in Hollywood terms was lunch money. To me at that time, it was manna—not the few dollars, but the sense it gave me of being back in another, more honorable kind of work, the kind I'd aspired to since being inspired at Columbia by professors like Mark Van Doren and Lionel Trilling.

It must have been DeWitt also who got me a gig teaching a writing course at Emerson, where at the end of the decade he secured me a three-year appointment as Writer-in-Residence. This cofounder of *Ploughshares,* whose genuine modesty and self-effacing nature have muted his contributions to our literature, has served as a guardian angel for many writers, including the late Richard Yates. Teaching writing at Emerson was yet another stepping stone for me back to a focus on books and away from the Tube that had nearly swallowed me.

These elements nurtured the new novel I'd been unable to complete in my L.A. exile, and helped me finish a work which I'm still proud of, *Under the Apple Tree,* and later that decade the fictionalizing of my Hollywood experience in *Selling Out.* DeWitt and *Ploughshares* and Emerson were crucial elements of my recovery to health of mind, body, spirit, and what I think of as "real writing."

A Profile by Liam Rector

Hall as Young Artist

Approaching his mid-seventies, Donald Hall is—as he fre-quently reminds people—an old man now. Yet the term *old* can encompass a long shelf life, and no American writer has done more to honor the reality of time and generation than has Donald Hall. He's given detail, definition, and dignity to the reality of old: old like his grandparents, whom he so poignantly evoked in his memoir *String Too Short to Be Saved;* old like many of the poets he met in his relative youth, whom he characterized so vividly in *Their Ancient Glittering Eyes;* old like the aging widower who con-templates the premature death of his forty-seven-year-old wife in books of poems such as *Without.* Old with real sentiment. Old without sentimentality. I don't think Donald Hall has physically enjoyed getting older (who the hell does?), but he has looked at aging with a cold, bloody eye, made animate and real by sympa-thy, and he has lyrically, in many forms, told it like it is. This is sublimely useful in a culture hellbent and insipidly based on some version of Forever Young.

Hall was born in New Haven, Connecticut, in 1928. By the age of twelve he was writing under the spell of Edgar Allan Poe. "I wanted to be mad, addicted, obsessed, haunted, and cursed," Hall remembers. "I wanted to have deep eyes that burned like coals—profoundly melancholic, profoundly *attractive.*" He wrote poems and stories throughout prep school at Exeter, and at the tender age of sixteen attended the Bread Loaf Writers' Conference, where he met Robert Frost.

Hall went to university at Harvard, Oxford, and Stanford. At Harvard, Archibald MacLeish was his teacher for a year, and his classmates included Robert Bly, Adrienne Rich, Frank O'Hara, John Ashbery, and Kenneth Koch. Hall and Bly worked together editing *The Harvard Advocate,* and angered T. S. Eliot when they published some of his juvenilia with a few typos.

While a student at Oxford, Hall was awarded the Newdigate

Linden Frederick

Prize in poetry, and his photograph appeared in *Time* magazine—honors that suddenly made things at home easier. After a year in Palo Alto and a three-year stint as a fellow at Harvard, Hall went to the University of Michigan to teach, and stayed in Ann Arbor for the next seventeen years. As lore now has it, Hall made his decision to abandon full-time work at the university after a campus visit by Robert Graves, who suggested Hall attempt to live by his wits. Abandoning tenure, with children in college, Hall and his second wife, Jane Kenyon, headed for the house in New Hampshire where he had spent summers with his grandparents. "It was Jane who gave me the nerve to make the move," he says.

Ever since, Hall has indeed lived by his wits, simply and handsomely, centering his life on writing. At his home in Danbury, he goes from desk to desk, pile to pile, starting with poetry first in the early morning and then heading on to essays, magazine pieces, short stories, memoirs, children's books, textbooks, editing tasks, letters, and the like. He has kept his overhead low, and he has been prolific, readily and gamely taking on many protean forms and shapes. He has lived deeply within the New England ethos of plain living and high thinking, and he has done so with a sense of humor and eros.

Hall as Teacher

The man who in his seminal 1980's essay "Poetry and Ambition" called for the abolishment of the M.F.A. degree in creative writing is today being honored by the Associated Writing Programs with a poetry publication award given in his name. Many of Hall's criticisms of writing programs in that essay still stand, and some have led to reform, particularly where more emphasis is now put upon reading.

Hall has taught as a visiting poet-in-residence at the low-residency graduate Writing Seminars at Bennington College for over seven years now, joined in the last few years by his friend and co-conspirator, Robert Bly. Part of their living by their wits has been keeping ties with colleges where they find rapport, audiences, and some money, helping them cobble together a freelance livelihood. Hall is often on the road doing readings, and his travels recently have involved flights to Pakistan, India, Ireland, the Czech Republic, and other ports far from New Hampshire.

Having Hall and Bly at Bennington is a bit like having Freud and Jung. Hall is the relentless monotheist who loves Freud because Freud's thinking and writing are as nasty as life itself is, and Bly is a whirling dervish of polytheistic and polyglot pandemonium, a one-man American Fourth of July parade of many gods and many voices. The friendship and argument of Donald Hall and Robert Bly is old, contrary, affectionate, and ferocious. The students and faculty love to see them going at it.

Jane Kenyon was also there at Bennington with Hall at the outset of the Writing Seminars, and gave the last public reading of her life in January of 1994, during the first residency of the program. Kenyon lectured on Keats, Akhmatova, and Bishop, and extolled the Keatsian "Fuck and Die School of Poetry," of which she counted herself a member.

Hall as Editor and Player

Hall was the first poetry editor of *The Paris Review*, and he's been an editor of something or other most of his adult life. He was on the editorial board at the beginning of the Wesleyan University Press poetry series, which delivered early books by James Wright, John Ashbery, James Dickey, Barbara Howes, Louis Simpson, Robert Bly, Robert Francis, Richard Howard, and Donald Justice. In addition, Hall brought Sylvia Plath and many others to Harper & Row, and his editing of the University of Michigan's "Poets on Poetry" series gave us a record of his generation and their poetics we might have missed otherwise.

In the 1950's, Hall, Louis Simpson, and Robert Pack edited an anthology called *New Poets of England and America,* which inspired Donald Allen's countervailent *The New American Poetry* and created what was then known as "the anthology wars." It's difficult to imagine the same thing happening now, when most anthologies appear and are not even reviewed, much less debated, few creating anything even vaguely resembling a stir.

A moment of synthesis soon set when Hall was the sole editor of *Contemporary American Poetry,* and in my judgment it remains one of the last anthologies of American poetry—alongside Mark Strand's and Al Poulin's—with any real intelligence, nerve, discernment, depth, history, and knowledge.

Behind and in front of the scenes, Hall has been acting to bring poetry to readers and readers to poetry, and in the 1990's was active on the National Council for the Arts, the group that oversees the National Endowment for the Arts. There, he was sometimes the sole voice that resisted censorship in public funding of the arts, and to his amusement he became something of a smutmeister in the process.

Hall as Writer

The One Day, to my mind, is Hall's masterwork so far, among the fourteen books of poems he's published, including *Exiles and Marriages, Kicking the Leaves, The Happy Man, Old and New Poems, The Museum of Clear Ideas, The Old Life,* and the forthcoming *The Painted Bed.* In the latter part of the twentieth century, *The One Day* took its place also among books such as Anne Carson's *Glass, Irony, and God* as an eloquent consummation of Modernism, marked by doing the polis in many voices through the phenomenology of montage form. Hall's most recent book, *Without*, rivals Hardy's poems to his wife as one of the finest, even practical enactments of elegy in English-speaking poetry. The fact that Hall is producing some of his best writing in his later years makes him a patron saint to all poets. Where there's this kind of long life in the art, there's hope.

Liam Rector's books of poems are American Prodigal *and* The Sorrow of Architecture. *He edited* The Day I Was Older: On the Poetry of Donald Hall. *He directs and teaches in the graduate Writing Seminars at Bennington College.*

*Books Recommended by
Our Advisory Editors*

Madeline DeFrees recommends *Overtime,* poems by Joseph Millar: "Take a sensibility of remarkable delicacy and precision, immerse it in the abrasive, often violent atmosphere of twentieth-century blue-collar America, and what you get is a chronicle of drink, debt, and divorce: a story not unlike that of Raymond Carver. Joseph Millar's *Overtime* includes some of the best poems about work since Philip Levine's. In some remarkable 'portrait poems,' the reader is introduced to the poet's father and to characters whose lives are furnished with the staples of poverty: secondhand clothes, bad food, worry, and broken-down cars." (Eastern Washington)

Marilyn Hacker recommends *Little Ice Age,* poems by Maureen Seaton: "There are very few poets of whom I might say, 'It is inexplicable why this work is not better known, celebrated for all it's worth.' Maureen Seaton is a poet like that. Her register is enormous, her verbal daring and wayfaring breathtaking; while the solidity of her skill—whether in renewing received prosody or in formal invention—underpins a worldview that might otherwise be vertiginously frightening. *Little Ice Age,* her fourth book, is a marvel. She writes so much that has not been written, that

has needed utterance—in poetry *or* prose: about violence and eroticism, about women's desire, about the intersection of emotions, mathematics, and history, and she writes it indelibly." (Invisible Cities)

Philip Levine recommends *Skirts and Slacks,* poems by W. S. Di Piero: "In his new book, the poet W. S. Di Piero manages to place the reader in specific places at particular times with such ease and authority that after a single reading I felt close to lives I'd known nothing about and cared nothing about until he introduced me to them. His poems have the texture of American cities, the sights, sounds, and especially the smells of where we've lived in the last thirty years, and he has caught our American voices in all their glory and banality, our diction and our inflections, even when we're talking to ourselves. By some magic—let's call it inspiration— he knows us even when there's almost nothing to know." (Knopf)

Gary Soto recommends *Star Apocrypha,* poems by Christopher Buckley: "Buckley has been the master of nostalgia in his previous eight collections, and once again he has distinguished himself with a sorrow for the Santa Barbara of his childhood, for music, for his late friend and inspiration Larry Levis, and—this is scary—for the middle age moving ever so quickly toward old. Here is humor, but also a quietness that stills the heart." (TriQuarterly)

Henry Bromell, *Little America*, a novel: A rousing, clever, and thoughtful tale that's part John Cheever and part John Le Carré, this novel follows historian Terry Hooper from Boston to Rome as he tries to clarify his CIA father's involvement in the assassination of a Middle Eastern king. (Knopf)

DeWitt Henry, *The Marriage of Anna Maye Potts*, a novel: This incisive novel heartbreakingly portrays Anna Maye Potts, whose life is upended by her widowed father's death and by her younger sister's subsequent attempt to take possession of the family house. The first winner of the Peter Taylor Prize for the Novel. (Tennessee)

Yusef Komunyakaa, *Pleasure Dome*, poems: A compelling twelfth collection that gathers work from the past twenty years, as well as some new and previously uncollected work. *Publishers Weekly* astutely predicts that readers will want this volume for its "heady mix of gothic foreboding, racial history and realpolitik, biblical and Attic allusion, and sexual longing." (Wesleyan)

Al Young, *The Sound of Dreams Remembered*, poems: Containing nearly one hundred fifty poems from the past ten years, this volume serves as a playful, shrewd, hip, and occasionally shocking record of millennial America. (Creative Arts)

POSTSCRIPTS

Miscellaneous Notes · Fall 2001

NEW WEBSITE Our new website—www.pshares.org—is now up and running. The new site has a dizzying amount of features, including free online access to over 2,750 poems, stories, essays, and reviews from *Ploughshares* issues, as well as Web-only news items, event listings, book recommendations, forums, links, and much more. The site was programmed by Juxta Digital with a major grant from the Wallace–Reader's Digest Funds.

COHEN AWARDS Each year, we honor the best short story and poem published in *Ploughshares* with the Cohen Awards, which are wholly sponsored by our longtime patrons Denise and Mel Cohen. Finalists are nominated by staff editors, and the winners—each of whom receives a cash prize of $600—are selected by our advisory editors. The 2001 Cohen Awards for work published in *Ploughshares* in 2000, Volume 26, go to Elizabeth Graver and Adrian C. Louis.

ELIZABETH GRAVER *for her story "The Mourning Door" in Fall 2001, edited by Gish Jen.*

Debi Milligan

Elizabeth Graver was born in 1964 and grew up in Williamstown, Massachusetts, where both her parents taught English at Williams College. She remembers spending most of her free time as a child "writing, drawing, or playing imaginary games." She went to Wesleyan University, where she studied with Annie Dillard, and after graduating worked as a temporary secretary in Boston for a year, and then spent the next year teaching English at a public high school in Paris, all the while trying to carve out time to write.

In 1988, she enrolled in the M.F.A. program at Washington University in St. Louis, where she worked with Stanley Elkin, Deborah Eisenberg, and Angela Carter. Her first published story, "Square Dance," appeared in *Story* in 1990, and her story collection, *Have You Seen Me?*, was chosen by Richard Ford for the Drue Heinz Literature Prize and published by the University of Pittsburgh Press in 1991. That same year, she also received an NEA grant for fiction, which gave her the courage—and money—to drop out of Cornell's Ph.D. program in literature. She moved back to Boston, where she had close friends and a writers' group, and began working on a novel, *Unravelling*, which was eventually published by Hyperion in 1997. Her second novel, *The Honey Thief*, followed in 1999, and she is currently at work on a third novel. Graver has been teaching creative writing and literature at Boston College since 1993, and lives outside of Boston with her husband, Jim Pingeon, a civil rights lawyer, and their daughter, Chloe. In addition to being granted the Cohen Award, "The Mourning Door" was selected for this season's *The Best American Short Stories, O. Henry Awards,* and *The Pushcart Prize.*

About the story, Graver writes: "I was making the bed one day and passed my hand over a bump which felt like a small fist. The story grew from there and seemed—in the way of a dream—almost to write itself. I was trying to get pregnant at the time, and while we ended up not having to enter the maze of reproductive technology, I had a number of friends who were deep inside that maze. The story came, I suppose, from watching them navigate a world that seemed as surreal as the world of my story, as well as from my own anticipatory anxiety. As a writer, I'm used to being able to *make* things, to spin them out of thin air—with enough hard work, enough deep attention. Trying to have a baby demands a kind of surrender to the body that I found at once difficult and moving. Our daughter, Chloe, was born a few weeks before 'The Mourning Door' appeared in *Ploughshares.*"

ADRIAN C. LOUIS *for his poem "This Is the Time of Grasshoppers and All that I See Is Dying" in Winter 2000–01, edited by Sherman Alexie.*

Adrian C. Louis was born in 1946 in Lovelock, Nevada, and is an enrolled member of the Lovelock Paiute Indian Tribe. His mother was a registered nurse, and his father, whom he never met, was an Army veteran and erstwhile student at the University of New Mexico. His parents never married, and Louis was raised by his mother and grandparents on the small Lovelock reservation.

He attended the University of Nevada from 1964–66 and

flunked out. He then migrated to San Francisco's Haight-Ashbury and spent—as he puts it—"some stoned years on the edge" before he resumed his education in the early seventies. He graduated from Brown University with both a B.A. and an M.A., the latter in creative writing. Louis says he began writing in high school at the urging of one of his English teachers. "I had a love of language, and in the folly of youth I thought that writing poems, being a poet, might well be the highest calling of mankind. I was a romantic fool and read everything I could get my  hands on, from Robert Frost to Robert Lowell to Jack Kerouac, but when I read *The City of Trembling Leaves* by Walter Van Tilburg Clark, I knew I truly wanted to be a writer."

Colleen Brewer

He has been the editor of five tribal newspapers, including a stint as the managing editor of the country's largest publication, *Indian Country Today.* From 1984–98, he taught at Oglala Lakota College on the Pine Ridge Reservation of South Dakota, and currently teaches at Southwest State University in Marshall, Minnesota. "I teach creative writing and literature," he says, "but I get more satisfaction from teaching freshman comp than I do from creative writing."

Louis has written nine books of poems, including *Fire Water World,* winner of the 1989 Poetry Center Book Award from San Francisco State University. In addition, he is the author of two works of fiction, *Wild Indians & Other Creatures,* a collection of short stories, and *Skins,* a novel, which has been adapted into a feature film, directed by Chris Eyre (director of the Sherman Alexie film *Smoke Signals*). The movie is scheduled for release in spring 2002.

Louis has received fellowships from the Bush Foundation, the NEA, and the Lila Wallace–Reader's Digest Fund, among other awards. In 1999 he was elected to the Nevada Writers' Hall of Fame. He is now completing another collection of poems, *Evil Corn.*

About "This Is the Time of Grasshoppers and All that I See Is Dying," he writes: "It's just another chapter in my life. That's all I write about—the world and my shambling place in it. The poem is basically about dealing with my wife's Alzheimer's disease.

Actually it was written almost three years ago, so a lot more dark water has run under the bridge, and my reality is much more grim now. It's from a collection called *Bone & Juice,* which will be published by Northwestern University in September of 2001."

MORE AWARDS Our congratulations to the following writers, whose work has been selected for the following anthologies:

BEST STORIES Four stories from *Ploughshares*—a record number from a literary journal—will be among the twenty in *The Best American Short Stories 2001:* Claire Davis's "Labors of the Heart," from the Spring 2000 issue edited by Paul Muldoon, and Peter Ho Davies's "Think of England," Elizabeth Graver's "The Mourning Door," and Jess Row's "The Secrets of Bats," all from the Fall 2000 issue edited by Gish Jen. The anthology is due out this October from Houghton Mifflin, with Barbara Kingsolver as the guest editor and Katrina Kenison as the series editor.

BEST POETRY James Richardson's "Vectors: 45 Aphorisms and Ten-Second Essays," from the Spring 2000 issue, will appear in *The Best American Poetry 2001* this September from Scribner, with Robert Hass as the guest editor and David Lehman as the series editor.

O. HENRY Elizabeth Graver's "The Mourning Door" has also been chosen for *Prize Stories 2001: The O. Henry Awards* by editor Larry Dark. The anthology will be published in October by Anchor Books.

PUSHCART Elizabeth Graver's "The Mourning Door," Jess Row's "The Secrets of Bats," and Pamela Painter's story "Grief" (from the Fall 2000 issue as well) have been selected for *The Pushcart Prize XXVI: Best of the Small Presses,* which will be published by Bill Henderson's Pushcart Press this fall.

DEDICATION This issue is dedicated to the hundreds of staff members, readers, and interns—almost all of them volunteers— who worked at *Ploughshares* over the last thirty years. We would like to pay special tribute to these former staff editors: Jessica Dineen, Jodee Stanley Rubins, Elizabeth Detwiler, Renee Rooks, Barbara Tran, Susannah Lee, and Jennifer Rose.

CONTRIBUTORS' NOTES

Fall 2001

DAVID BARBER's collection of poems, *The Spirit Level,* was awarded the 1995 Terrence Des Pres Prize and published by TriQuarterly Books. His poetry and prose have recently appeared in *The Atlantic Monthly, The New Criterion, The New Republic, The Paris Review,* and *Parnassus.*

ANN BEATTIE's seventh novel, *The Doctor's House,* will be published by Scribner in February 2002. She is the author of seven collections of stories, most recently *Perfect Recall.* She is a professor of literature and creative writing at the University of Virginia in Charlottesville, where she lives part of the year with her husband, Lincoln Perry. She edited *Ploughshares* Vol. 21/2&3.

APRIL BERNARD is the author of two poetry collections, *Blackbird Bye Bye* and *Psalms,* as well as a novel, *Pirate Jenny.* Her third collection, *Swan Electric,* will be published next year.

ANNE BERNAYS is the author of eight novels and the co-author of three non-fiction books, including the forthcoming *Back Then,* a double memoir of life in New York City in the 1950's, written with her husband, Justin Kaplan. She co-edited *Ploughshares* Vol. 10/2&3 with Kaplan.

WENDELL BERRY's most recent books are *Selected Poems,* the essay *Life Is a Miracle,* and the novel *Jayber Crow,* all from Counterpoint.

FRANK BIDART's most recent book of poems, *Desire,* was published by Farrar, Straus & Giroux in 1997. He edited *Ploughshares* Vol. 2/4.

GEORGE BILGERE's poems have appeared recently in *Poetry, The Iowa Review, Shenandoah,* and *The Best American Poetry,* and are forthcoming in *The Southern Review, Denver Quarterly,* and *Field.* His newest book of poems is *Big Bang* (Copper Beech). He teaches at John Carroll University in Cleveland, Ohio.

ROBERT BLY's most recent book of poems, *The Night Abraham Called to the Stars,* appeared this year from HarperCollins. With Sunil Dutta, he translated *The Lightning Should Have Fallen on Ghalib: Selected Poems of Ghalib* (Ecco). Harper-Collins has also published his *Eating the Honey of Words: New and Selected Poems.*

DON BOGEN is the author of two books of poetry, *After the Splendid Display* and *The Known World,* from Wesleyan University Press. A third is forthcoming in 2003. He teaches at the University of Cincinnati.

LAURE-ANNE BOSSELAAR is the author of *The Hour Between Dog and Wolf.* Her second poetry collection, *Small Gods of Grief,* won the Isabella Gardner Prize for Poetry for 2001. She is the editor of *Outsiders: Poems About Rebels, Exiles, and Renegades* and *Urban Nature: Poems About Wildlife in the City.*

AMY BOTTKE is a teacher at the Hampden County Correctional Center in Ludlow, Massachusetts. Her poems have been published in anthologies by Graywolf Press, Milkweed Editions, and Iowa Press. Her work has also appeared in *Quill, Many Mountains Moving,* and *Louisiana Literature.*

ROSELLEN BROWN's novel *Half a Heart* (Picador) is now in paperback, and her 1974 story collection *Street Games* was republished—its fourth incarnation—this past summer by Norton. She teaches in the M.F.A. program at the School of the Art Institute of Chicago. She edited *Ploughshares* Vol. 4/2 and 20/2&3.

HAYDEN CARRUTH has published forty-five books, chiefly of poetry but including also a novel, four books of criticism, and two anthologies. His most recent books are *Reluctantly, Beside the Shadblow Tree, Three New Poems,* and *Dr. Jazz.* He has received the National Book Critics Circle Award, the Lannan Award, the National Book Award, and many other honors.

TOM CLARK's latest books are *White Thought* (The Figures) and *The Spell: A Romance* (Black Sparrow). He is at work on a biography of the American poet Edward Dorn.

VICTORIA CLAUSI received her M.F.A. in poetry from Bennington College, where she currently teaches poetry in the July Program. She has published poems in various journals and anthologies, including *Roots and Flowers* (Henry Holt, 2001). Her limited-edition chapbook, *Boarding House,* was published through Bennington's Alumni Chapbook Series.

MARK CONWAY has work appearing in *The Paris Review, The Gettysburg Review, The Journal,* and *Prairie Schooner.* He lives in Avon, Minnesota.

JUSTINE COOK is a graduate of Wesleyan University and works as the managing editor of *Zoetrope: All-Story.* She has published poetry in *The New Yorker, Poetry,* and *The Southwest Review,* and written variously on fashion, art, and books.

MARY CROW is the author of nine collections of poetry, most recently *I Have Tasted the Apple.* Her translations of Olga Orozco's and Enrique Lihn's poems are forthcoming next year. Her work has appeared in *The American Poetry Review, Ploughshares, The American Voice, New Letters,* and elsewhere. Poet Laureate of Colorado, she teaches in the creative writing program at Colorado State University.

NICOLE CUDDEBACK's poems have most recently appeared in *The Paris Review, Quarterly West,* and *River Styx.* She lives in Florence, Italy, where she teaches prose writing at NYU's Villa La Pietra.

MADELINE DEFREES's *Blue Dusk: New and Selected Poems* will be published this fall by Copper Canyon Press. Her poems have recently appeared in *Urban Nature, Visiting Emily, The Ohio Review,* and *The Extraordinary Tide.* She co-edited *Ploughshares* Vol. 12/4 with Tess Gallagher.

MARK DOTY is a 2001–02 fellow at the Center for Scholars and Writers at the New York Public Library. His new collection of poems, *Source,* will be published this winter by HarperCollins. He edited *Ploughshares* Vol. 25/1.

RITA DOVE is a Pulitzer Prize winner and former U.S. Poet Laureate. Her latest poetry collection, *On the Bus with Rosa Parks,* was published in 1999. She is Commonwealth Professor of English at the University of Virginia in Charlottesville and writes a weekly column, "Poet's Choice," for *The Washington Post.* She co-edited *Ploughshares* Vol. 16/1 with Fred Viebahn.

EMILIA DUBICKI exhibits paintings in Wellfleet and Provincetown, Massachusetts. In the spring of 2000, she had a residency at the Wurlitzer Foundation in Taos, New Mexico. She is completing a novel.

MARTÍN ESPADA's sixth book of poems is *A Mayan Astronomer in Hell's*

Kitchen (Norton). His previous collection, *Imagine the Angels of Bread* (Norton), won an American Book Award and was a finalist for the National Book Critics Circle Award. Espada teaches in the English department at the University of Massachusetts, Amherst.

ANGIE ESTES is the author of *The Uses of Passion*, which won the Peregrine Smith Poetry Prize. Her new manuscript, *Voice-Over*, was awarded the 2001 Alice Fay di Castagnola Prize by the Poetry Society of America. Recent work appears in *The Paris Review*, *TriQuarterly*, *Field*, and *Chelsea*.

ROBERT FARNSWORTH lives and teaches in Maine. Wesleyan University Press published his two collections, and new poems have been appearing in *The Southern Review*, *Michigan Quarterly Review*, *The Hudson Review*, and elsewhere.

CAROLINE FINKELSTEIN is the author of the poetry collections *Windows Facing East* (Dragon Gate, 1986), *Germany* (Carnegie Mellon, 1995), *Justice* (Carnegie Mellon, 1999), and the forthcoming *The Moment*. She spent 1999 as an Amy Lowell Traveling Scholar in Florence, Italy, and now lives in Westport, Massachusetts.

TERRI FORD is a graduate of the M.F.A. Program for Writers at Warren Wilson College. Her first book of poems, *Why the Ships Are She*, was issued by Four Way Books in May. She lives in Cincinnati, Ohio.

CHRIS FORHAN won the Bakeless Prize for his first book of poetry, *Forgive Us Our Happiness* (New England, 1999), and his work has appeared in *Poetry*, *Parnassus*, *New England Review*, and elsewhere. He teaches in Warren Wilson College's M.F.A. Program for Writers.

ELIZABETH KEMPER FRENCH's stories have appeared in *The North American Review*, *StoryQuarterly*, *Sundog: The Southeast Review*, and the anthology *Microfiction* (Norton, 1996). She received a special mention in *The Pushcart Prize XXIII*. She lives in southern Massachusetts, where she is working on a collection of stories.

LORRIE GOLDENSOHN's *Elizabeth Bishop: The Biography of a Poetry* was nominated for a Pulitzer Prize in 1992. Her current projects include a collection of poems, *Occupying Forces*, and a study of twentieth-century war literature, *Dismantling Glory*. She co-edited *Ploughshares* Vol. 5/1 with Ellen Bryant Voigt and Vol. 6/4 with Jayne Anne Phillips.

DAVID GULLETTE teaches writing and literature at Simmons College and is Literary Director of the Poets' Theatre. He has written two books about the confluence of poetry and revolution in Nicaragua: *Nicaraguan Peasant Poetry from Solentiname* and *¡GASPAR!: A Spanish Poet/Priest in the Nicaraguan Revolution*. He edited *Ploughshares* Vol. 2/3.

MARILYN HACKER is the author of nine books, including *Winter Numbers*, *Selected Poems*, and *Squares and Courtyards*. She also recently translated Claire Malroux's *Soleil de Jadis* and Vénus Khoury-Ghata's *Here There Was Once a Country*. She lives in New York and Paris, and is director of the M.A. program in English literature and creative writing at the City College of New York. She edited *Ploughshares* Vol. 15/4 and 22/1.

JEFFREY HARRISON was a Guggenheim fellow last year. His third book of poems, *Feeding the Fire*, will be published by Sarabande Books in November. He lives in Andover, Massachusetts, where he was the Roger Murray Writer-in-Residence at Phillips Academy for three years.

DEWITT HENRY's novel, *The Marriage of Anna Maye Potts*, will appear in September from the University of Tennessee Press as the inaugural winner of the Peter Taylor Prize for the Novel. His latest anthology is *Sorrow's Company: Writers on Loss and Grief* from Beacon Press (for details, see www.dewitthenry.com). He is the cofounder and founding editor of *Ploughshares*. He edited or co-edited fourteen issues.

JIM HEYNEN is currently writer-in-residence at St. Olaf College in Northfield, Minnesota. Three of his books will be released this fall: *The Boys' House: New and Selected Stories; Standing Naked: New and Selected Poems;* and *Fishing for Chickens: Stories about Rural Youth*. Earlier books include *The One-Room Schoolhouse*. He lives in St. Paul with his wife, the journalist Sarah T. Williams.

JANE HIRSHFIELD's fifth collection, *Given Sugar, Given Salt*, appeared earlier this year from HarperCollins. Recipient of fellowships from the Guggenheim and Rockefeller foundations, the Poetry Center Book Award, the Bay Area Book Reviewers Award, and other honors, she co-edited *Ploughshares* Vol. 24/1 with Stuart Dybek.

FANNY HOWE's *Selected Poems* has just been published by the University of California Press. Her other books of poetry include *One Crossed Out* (Graywolf), *The End* (Littoral), and *The Vineyard* (Lost Roads). Her most recent novels include *Nod* (Sun & Moon) and *Indivisible* (Semiotext(e)/MIT). She edited *Ploughshares* Vol. 2/1.

CYNTHIA HUNTINGTON has published two books of poems, *The Fish-Wife* (1986) and *We Have Gone to the Beach* (1996). A prose memoir, *The Salt House,* was published by the University Press of New England in 1999. Her work has recently appeared in *Agni, TriQuarterly, The Virginia Quarterly Review,* and elsewhere.

COLETTE INEZ has authored eight collections, including *Clemency* (Carnegie Mellon, 1998). She has received fellowships from the Guggenheim and Rockefeller foundations, and twice from the NEA. She is on the faculty of Columbia University's Writing Program in the School of General Studies.

KATIA KAPOVICH is a bilingual poet writing in English and Russian. Her poems have appeared in *The London Review of Books, Harvard Review, The Antioch Review, The American Scholar, The Massachusetts Review, Press, Slate, Salamander,* and *The Dark Horse,* and are forthcoming in *Verse* and *Stand.*

MEG KEARNEY's first collection of poetry, *An Unkindness of Ravens,* will be published by BOA Editions in October 2001. Her poems have appeared in *Agni, The Gettysburg Review, DoubleTake, Black Warrior Review,* and the anthology *Urban Nature.* She is Associate Director of the National Book Foundation in Manhattan.

X. J. KENNEDY has had verse lately in *The Hudson Review* and *The Sewanee Review.* Two new children's books, *Elefantina's Dream* (Philomel) and *Exploding Gravy* (Little, Brown), are forthcoming. The X. J. Kennedy Poetry Prize, which includes book publication by Texas Review Press, is now in its fourth year.

MAXINE KUMIN's thirteenth collection of poems, *The Long Marriage,* is out this fall from W.W. Norton, which also published her memoir, *Inside the Halo and Beyond: Anatomy of a Recovery.* A Pulitzer Prize–winning poet, she was awarded the Ruth Lilly Prize in 1999. She and her husband live on a farm in New Hampshire. She edited *Ploughshares* Vol. 14/1.

LAURIE LAMON is an associate professor of English at Whitworth College in Spokane, Washington. Her poems have appeared in many journals and magazines, including *The Atlantic Monthly* and *The New Republic.*

DON LEE is the author of a collection of short stories, *Yellow,* which was published this past April by W.W. Norton. He co-edited *Ploughshares* Vol. 20/4 with David Daniel.

DAVID LEHMAN's most recent book, *The Daily Mirror,* consisted of one hundred fifty of the poems he wrote after resolving to write one every day as an experiment. He has continued the practice, and "March 30" is from a new year of daily poems, *The Evening Sun,* which Scribner will publish in 2002.

PHILIP LEVINE is the author of sixteen books of poetry, most recently *The Mercy.* He edited *Ploughshares* Vol. 14/4.

TIMOTHY LIU's new book of poems is *Hard Evidence* (Talisman, 2001). He lives in Hoboken, New Jersey.

MICHAEL LONGLEY's most recent collection, *The Weather in Japan,* won both the T. S. Eliot Prize and the Hawthornden Prize for 2000. In 2001, he was awarded the Queen's Gold Medal for Poetry. He and his wife, the critic Edna Longley, live and work in Belfast.

ALICE MATTISON's most recent book is the novel *The Book Borrower.* This fall, Harper Perennial will bring out a paperback edition of her 1995 novel *Hilda and Pearl.* She lives in New Haven and teaches in the M.F.A. program at Bennington College.

WESLEY MCNAIR's most recent book of poetry is *Talking in the Dark.* Early next year Godine will publish his sixth collection, *Fire.*

JEAN MONAHAN is the author of three books of poetry: *Hands,* chosen by Donald Hall for the 1991 Anhinga Prize; *Believe It or Not* (Orchises, 1999); and *Same Difference* (unpublished). She is currently working on a fourth collection, *18th Century Zebra.*

PAUL MULDOON is the author of eight collections of poetry, most recently *Poems 1968–1998.* He is Howard G.B. Clark '21 Professor in the Humanities at Princeton University and Professor of Poetry at the University of Oxford. He edited *Ploughshares* Vol. 26/1.

JAY NEUGEBOREN is the author of thirteen books, including two novels, *The Stolen Jew* and *Before My Life Began;* two collections of stories, *Corky's Brother* and *Don't Worry About the Kids;* and two books of nonfiction, *Imagining Robert* and *Transforming Madness.* He lives in New York City. He edited *Ploughshares* Vol. 6/3.

CORNELIA NIXON is the author of two novels, *Now You See It* and *Angels Go Naked,* as well as a study of D. H. Lawrence. She won first prize in the 1995 O. Henry Awards. She teaches in the M.F.A. program at Mills College, near San Francisco.

JOYCE CAROL OATES's most recent books are the collection of stories *Faithless: Tales of Transgression* and the novel *Blonde.*

GEOFFREY G. O'BRIEN's first book, *The Guns and Flag Project,* will be published by the University of California Press in February 2002.

SHARON OLDS's books are *Satan Says, The Dead and the Living, The Gold Cell, The Father, The Wellspring,* and *Blood, Tin, Straw.* She teaches at NYU and helps run the NYU workshop at a state hospital for the severely physically challenged. She was New York State Poet Laureate from 1998–2000.

GREGORY ORR is the author of seven collections of poetry, the most recent of which is *Orpheus and Eurydice* from Copper Canyon Press, which will release *The Caged Owl: New and Selected Poems* in 2002.

JOYCE PESEROFF's three books of poems are *The Hardness Scale, A Dog in the Lifeboat,* and *Mortal Education.* She is Visiting Professor and Poet in Residence at the University of Massachusetts, Boston. She was the first Managing Editor of *Ploughshares,* as well as Associate Poetry Editor from 1988–1991. She edited Vol. 8/1, and co-edited Vol. 17/2&3 with DeWitt Henry.

DONALD PLATT's second book, *Cloud Atlas,* will appear this winter from Purdue University Press as a winner of the Verna Emery Poetry Prize. His chapbook *Leap Second at the Turn of the Millennium* was published in the spring of 2000 by the Center for Book Arts in New York City. He is an associate professor of English at Purdue University.

JAMES RANDALL cofounded Pym-Randall Press with his wife, Joanne. He also founded the writing program at Emerson College, at which he is now Emeritus Professor. He edited *Ploughshares* Vol. 1/3, 5/3, and 7/1, and co-edited Vol. 4/1 with DeWitt Henry and Tim O'Brien.

LIAM RECTOR is the author of two books of poems, *American Prodigal* and *The Sorrow of Architecture.* He is the director of the graduate Writing Seminars at Bennington College.

LEE ANN RORIPAUGH's first volume of poetry, *Beyond Heart Mountain* (Penguin, 1999), was a 1998 winner of the National Poetry Series, and was selected as a finalist for the 2000 Asian American Literary Awards. She is currently an assistant professor of English at the University of South Dakota.

GIBBONS RUARK's books include *Keeping Company, Rescue the Perishing,* and *Passing Through Customs: New and Selected Poems* (LSU, 1999). A recipient of three NEA fellowships and a Pushcart Prize, he has new work in *The New Criterion, Shenandoah,* and *The Cortland Review.*

STEPHEN SANDY's most recent collection of poems is *Black Box* (LSU, 1999). His long poem *Surface Impressions* will be published next March by LSU Press. His work appears in recent or forthcoming issues of *The Atlantic Monthly, Fence, The Paris Review, The Partisan Review, Salamander,* and *Salmagundi.*

LLOYD SCHWARTZ directs the creative writing program at the University of Massachusetts, Boston, and reports on classical music for NPR's *Fresh Air* and *The Boston Phoenix,* for which he received the 1994 Pulitzer Prize for criticism. His most recent poetry collection is *Cairo Traffic.* He is currently co-editing Elizabeth Bishop's collected works for the Library of America. He co-edited *Ploughshares* Vol. 2/4 with Frank Bidart and Robert Pinsky, and edited Vol. 5/2.

REBECCA SEIFERLE's third poetry collection, *Bitters,* is forthcoming from Copper Canyon Press this fall. Poems from her previous book, *The Music We Dance To,* won the Hemley Award from the Poetry Society of America and were included in *The Best American Poetry 2000.* She is the editor of *The Drunken Boat* (www.thedrunkenboat.com).

NEIL SHEPARD has published two books of poetry, *Scavenging the Country for a Heartbeat* (1993) and *I'm Here Because I Lost My Way* (1998), both from Mid-List Press. His poems have recently appeared in *The Paris Review, Boulevard, The Notre Dame Review, TriQuarterly,* and *Ontario Review.* He teaches at Johnson State College in Vermont and edits *The Green Mountains Review.*

REGINALD SHEPHERD's third book, *Wrong* (1999), was published by the University of Pittsburgh Press, which also published his previous two books, *Some Are Drowning* (1994) and *Angel, Interrupted* (1996). The poem in this issue is from his fourth book, *Otherhood,* forthcoming from Pittsburgh. He has received grants from the NEA, the Illinois Arts Council, and the Constance Saltonstall Foundation.

SARAH SILBERT has published stories and essays in *Agni, Hope Magazine, Spectacle, The Georgetown Law Journal Against Poverty, An Intricate Weave,* and elsewhere. She teaches writing at Vermont Technical College, New England Medical Center, and Ucross Artists Colony.

TAIJE SILVERMAN graduated from Vassar College and is currently enrolled in the University of Houston's M.F.A. program. She is from Charlottesville, Virginia.

LOUIS SIMPSON's most recent publications are a collection of poems, *There You Are,* and a translation from the French of François Villon's *The Legacy & The Testament.* He is at work on his *New and Selected Poems* and a collection of essays. He lives in Stony Brook, New York.

JOHN SMELCER's recent poetry books include *Songs from an Outcast* (UCLA, 2000), *Riversongs* (CPR, 2001), and *Changing Seasons.* His nonfiction books include *Durable Breath: Contemporary Native American Poetry, In the Shadows of Mountains,* and *The Raven and the Totem.*

BRUCE SMITH is the author of four books of poetry, most recently *The Other Lover* (Chicago), which was a finalist for the National Book Award and a nominee for the Pulitzer Prize. He teaches in the University of Alabama's graduate writing program.

W. D. SNODGRASS is the author of more than twenty books of poetry, including *The Fuehrer Bunker: The Complete Cycle, Each in His Season,* and *Selected Poems 1957–1987.*

ELIZABETH SPIRES is the author of four collections of poetry, most recently *Worldling,* and four books for children, including *The Mouse of Amherst* and *I Am Arachne.* "Ghazal" will be included in her new book of poems, *Now the Green Blade Rises,* forthcoming from W.W. Norton in 2002. She co-edited *Ploughshares* Vol. 25/4 with Madison Smartt Bell.

MAURA STANTON's most recent book of poetry, *Glacier Wine,* is just out from Carnegie Mellon University Press. Her book of stories *Do Not Forsake Me, Oh My Darling* won the Sullivan Prize, and will be published by the University of Notre Dame Press in 2002. She teaches in the creative writing program at Indiana University, Bloomington. She edited *Ploughshares* Vol. 15/1.

GERALD STERN is the author of *This Time: New and Selected Poems,* which won the National Book Award, and *Last Blue,* both from W.W. Norton. He has a new book, *59 American Sonnets,* coming out in the spring of 2002. He lives in Lambertville, New Jersey. He edited *Ploughshares* Vol. 16/4.

MARK STRAND is the author of ten books of poems, the most recent of which are *Blizzard of One* and *Chicken, Shadow, Moon, and More.* He teaches in the

Committee on Social Thought at the University of Chicago. He co-edited *Ploughshares* Vol. 21/4 with Tim O'Brien.

BRIAN SWANN has published numerous books of poetry, fiction, children's literature, translations, and Native American literature. He lives in New York City and Delaware County, New York.

DEBORAH TALL's fourth book of poems, *Summons,* was chosen for the Kathryn A. Morton Poetry Prize by Charles Simic and published by Sarabande Books. She is also the author of two books of nonfiction, co-editor of *The Poet's Notebook* from W.W. Norton, and editor of *Seneca Review.*

SUSAN TERRIS's recent books of poetry are *Curved Space* (La Jolla Poets, 1998), *Eye of the Holocaust* (Arctos, 1999), and *Angels of Bataan* (Pudding House, 1999). She is also the author of seventeen young adult novels, including *Nell's Quilt* (FSG). With C. B. Follett, she is co-editor of a new journal, *RUNES: A Review of Poetry.*

ALPAY ULKU's first book, *Meteorology* (BOA, 1999), was selected as a Notable Debut by the Academy of American Poets. His poems have appeared recently in *Witness, The Malahat Review,* and *The Gettysburg Review,* and previously in *Ploughshares.* He works as a technical writer in Chicago.

FRED VIEBAHN has published extensively in his native Germany, where he also worked as a journalist and editor before coming to the U.S. in 1976 as a Fulbright Fellow in the University of Iowa's International Writing Program. *The Stain,* the revised American version of one of his German novels, was published in 1988. He co-edited *Ploughshares* Vol. 16/1 with his wife, Rita Dove.

ELLEN BRYANT VOIGT's sixth volume of poetry, *Shadow of Heaven,* is forthcoming from W.W. Norton in February 2002. Most recently, she published *The Flexible Lyric,* a collection of craft essays. She teaches in Warren Wilson College's M.F.A. Program for Writers, and is currently the Vermont State Poet. She co-edited *Ploughshares* Vol. 5/1 with Lorrie Goldensohn, and Vol. 22/4 with Robert Boswell.

DAN WAKEFIELD is a novelist, journalist, and screenwriter whose books include the memoir *New York in the Fifties* and the novel *Going All The Way.* He can be reached at his website, www.danwakefield.com. He edited *Ploughshares* Vol. 7/3&4.

REBECCA WEE's first book, *Uncertain Grace,* won the Hayden Carruth Award for New and Emerging Poets in 2000 and was published by Copper Canyon Press in May 2001. Her poem in this issue is dedicated to her husband, Michael Hudson, who died in 1998 of leukemia. Her recent work also appears in *The Mid-America Poetry Review* and the anthology *The Cancer Poetry Project,* edited by Karin Miller. She teaches at Augustana College in Rock Island, Illinois.

ANN JOSLIN WILLIAMS is a former Wallace Stegner Fellow and a graduate of the Iowa Writers' Workshop. Her work has appeared in *Story, The North American Review, The Missouri Review, Willow Springs, The Chattahoochee Review,* and elsewhere. She lives in San Francisco.

JONAH WINTER is a children's book author and illustrator whose most recent book is called *¡BEISBOL! Latino Baseball Pioneers and Legends.* He currently teaches at George Mason University.

CHARLES WRIGHT lives in Charlottesville, Virginia, and teaches at the University of Virginia. His most recent book is *Negative Blue: Selected Later Poems.* His poem in this issue is from a projected collection called *A Short History of the Shadow.*

∼

GUEST EDITOR POLICY *Ploughshares* is published three times a year: mixed issues of poetry and fiction in the Spring and Winter and a fiction issue in the Fall, with each guest-edited by a different writer of prominence, usually one whose early work was published in the journal. Guest editors are invited to solicit up to half of their issues, with the other half selected from unsolicited manuscripts screened for them by staff editors. This guest editor policy is designed to introduce readers to different literary circles and tastes, and to offer a fuller representation of the range and diversity of contemporary letters than would be possible with a single editorship. Yet, at the same time, we expect every issue to reflect our overall standards of literary excellence. We liken *Ploughshares* to a theater company: each issue might have a different guest editor and different writers—just as a play will have a different director, playwright, and cast—but subscribers can count on a governing aesthetic, a consistency in literary values and quality, that is uniquely our own.

∼

SUBMISSION POLICIES We welcome unsolicited manuscripts from August 1 to March 31 (postmark dates). All submissions sent from April to July are returned unread. In the past, guest editors often announced specific themes for issues, but we have revised our editorial policies and no longer restrict submissions to thematic topics. Submit your work at any time during our reading period; if a manuscript is not timely for one issue, it will be considered for another. We do not recommend trying to target specific guest editors. Our backlog is unpredictable, and staff editors ultimately have the responsibility of determining for which editor a work is most appropriate. Mail one prose piece or one to three poems. No e-mail submissions. Poems should be individually typed either single- or double-spaced on one side of the page. Prose should be typed double-spaced on one side and be no longer than thirty pages. Although we look primarily for short stories, we occasionally publish personal essays/memoirs. Novel excerpts are acceptable if self-contained. Unsolicited book reviews and criticism are not considered. Please do not send multiple submissions of the same genre, and do not send another manuscript until you hear about the first. *No more than a total of two submissions per reading period.* Additional submissions will be returned unread. Mail your manuscript in a page-size manila envelope, your full name and address written on the outside. In general, address submissions to the "Fiction Editor," "Poetry Editor," or "Nonfiction Editor," not to the guest or staff editors by name, unless you have a legitimate association with them or have been previously published in the magazine. Unsolicited work sent directly to a guest editor's home or office will be ignored and discarded; guest editors are formally instructed not to read such work. All manuscripts and correspondence regarding submissions should be accompanied by a self-addressed, stamped envelope (s.a.s.e.) for a response; no replies will be given by e-mail or postcard. Expect three to five months for a decision. We now receive well over a thousand manuscripts a month. Do not query us until five months have passed, and if you do, please write to us, including an s.a.s.e. and indicating the postmark date of submission, instead of calling or e-mailing. Simultaneous submissions are amenable as long as they are indicated as such and we are notified immediately upon acceptance elsewhere. We cannot accommodate revisions, changes of return address, or forgotten s.a.s.e.'s after the fact. We do not reprint previously published work. Translations are welcome if permission has been granted. We cannot be responsible for delay, loss, or damage. Payment is upon publication: $25/printed page, $50 minimum and $250 maximum per author, with two copies of the issue and a one-year subscription.

~

THE NAME *Ploughshares* **1.** The sharp edge of a plough that cuts a furrow in the earth. **2 a.** A variation of the name of the pub, the Plough and Stars, in Cambridge, Massachusetts, where the journal *Ploughshares* was founded. **2 b.** The pub's name was inspired by the Sean O'Casey play about the Easter Rising of the Irish "citizen army." The army's flag contained a plough, representing the things of the earth, hence practicality; and stars, the ideals by which the plough is steered. **3.** A shared, collaborative, community effort that has endured for thirty years. **4.** A literary journal that has been energized by a desire for harmony, peace, and reform. Once, that spirit motivated civil rights marches, war protests, and student activism. Today, it still inspirits a desire for beating swords into ploughshares, but through the power and the beauty of the written word.

~

SUBSCRIBERS Please feel free to contact us by letter or e-mail with comments, address changes (the post office will not forward journals), or any problems with your subscription. Our e-mail address is: pshares@emerson.edu. Also, please note that on occasion we exchange mailing lists with other literary magazines and organizations. If you would like your name excluded from these exchanges, simply send us an e-mail message or a letter stating so.

Ploughshares Patrons

This nonprofit publication would not be possible without the
support of our readers and the generosity of the following
individuals and organizations.

COUNCIL
Denise and Mel Cohen
Eugenia Gladstone Vogel
Marillyn Zacharis

PATRONS
Anonymous
William H. Berman / Houghton Mifflin
Johanna Cinader
Jacqueline Liebergott
JoAnne Trafton
Turow Foundation

FRIENDS
Anonymous (2)
R. B. Bloxom
Tom Jenks and Carol Edgarian
Mr. and Mrs. John L. Lindsey

ORGANIZATIONS
Emerson College
Wallace–Reader's Digest Funds
Massachusetts Cultural Council
National Endowment for the Arts

COUNCIL: $3,000 for two lifetime subscriptions and
acknowledgement in the journal for three years.
PATRON: $1,000 for a lifetime subscription and
acknowledgement in the journal for two years.
FRIEND: $500 for a lifetime subscription and
acknowledgement in the journal for one year.
All donations are tax-deductible.

THE 2002 BAKELESS LITERARY PUBLICATION PRIZES

FOR FICTION, POETRY, AND CREATIVE NONFICTION

By authors who have not yet published
a book in their entry's genre

Prize winners to be published by Houghton Mifflin in Mariner Paperback Original

Winners are also awarded a fellowship to
attend the Bread Loaf Writers' Conference

Judges for the Year 2002 Prizes:

URSULA HEGI, fiction
YUSEF KOMUNYAKAA, poetry
VIVIAN GORNICK, creative nonfiction

Dates for Submission: October 1 to November 15, 2001

For guidelines to the Katharine Bakeless Nason
Literary Publication Prizes, please send a SASE to:

Mr. Ian Pounds, Contest Coordinator
The Bakeless Contest
c/o Bread Loaf Writers' Conference
Middlebury College
Middlebury, VT 05753

or find guidelines at our website:
www.middlebury.edu/~blwc

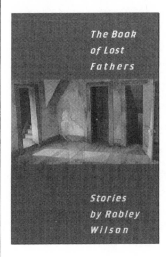

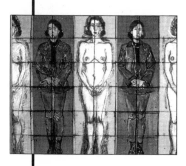

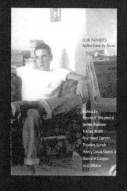

Our Fathers
Reflections by Sons
Steven L. Shepherd, editor

The first anthology of nonfiction prose to explore
issues surrounding fathers and sons in depth.
Fourteen of our most powerful writers illuminate
this relationship and offer valuable insights that help
untangle the beautiful and terrible threads which tie
sons to their fathers.

Contributors include **JAMES BALDWIN, TOBIAS WOLFF,
THOMAS LYNCH**, and **HENRY LOUIS GATES, JR.**

Resurrecting Grace
Remembering Catholic Childhoods
Marilyn Sewell, editor

Personal recollections, both painful and sweet,
from some of our very finest literary writers—
their candid confessions about growing up in the
Catholic church. With them, we return to their
youthful experience of the ritual, the saints, the
nuns, the hidden desires, the overt transgres-
sions, and of course the omnipresent guilt.

Features the work of **JAMES CARROLL, SANDRA
CISNEROS, SIMONE DE BEAUVOIR, ROSEMARY L.
BRAY, ANNA QUINDLEN**, and **TOBIAS WOLFF.**

BEACON PRESS   www.beacon.org

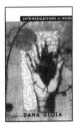

Ploughshares

Stories and poems for literary aficionados

Known for its compelling fiction and poetry, *Ploughshares* is widely regarded as one of America's most influential literary journals. Each issue is guest-edited by a different writer for a fresh, provocative slant—exploring personal visions, aesthetics, and literary circles—and contributors include both well-known and emerging writers. In fact, *Ploughshares* has become a premier proving ground for new talent, showcasing the early works of Sue Miller, Mona Simpson, Robert Pinsky, and countless others. Past guest editors include Richard Ford, Derek Walcott, Tobias Wolff, Carolyn Forché, and Rosellen Brown. This unique editorial format has made *Ploughshares,* in effect, into a dynamic anthology series—one that has established a tradition of quality and prescience. *Ploughshares* is published in quality trade paperback in April, August, and December: usually a fiction issue in the Fall and mixed issues of poetry and fiction in the Spring and Winter. Inside each issue, you'll find not only great new stories and poems, but also a profile on the guest editor, book reviews, and miscellaneous notes about *Ploughshares,* its writers, and the literary world. Subscribe

Visit *Ploughshares* online: www.pshares.org